WOLFRAM

WOLFRAM

THE BOY WHO
WENT TO WAR

GILES
MILTON

SCEPTRE

First published in Great Britain in 2011 by Sceptre
An imprint of Hodder & Stoughton
An Hachette UK company

1

Maps by Rosie Collins
Family tree by Craig Burgess

Endpapers in hardback edition: Drawing by Wolfram, aged 11.
Courtesy of Wolfram Aïchele.

Hardback ISBN 978 0 340 83788 7
Trade Paperback ISBN 978 1 444 71627 6

Typeset in Miller Text by Hewer Text UK Ltd, Edinburgh

Printed and bound by Clays Ltd, St Ives plc

Hodder & Stoughton policy is to use papers that are natural, renewable
and recyclable products and made from wood grown in sustainable
forests. The logging and manufacturing processes are expected to
conform to the environmental regulations of the country of origin.

Hodder & Stoughton Ltd
338 Euston Road
London NW1 3BH

www.hodder.co.uk

For Martin

'I'd rather be anywhere in the world.'

Wolfram, Ukraine, 1942. Letter to his parents

'It is not enough for people to be more or less
reconciled to our regime, to be persuaded to adopt
a neutral attitude towards us; rather, we want to
work on people until they have capitulated to us.'

Joseph Goebbels, 1933. Press conference.

CONTENTS

Foreword   1

Prologue   5

1 The Gathering Storm   9
2 Enemy of the State   28
3 A Visit from the Führer   44
4 Flying the Nazi Flag   61
5 War of Words   81
6 Deporting the Jews   101
7 Training for Victory   116
8 Dirty War   132
9 A Matter of Life or Death   148
10 Surviving the Home Front   165
11 Slaughter from the Air   179
12 Prisoner at Last   207
13 Working with Cowboys   224
14 Firestorm   236
15 Counting the Cost   258
16 Escape to Freedom   278

Epilogue   303
Notes and Sources   319
Picture Acknowledgements   326
Index   327

WOLFRAM'S WARTIME JOURNEY

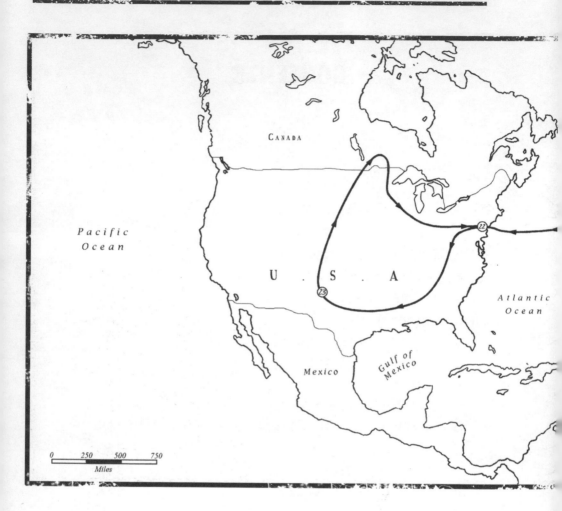

KEY

1 Pforzheim
2 Oberammergau
3 Niederbayern training camp
4 Brest-Litovsk
5 Kursk
6 Dnepropetrovsk
7 Mariupol
8 Feodosia
9 Kerch
10 Cherson
11 Nikolaev

12 Lvov
13 Marienbad
14 Strasbourg
15 Münsingen
16 Chateau Audrieu
17 St Brieux
18 Utah Beach
19 Southampton
20 Driffield
21 Liverpool
22 New York
23 Oklahoma

THE AÏCHELE & RODI FAMILIES

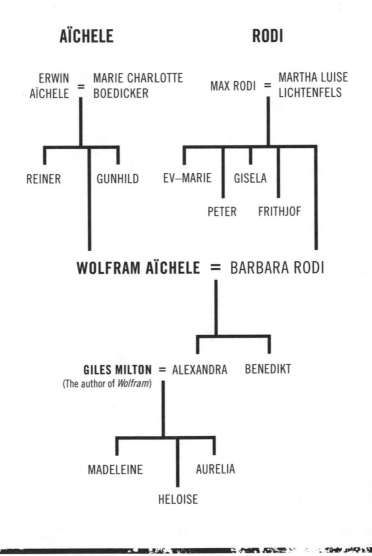

AÏCHELE

ERWIN AÏCHELE = MARIE CHARLOTTE BOEDICKER

REINER   GUNHILD

RODI

MAX RODI = MARTHA LUISE LICHTENFELS

EV—MARIE   GISELA
          PETER   FRITHJOF

WOLFRAM AÏCHELE = BARBARA RODI

GILES MILTON = ALEXANDRA   BENEDIKT
(The author of *Wolfram*)

MADELEINE   AURELIA
          HELOISE

FOREWORD

Wolfram: *The Boy Who Went to War* was born out of an incident that might have been amusing, had it not been so disquieting.

My seven-year-old daughter, Madeleine, had been set a school project to design an heraldic shield that represented the most important elements in her family background.

Aware that one set of her grandparents was German, she proudly decorated her shield with the only German symbol she knew: a giant swastika.

My wife was horrified and swiftly suggested that she change it but this left Madeleine perplexed. She was proud of her German roots and wanted to celebrate the fact in her heraldic shield. She knew nothing of the swastika's evil associations. To her innocent eyes, it meant nothing bad.

We knew that it would be only a matter of time before Madeleine and her sisters would discover the horrors of the Third Reich. They would also soon discover all the shibboleths and stereotypes that people held about Germany.

Would they therefore choose to distance themselves from their German roots?

To do so would be sad and misplaced. Their German grandfather had an extraordinary wartime story to tell: one that overturned all the clichés.

The war and the Third Reich were rarely mentioned when I stayed with my parents-in-law at their apartment in Paris. For years after first meeting Wolfram, I had little idea about what he had done during the war. I was reticent about asking any questions. Wolfram is a deeply private person and I had no wish to intrude on that privacy.

Yet he loved to talk, especially in the evenings when dinner was finished and a bottle of rare, home-distilled *kirschenwasser* was brought to the table. He would speak about Swabian folk art, Byzantine icons and his footsore pilgrimage through Serbia and Kosovo in the 1950s. These were some of the subjects that had fired him with enthusiasm and inspired his life as a celebrated artist.

He talked with great intensity and dynamism – vivid stories that were gilded with the rich experience of a lifetime's reading. One anecdote would spill into another, colourful and immediate, until the evening became a kaleidoscopic voyage into another world.

Kandinsky, the Russian hymnographer Kovalevsky and the soaring peaks of the high Wetterstein: one minute I'd be standing in the glittering twilight of an Athonite monastery, the next I'd find myself traipsing over the ice-bound crag of the Bavarian Zugspitze.

It was my daughter's swastika incident that led me, tentatively, to ask Wolfram about his childhood during the Third Reich. He seemed surprised that I was interested: after all, it was all a long time ago and it had not been the happiest time of his life.

He nevertheless began to answer my questions, remembering events with all the clarity of an eyewitness, his perception having been sharpened by his artistic powers of observation. With his heightened visual memory he was able to transport me in an instant to the places he had been: Brest-Litovsk, the Crimea, the beaches of Normandy.

I found myself listening to a story that had moments of horror and profound darkness, but was also extraordinarily touching and poignant. It proved a revelation: I had never considered the Second World War from a German perspective.

And thus, slowly, the book was born. Wolfram described at length what it was like to grow up under the Third Reich, talking into my ever-turning Dictaphone. He spoke in long monologues: he has never cared for interruptions lest he lose his train of thought. Yet they were monologues from another world – one that was infinitely more sinister than I had ever imagined.

Wolfram told me how he had always dreamed of being an artist, even when he was a young boy. His artistic dreams would keep him alive on the Russian front and sustain him during his terrible months in Normandy in 1944. Scarcely had he been imprisoned by the Allies than he was able to resume his sculpting, having made an ad hoc chisel from a stolen metal bed-slat.

Life was too precious to squander in the years that followed the war. Wolfram returned from the battlefront and consecrated his life to his art. His Orthodox iconostasis, painted in the 1950s, can still be seen in the Russian church in Düsseldorf.

His more recent work – semi-abstract watercolours – now hang in national museums and are eagerly sought after by private collectors. Wolfram is now eighty-six and he still paints every day.

My daughters have now learned that the Third Reich committed unspeakable atrocities in the name of the Führer. They also know that the swastika stands as a symbol of mass murder.

However, they can take a quiet pride in their German ancestry for they have learned, too, something that they have never been taught at school: that even in times of exceptional darkness, when morality has been twisted and defaced beyond recognition, there remains a brilliant spark of humanity that can never be totally extinguished.

One of those sparks was carried by their grandfather.

PROLOGUE

The fighter-bombers appeared from nowhere.

Wolfram and his comrades were making their way along a narrow country lane in Normandy when there was an ominous rumble in the sky to the east. They scarcely had time to look upwards before scores of Allied aircraft were upon them, screaming in low and fast towards their exposed positions. They were flying in so close to the ground that their underbellies were almost touching the treetops.

Wolfram, a wireless operator serving with the 77th German Infantry Division, looked for cover, dropped his communications equipment and flung himself into a nearby ditch, as did the hundreds of men around him, scattering in panic as they sought somewhere to hide. *Schnell . . . schnell! Quick! Take cover!*

There was no time to think about firing back, nor even to unharness the horses pulling the artillery. They were whinnying in panic as the first of the machine-guns burst into action from above, unleashing a hail of deadly fire.

Wolfram buried his head in his arms as the opening salvo

exploded all around him. The ground shuddered and jolted as heavy weaponry thumped into the soil. It was like a giant fist punching the ground. Explosion after explosion. Thump – thump – thump.

A mortar landed close by, flinging upwards a shower of mud. Machine-gun fire zipped across the country lane, twanging as it hit the metal shafts of the stalled artillery. Shrapnel and glass were sent flying through the air.

The blitz of fire came to a temporary halt, bringing a few seconds of silence. Wolfram briefly lifted his head as the planes traced a circle in the sky and was appalled by the scene of destruction around him. The ground was on fire, strewn with the dead and the dying. There were bodies everywhere.

A young student artist, with a powerful visual memory, he found himself gazing on a canvas that would remain with him for ever. His comrades lay wounded and bleeding, their bodies punctured by bullets, their limbs torn to shreds by shards of metal. The horses, still harnessed to the big field guns, let out strange screams of pain from the shrapnel that had buried itself deep in their flesh. The narrow country lane, a scene of sunny calm just a few seconds earlier, had been transformed into a picture of carnage.

It was 17 June 1944, and eleven eventful days had passed since *invasionstag* or D-Day, when the Allies had first landed in Normandy. Wolfram and his men had experienced a world of dangers as the American forces fought their way inland from their landing zone on Utah Beach. However, the German soldiers had not realised, until it was far too late, that they had pushed dangerously close to the American front line. Nor did they know that the little village of Le Vretot, their goal on that sunny afternoon, had already fallen into Allied hands. Wolfram, along with all the other men of the 77th Infantry Division, had inadvertently become trapped inside the American beachhead.

Now, they were sitting ducks.

There is a photograph of Wolfram Aïchele from about 1934, shortly before his life was to be turned upside down by the megalomaniac ambitions of the Führer. With his freckles and toothy grin, he looks like a typical happy-go-lucky ten-year-old, yet his contemporaries remember the young Wolfram as something of an oddball, albeit an endearing one. He was a dreamer who was perpetually lost in his own imaginary world.

He still has his *zeitglöcklein* or 'birthday book' from this time: a daily calendar in which to note the birthdays of aunts, uncles, brothers and sisters. This particular book is filled instead with the birthdays of his childhood heroes – and they are not the ones you might expect from a young boy. No footballers, no heavyweight boxers. Instead, he lists, among others, Johannes Gutenberg, Albrecht Dürer and Tilman Riemenschnieder, master-craftsman of the late German gothic.

Wolfram was quite unlike other boys of his age. Each weekend, he would clamber on to his trusty boneshaker and set off into the rolling countryside, cycling enthusiastically from church to church in order to marvel at the glittering diptychs and triptychs of medieval Swabia. Overlooked by most adults – and certainly by children, these fantastical painted landscapes fired the imagination of young Wolfram. Their gilded twilights and luminous trees transported him into another world and he would dash home to make faithful copies of everything he had seen while out on his bicycle.

He had inherited his eccentricities from his parents, who encouraged him in his medieval fantasies. They also encouraged him always to think for himself – a pedagogy that would sit very uncomfortably with the Nazi ideology of the 1930s. His primary-school teacher, Frau Philip, was exasperated by his lack of interest in the team spirit, although others, close friends of the family, saw his precocious nonconformity as a cause for celebration.

'My sons are interested only in following the crowd,' bemoaned the family's physician, Dr Vögtle, just a few months before the Nazis came to power. 'I just wish they could be like Wolfram.'

Wolfram was born in 1924, an inauspicious time in which to arrive in the world. His most impressionable years would be spent in the shadow of the Third Reich, with its marching, drilling and obligatory attendance at gatherings of the Hitler Youth. He would turn eighteen, the age for compulsory drafting into the Reich Labour Service, in 1942. It was the year in which Hitler's invasion of Soviet Russia crumbled into disaster. There was never any doubt that Wolfram would be sent to the eastern front.

Nor was there to be any escape from serving in Normandy, where he would witness, from his German foxhole, the biggest amphibious assault in the history of warfare.

However, both war and defeat lay many years in the future for that young Swabish lad with his passion for bicycle rides and gothic altarpieces. In those childhood days before the Nazis came to power, life seemed filled with infinite possibility.

CHAPTER ONE

THE GATHERING STORM

'You mustn't join the Nazi Party.'

I t is a bright spring day in 1931: Wolfram's parents, Erwin and Marie Charlotte, have just moved into their extraordinary new home. While the grown-ups busy themselves with unpacking books and paintings, the children are left to amuse themselves.

The corridors and interconnecting salons of the Eutingen villa are alive with giggling and merriment as seven-year-old Wolfram cavorts around with Gretel, his pet wild boar. Together with his brother and sister, he has made an obstacle course out of upturned boxes and half-filled crates. And they have perfected the art of persuading Gretel to pursue bowls of milk balanced precariously in the cupped palms of their hands. As the liquid splashes to the floor and Gretel emits a contented grunt, the eighty-year-old parrot glares at them with disdain, expressing his irritation by plucking out his feathers and dropping them on to the polished parquet flooring.

'Raus! Out you go!' A sharp word from the maid sends children and boar scuttling outside, where they continue

their pursuit in the long grass of the lower garden. In the family menagerie, the tame wolf, deer and owls look on with bemused indifference as Wolfram, his siblings and a highly excited Gretel end up in a tangled heap of arms, legs and boar snout.

For many months, the construction of the Aïchele family's villa had been a source of curiosity to the townsfolk of nearby Pforzheim, in the Black Forest region of south-west Germany. People watched, wide-eyed, as a veritable army of masons and roofers set off for the building site each morning. Everyone in the neighbourhood was talking about the house and asking themselves who had the money to build such a place.

And with good reason. Germany was in the grip of a financial depression so catastrophic that many had seen their life's savings lost to hyperinflation. Pforzheim's prattling housewives were no less shocked by the outlandish style of the villa. Its unusual architecture owed nothing to the familiar homesteads of rural Swabia – an area of southern Germany with a particularly rich history and traditions – and the construction site soon became the goal of many a Sunday-afternoon promenade. Pforzheimers would put on their capes and boots to traipse the three miles along the muddy byways that led uphill to the little village of Eutingen in order to catch a glimpse of the stucco façade, the plate-glass windows and the grand porch built in the squat style of the Italian romanesque.

Aloof on a hilltop, as if at a physical remove from the rest of the world, Wolfram's childhood home would become a place for artistic expression and classical music, its hall and salons brilliant with freshly cut blooms from the flower garden.

It was assumed by everyone that the mysterious new owners must belong to the town's snooty bourgeoisie, which could hardly have been further from the truth. The Aïcheles were neither snooty nor bourgeois – in fact, they were so idiosyncratic and unconventional that it was well nigh impossible to pin any one label on them. Nor were they rich. Their new home was a luxury they could ill afford, requiring Erwin to work long hours in order to pay the builders.

Wolfram's mother could not have been more different from the archetypal German hausfrau with her smart blouse and sensible footwear. Marie Charlotte had holes in her stockings and cardigans. Although extremely cultivated, of that there was no question, it did not stop her from walking around the house in her gardening boots.

The rigid formality adhered to by so many middle-class German families was wholly absent in the Aïchele household. Wolfram's parents had taken the decision to to bring up their children in an environment that was devoid of all the norms and conventions of 1930s bourgeois Germany. There were no strictures from starched aunts in outmoded crinolines, and no sense that children should be seen and not heard.

Wolfram's mother liked to break with conventions. Luncheon in the Aïchele household was always served at 1 p.m. and not at noon, in marked contrast to their neighbours. It was a subtle way of letting it be known that they were cultured and open to outside influences.

Wolfram's father Erwin, a distinguished animal artist, was so preoccupied with paying off the debts incurred by the new house that he kept only a cursory eye on the newspapers in these difficult economic times. Yet it did not pass unnoticed that, in the wider world beyond Eutingen, good news seemed to be constantly outweighed by bad. Erwin was delighted when the octogenarian war hero, General Paul von Hindenburg, beat the young Adolf Hitler to the presidency in the elections of spring 1932. Nevertheless, in the nationwide ballot that followed in July, he was disquieted to learn that the Nazis had scored an unprecedented 37 per cent of the vote. People were already beginning to say that Hitler was the only man who could save Germany from disaster.

For the children, the political chicanery in Berlin belonged to another world. Here in Eutingen, the youngsters were healthy and the family had a steady income. Summer was a time for bicycle rides, country walks, and picking plums and cherries. The fears and troubles that lay at the back of everyone's minds did not yet impinge on the private domain of the Aïcheles.

Wolfram was an inquisitive child, even at an early age. On Sunday afternoons, when his father was busy painting in his garden atelier, he would creep to the landing at the very top of the house. This was his own place of enchantment, a little corner where his imagination could run riot. His father had an old wooden secretaire – his personal cabinet of curiosities – that had dozens of keys, handles and secret drawers. Each one contained a relic, a feather or a piece of fur or an unhatched bird's egg. Erwin kept such things as reminders of all the animals he had nurtured in the family menagerie.

Here, too, were his freemasonry magazines. When

Wolfram had tired of exploring the secret drawers, he would hide himself away with these journals and read stories of adventure from the outside world. There were articles about faraway countries, of the exotic Orient and the Dark Continent, as well as stories of films and artists from around the globe. Wolfram would enter another world, unimaginably distant from rural Swabia, and he was spellbound.

Alas, his reveries would never last for long. A shout from the hall would send him scuttling downstairs: it was his father, once again calling him to help in his atelier. For the next two hours, Wolfram would sit there, holding one of the dogs that Erwin was painting. It was an irksome task. He and his brother continually complained of it to their mother, but she would brush off their moaning with a joke, saying, 'I'd sooner he painted dogs than naked women.'

Wolfram's father belonged to a generation of Germans with first-hand experience of the brutality of war. Like so many of his contemporaries, he had volunteered for service in the First World War, but he was *untauglich* – unsuitable – for he had a weak constitution and was turned down by the army. After much persistence he finally got accepted as a war artist, producing vivid sketches of artillery battles, bomb-damaged churches and villages that had been destroyed by war.

His work carried him to the front line and he was gravely wounded in the slaughter-fields of Picardy in northern France. Hit by shrapnel – his shoulder was shattered into fragments – he slipped into a deep coma. He awoke many days later to find himself in a military hospital in Pomerania, some 800 miles from the battlefront.

By the time he was fully recovered, Germany was a

different country. The war was lost and the victorious allies were determined to impose a harsh penalty on the vanquished. As Erwin made his way back to the house of his parents, he witnessed the first signs of the street violence that was to lead Germany to revolution. Radicals clashed with Nationalists, and Communists fought with soldiers returning from the front.

Many of these returning servicemen were deeply shocked by the hostility shown them. 'I shall never forget the scene,' wrote one, 'when a comrade without an arm came into the room and threw himself on his bed crying. The red rabble, which had never heard a bullet whistle, had assaulted him and torn off his insignia and medals.'

Erwin was himself a target for abuse, albeit verbal. Knowing little of the political revolution that had taken place, he arrived in Berlin still wearing the insignia of the Kaiser. It provoked a tongue-lashing from a shopkeeper, who told him to remove the monarchical colours. Erwin was deeply disturbed. Like his yeomen antecedents, he was a German Nationalist – a staunch believer in the old order, preferring Germany under the firm rule of the Kaiser. He had no time for the 'red rabble' who were attempting to sow the seeds of revolution. And he had no time for democracy.

Erwin was fortunate to have a job in the aftermath of the First World War. He had found employment as an art teacher at a jewellery school in the provincial town of Pforzheim shortly before August 1914. It was to Pforzheim that he now returned, along with the young woman who was shortly to transform his life. Marie Charlotte was bright, highly educated and physically striking.

Although not conventionally beautiful, she could turn men's heads, perhaps because she looked so unusual, with wide almond eyes and such uncommonly high cheekbones that throughout her life people would assume that she had Slav blood.

In fact, she was a thoroughbred German like Erwin, but she hailed from very different stock. She was the daughter of a distinguished military family who had first won their spurs fighting alongside Napoleon during his 1812 invasion of Russia.

The couple wedded in 1919 and Erwin resumed his job at Pforzheim's jewellery school. It was a difficult time to be starting a new life: rioting, political assassinations and running gun battles were commonplace, and there were constant clashes between rival militia and paramilitary gangs.

Amid such scenes, it was a miracle that a parliamentary democracy of sorts was born. By the summer of 1919, Germany had a constitution, a plethora of political parties and a democratically elected president. However, the constitution, drawn up in the city of Weimar, contained a defect that was to undermine the democratic process from the very outset. Article 48 allowed the president to rule by decree in times of trouble. President Friedrich Ebert was to use this prerogative on no fewer than 136 occasions – a worrying precedent for the country's fledgling democracy.

The young Aïchele couple had precious little money at this time. As Erwin was paid a pittance, he and his new wife had to live in a series of damp and inadequate rented lodgings, with no heating and many broken windows, which they had no spare money to repair. In the winter chill, Marie

Charlotte was so cold that she would buy cheap, oven-hot bread buns and put them into her coat pockets to warm her hands as she walked home from the shops.

In 1921, Marie Charlotte gave birth to her first son, a plump and healthy baby named Reiner. Three years later, Wolfram was born. The extra mouths further stretched their hard-pressed finances and the family subsisted on a diet of bread and potatoes. When Erwin began to make a name for himself as an animal artist, he supplemented his income by selling his paintings to the hunting fraternity. He had soon saved enough spare cash to employ Ilse, the first in a series of increasingly bohemian maids.

The young Wolfram – he was just five years old – would clamber atop the kitchen cupboard, where an air vent provided a clandestine view into the bathroom. From this vantage point, he and his brother were able to spy on Ilse as she lay naked in the bath. Her unclothed body was not the only attraction for the young voyeurs. Ilse had arrived to take up employment at the Aïchele household accompanied by her pet snake and every time she had a bath she did so with the reptile coiled around her neck.

Wolfram decided that he was going to marry her. Her hair was cut into a fashionable bob and she always wore the latest fashions. To his discerning young eyes, the exotic Ilse seemed to be a perfect choice of wife and he was most upset to discover that his affection was not reciprocated. Ilse soon left, to be replaced by a new maid named Clara.

Pforzheim was an unusual choice of home for a young artist. The free-spirited bohemianism of Berlin was wholly absent in provincial Swabia, and the capital's jazz clubs and freewheeling subculture might have belonged to another world. Pforzheim, home to thriving jewellery and watch-making industries, was staid and deeply provincial.

There was a Bismarckian solidity to the architecture of streets like Goethestrasse and Bleichstrasse that perfectly mirrored the oppressive spirit of the place. Ponderous buildings stood shoulder to shoulder like a row of well-heeled *bürgermeisters*. Built out of dark-russet sandstone and blackened by pollution, they were singularly lacking in frivolity.

In the late nineteenth century, the town's merchants had amassed sizeable fortunes from their jewellery businesses. With this money they built solid *fin-de-siècle* mansions on the leafy fringes of town, adorned with pinnacles, turrets and crenellated battlements in homage to Germany's Teutonic past. Yet there was nothing whimsical about the families that lived here, profoundly conservative and deeply conventional, in marked contrast to Wolfram's parents.

A number of the wealthiest local dynasties were Jewish. The Rothschilds and Guggenheims were among the more prominent, along with many of the town's leading doctors and lawyers.

Wolfram's father would soon socialise with many of these wealthy Jews. Like them, he was a freemason – a member of the prosperous Reuchlin lodge. Every week, he would put on his smartest suit and stroll down to the Villa Becker, the lodge's headquarters, for an evening of debate, classical music and intellectual discussion.

Wolfram's mother was always at her happiest on the evenings when he went to his Masonic meetings because beforehand he washed, shaved and put on a top hat, although she could never understand why he insisted on leaving his wet shaving bowl and razor on the piano. She would let out a weary sigh when – as always happened – she would find him asleep in the bath with the newspaper floating all around him. Having fished out the pages, she would hang them on the radiators to dry.

All would be forgiven when Erwin emerged clean-shaven and dressed in his smartest clothes, bringing back fond memories of Marie Charlotte's comfortable bourgeois childhood; her father, a general, was always impeccably turned out.

The town's Jewish bourgeois elite quickly warmed to Erwin's eccentricities and awkward mannerisms, excusing him because he was an artist. He, in turn, found them stimulating company.

The overt anti-Semitism that was so prevalent in other parts of Germany was less visible in Pforzheim. Although there were sometimes tensions between the two communities, Jews played an important role in local society and several leading members of the Chamber of Commerce were Jewish. The town's two principal department stores were also owned by Jews and when the community came to build a new synagogue in 1893, they were offered a site in the very heart of the town. Its architecture was conspicuously Western; with its stocky tower and gilded cupola, it could easily have been mistaken for a church.

There were the occasional unpleasant incidents. In 1922 a couple of the synagogue's windows were smashed, and in 1926 some tombs in the Jewish cemetery were daubed with paint. Yet these were isolated cases, swiftly dealt with by the authorities. In Pforzheim, the Jews had nothing to fear.

* * *

Wolfram was not yet born when the German economy suffered its first spectacular crash. In April 1923, exactly twelve months before his birth, it cost 24,000 Deutschmarks to buy one American dollar. By Christmas, that same dollar cost a staggering 4,200 trillion Deutschmarks. Reparation payments together with the loss of both the industrialised Lorraine and Silesia, had created an underlying instability. Inflation, soon to become hyperinflation, started to spiral out of control.

As instability led to catastrophe, the German mark was rendered worthless. Prices rose so rapidly that, when Marie Charlotte took her mother to Café Brenner in the centre of Pforzheim, she joked that she should pay for the drinks immediately lest she could not afford them by the time they had finished.

When the German economy crashed for the second time, in 1930, Wolfram was six years old and had just started his education in a state school that catered for the children of both rich and poor. While the wealthy still managed to make ends meet, the impoverished underclass suddenly found themselves reliant on canteens run by Quaker charities from America.

Life for the downtrodden became a succession of miseries. Wolfram paid an occasional visit to a neighbouring family where everyone was out of work and had to sit in pitch darkness every evening because they could no longer afford electricity.

In the face of adversity, some people became inventive in their quest to earn money. A long rap at the Aïchele front door signalled the arrival of the woman who called every few days with baskets of kindling wood for sale. She used to ask the forest lumberjacks for thin slices from the stumps of trees that had been felled, then split these into tiny pieces and go from house to house, trying to earn a little cash.

By the winter of that year, thousands of the town's workers were without a job. Every morning, long before it was light, bands of ragged and hungry individuals would head for the Work Bureau in the hope of getting temporary employment. They would stand close together in an orderly queue, waiting for it to open and taking extreme care not to lose their place lest someone else be given the work they desperately needed.

In apartment blocks in and around Pforzheim, men would gather in the stairwell each evening for heated discussions about which political party was best equipped to save the German economy. Some were Communists. Others threw their support behind those at the other end of the political spectrum, Adolf Hitler's National Socialist Party.

Such discussions frequently took place in the Pforzheim block where the young Wolfram was living at the time. The building was owned by a committed Socialist whose tenants included a Nationalist, a Jew and a Nazi, making it a microcosm of the new Germany. The Nazi occupant, Herr Kraft, used to wag his finger at Wolfram's father and tell him that Hitler was the only leader strong enough to impose his ideas on the country. Erwin, however, vehemently disagreed; he had no time for the jumped-up Austrian corporal, and remained a German Nationalist who believed that President Hindenberg alone could lead the country out of these difficult times.

Herr Kraft, an early enthusiast for Nazism, was

particularly proud of his role in establishing the Pforzheim branch of the party in the autumn of 1920, one of the first local offices in Germany. He also knew Wolfram's father well enough to realise that he would never support the Nazis and even cautioned him against signing up for membership. 'You mustn't join,' he used to say. 'They've got nothing to offer you. And they're too rough.' Having said that, he secretly confessed that he had joined because he relished the pub brawls in which Nazi thugs played a prominent role.

Herbert Kraft's enthusiasm for Hitler was not shared by many in Pforzheim. The notion of the Nazi Party coming to power seemed fanciful, for it was still very much on the margins of political life. Hitler had briefly shot to prominence in the wake of his abortive coup in 1923 when he had held hostage the ruling triumvirate of Bavaria in a Munich beer hall. This incident, later to be celebrated in Germany as the Beer Hall Putsch, was a failure. The army moved in to crush Hitler's 600 storm-troopers, killing sixteen of them in the process. Hitler himself was arrested three days later. Although he won many plaudits at his showcase trial and managed to escape the gallows, he realised that attempting to seize power by force was doomed to failure. Henceforth, he would attempt to win through the ballot box.

Yet even this strategy seemed unlikely to succeed. In the elections of May 1928, the Nazi Party had won a derisory 2.6 per cent of the vote. Although they managed to get twelve deputies into the Reichstag – among them Joseph Goebbels and Hermann Goering – it was cold comfort to the party leadership. The stark truth was that fewer than three out of every hundred Germans agreed with Hitler's conviction that he was the saviour of their nation.

To maximise their chances of success the Nazi political programme of 1930 had been carefully worded to tap into all the grievances of the day. Nationalistic, anti-Semitic and written in unadorned language, it was designed to appeal not just to men like Herbert Kraft, but right across the social spectrum. Point one, 'We demand the union of all Germans in a Great Germany,' was a view held by the great majority of the electorate. Point two, 'We demand . . . revocation of the peace treaties of Versailles,' was also a vote winner. Other points addressed immigration, corruption and land reform, issues that struck a chord with the overwhelming majority of the population.

The fifth point of the programme was more contentious. 'Only those of German blood . . . may be members of the nation. Accordingly, no Jew may be a member of the nation.' In a town where the Jewish population was well integrated into society, this seemed neither feasible nor fair.

Although Wolfram's father had no truck with such dogma, he, like so many of his contemporaries, had learned to despise the fledgling democracy of the Weimar Republic. Indeed, he increasingly blamed democracy for the chaotic state of affairs in Germany.

Hitler used every possible occasion to stress his intention of coming to power through the ballot box. In March 1930, he finally got his chance. The right-wing German chancellor, Heinrich Brüning, dissolved the Reichstag and called national elections, confident that the electorate would blame the centre parties for the economic crisis and vote, in their millions, for the German Nationalist Party.

It was a catastrophic error of judgment and one that was fully exploited by Hitler. The Nazis threw everything into the campaign, aware that if they could not succeed in a time of economic crisis, they would never manage to win an election.

In Pforzheim there was a feeling that change was on its way. In Wolfram's tenement, Herbert Kraft felt certain that the Nazis would at long last achieve a breakthrough. Even those tenants who did not support Hitler agreed that a radical solution was necessary. People were saying that things could not carry on as they were and that life could not get any worse, even under Hitler or the Communists. What everyone agreed upon was that Germany needed a strong leader.

The prospect of Communist rule terrified Pforzheim's middle classes. Whilst also unhappy about the anti-Semitism of the Nazis, most of them thought that this did not have to be taken too seriously. Being prepared to try anything, they felt that Hitler should at least be given the opportunity to show what he could do.

It was an opinion shared by 6.4 million Germans. When the election results were announced, the Nazi Party was revealed to have achieved a stunning success. With 18.3 per cent of the electorate and 107 seats in the Reichstag, it had become the second-largest party.

Wolfram, who was far too young to care about such matters, spent his spare time seated at the family table, producing intricate drawings of medieval village life. Every now and then, his mother would glance into the dining room and smile as she watched her young son hunched over a sheet of paper, lost in his own miniature world.

The farmsteads and churches in his drawings were inspired by trips to his relatives in the countryside around Freiburg, but the crowds of villagers who inhabited the pictures were conjured to life in young Wolfram's imagination – rough farmhands, hawkers and pedlars, burghers and merchants in floppy galliskins.

The quality of the draughtmanship astonished his parents' friends; indeed, they did not quite believe that Wolfram could have produced them without help. One of these visitors, Herr Tiehl, visited the family villa regularly to select one of Erwin's paintings to print in the magazine he owned. When he paused one day to look at what the young Wolfram was drawing, he was taken aback by his confident technique. The illustration in question depicted a Christmas market with festive stalls and decorations, and cauldrons of steaming food. In the background were half-timbered mansions blanketed with snow.

Herr Tiehl immediately asked whether he could print it in the Christmas issue of the magazine, paying Wolfram the princely sum of 25 Deutchsmarks.

These childhood pictures also provide a glimpse of the village of Eutingen as it appeared to a young boy. The surrounding hillsides were covered in orchards and tidy vineyards that stretched up the slopes in orderly parallel lines.

The centre of the village, a sleepy single street called Hauptstrasse, lay at the bottom of the hill, with a parish church and a handful of stores selling household goods, haberdashery and sweets. Here, too, was the local primary school attended by Wolfram, his brother and sister. There was also a *rathaus* or town hall – a grandiose description for the village offices.

From the centre of the village, a steep path called the Hohe Steig or High Path led up to the *künstler colonie* or artists' colony at the top of the hill. There were only six houses here, each encircled by large gardens. They were so off the beaten track that no one went there unless they were invited, which meant that the Eutingen hilltop could become the Aïcheles' private domain – isolated in its own bubble from the rest of Germany.

Over the years to come, a stream of eclectic friends, acquaintances and clients of Erwin would visit, safe in the knowledge that, once they were inside this magnificent home, conversation was free and open. Among them was Dr Schnurmann, a Jewish physician whose penchant for Hitler jokes would soon land him in hot water, and August Zorn, whose headstrong daughter would get into serious trouble after falling in love with an enforced Polish labourer. Yet another was Karl Weber, a senior public attorney, who would soon join the Nazi Party only to find himself prosecuting individuals who were good friends of the Aïcheles.

On their visits, Dr Schaaff and his Japanese wife captivated the children with tales of miniature artwork from from Schaaff's native land. Another visitor was a great-aunt with a huge collection of African spears and lances. Another was Dr Hillenbrandt, who had hacked through the jungles of equatorial Africa like some latter-day Livingstone.

Wolfram loved to chat with the adults and listen to their tales, and they, bemused to find a young lad so interested in their stories, would talk to him as if he were already a grown-up. Wolfram's parents were pleased to see their children conversing with these adult visitors. They wanted them to form their own opinions about the world.

Among the occasional guests at the Eutingen villa was an attractive young mother and her four young children. Martha Luise Rodi was very different to most guests of the Aïcheles. The daughter of one of the influential jewellery dynasties of Pforzheim, she had been brought up in bourgeois comfort in the centre of Pforzheim.

She might never have met Wolfram's parents had it not been for the fact that she and her husband, Max, attended the same parish church. The Christengemeinschaft, or Christian Community of Pforzheim, was centred on the teachings of the esoteric Austrian philosopher Rudolf Steiner, who held that the spirit in human beings could be guided towards the spirit in the universe.

The Pforzheim community was a tiny one, rarely more than thirty souls, and people knew one another well. Although Wolfram's father refused to attend, all the other members of the two families would go to the services most Sundays. On occasions, Frau Aïchele would invite Frau Rodi and her children back to her house for coffee and cake.

Those children were entranced by their visits to Eutingen – a little island that seemed to be adrift from the rest of the globe. Visual harmony meant everything to Wolfram's mother; even the children's toys were objects of beauty. And the family lit their house with candles, which in those days was deemed to be highly eccentric. Visitors were left with the impression that they were entering a very cultured atmosphere.

The Rodi boys, Frithjof and Peter, found it difficult to get to know Wolfram, with his funny interests and strange stockings. He seemed like a child who had dropped from another planet. The two brothers wanted to play hide-and-seek and other boyish games, but the young Wolfram was keener to tell them about the gothic altarpieces he had seen while out on his bike rides.

In the twilight years of the Weimar Republic, a shared outlook on life had already brought the Aïcheles and the Rodis into each other's orbit. Each night, the Rodi children would drift off to sleep as their father played his beloved Schumann on the piano, while in a little village on the other side of Pforzheim, Wolfram and his siblings would listen to Bach arias on their father's wind-up gramophone.

As darkness closed in, both families shared the feeling that difficult times lay just around the corner. Yet no one foresaw the fact that their idyllic world, so carefree and tolerant, was about to be thrust into a brutal and terrible future.

CHAPTER TWO

ENEMY OF THE STATE

'Anyone who stands in our way will be butchered.'

O n a sharp autumn dawn with a clear cobalt sky, Wolfram's mother could be heard calling down the corridor, urging her young sons to put on their boots. It was a beautiful Saturday morning, the perfect weather for a hike in the countryside.

On most days, the family would take the little lane that led downwards towards the centre of Eutingen, but on this particular morning they turned right, following the lane in a northerly direction. It curved upwards to the brow of the hill, which offered an open vista of apple orchards, meadows and gently undulating pastureland. It looked as if a great tapestry of greenery had been flung across the landscape and allowed to settle into natural bumps and vales.

In the early 1930s, the only noise to be heard from this hilltop was the twittering of birdsong and the whisper of the wind in the trees. The E52 motorway from Karlsruhe to Stuttgart, one of Hitler's more ambitious engineering projects, was not even on the drawing board.

Wolfram was eight years of age when he started to

accompany his mother on hikes to the nearby villages of Dürrn, Bauschlott and Ottisheim. These little farming communities seemed to belong to another century than the mechanised industries of nearby Pforzheim. In these years of economic decline (it was just two years after the Wall Street Crash) tractors and combine harvesters were still an unafford-able novelty. Wolfram recalls farmers traipsing out to the fields at harvest time accompanied by flocks of young children. The menfolk would scythe the sun-ripened corn by hand; it would then be chaffed and winnowed by their wimpled wives and adolescent daughters, just as it had been for centuries.

A few of the more prosperous farmers used oxen to haul their wagons back from the fields, but most were too poor to afford such a luxury. They would harness their milking cows to the yoke and stir the reluctant animals to motion with a strong crack of the whip.

Motor cars were a rare sight indeed during these walks in the countryside. Adolf Hitler's vision of every German family having its own vehicle must have seemed like a distant pipe dream to the inhabitants of Dürrn, Bauschlott and Ottisheim.

The massive Swabian farmsteads in these villages were a source of fascination to Wolfram. Framed from gigantic oak timbers, and held together by an elaborate jigsaw of mortise-joints and wooden pegs, they looked for all the world like upturned galleons. Their vast keels pointed upwards towards the clouds; their timber forecastles jutted forth at improbable angles, in defiance of gravity and logic. It was as if they had been left high and dry by the passing of some biblical flood.

The kitchens of these farms, blackened by centuries of soot, would set off a hungry rumble in young Wolfram's belly. Strings of smoked sausages hung from the beams and great knuckles of ham swung from the fireplace. There were jars of pickled beans, flagons of crisp Riesling and vats of fermenting sauerkraut; most of the villagers were self-sufficient in all but luxury goods.

Wolfram was particularly fascinated by the customs and traditions of village life, and he tried to remember every detail that he had seen – every vista and every farmstead. Then, upon returning home, he would sit himself at the dining-room table and, in painstaking detail, set them down on paper.

His passion for drawing consumed all his energies. In the classroom, he was a hapless pupil. Wolfram excelled at only one subject, handwriting, producing page after page of beautiful gothic script, but he was incapable of learning by rote the flighty poesies of Ludwig Uhland. Instead, he would stare into space and try to conjure images of the farmsteads he had seen on the previous weekend. So compulsive was his daydreaming that his teacher, Hulde Philip, despaired of his passing a single exam. She could not understand how he could spend hour after hour looking blankly at the ceiling.

Her attitude changed one day in the winter of 1932, when she was invited to the family villa and shown some of Wolfram's artwork. Like all the Aïcheles' other adult visitors, she was amazed by what she saw, suddenly realising that those long hours of daydreaming had brought forth rich fruit.

Peter and Frithjof Rodi, those occasional visitors to Eutingen, lived in an apartment in the centre of Pforzheim. Each evening, as twilight fell, they would lean out of the window to watch the political marches and processions that were becoming more and more a part of daily life.

The Pforzheim marches were small and provincial compared with those taking place in the capital and usually did not involve more than about one hundred men from the SA. The first part of the procession consisted of pipers and drummers, followed, at the back, by the brass band. It made quite a spectacle for the two young boys, who always hoped that the band would strike up a tune as it passed underneath the family window.

Peter, who was four years older than Frithjof, was allowed to go to bed that much later. At night, when it was completely dark, he would watch the torchlit processions making their way through the streets. One evening, he noticed that swastikas had started appearing on every building. There was a sudden emphasis on the populace coming together and uniting behind Hitler.

Hitler's star was indeed in the ascendant, a consequence of the profound political crisis now overtaking Germany. The Weimar Republic, which had become progressively unstable over the previous three years, seemed on the point of complete collapse.

'Will Schleicher Resign?' asked Pforzheim's local newspaper on Saturday, 28 January 1933 – a reference to the chancellor, Kurt von Schleicher, and his increasingly untenable hold on power. 'Hitler again in Berlin: today there will be extremely important talks at the offices of the German president.'

This was not the first time that Adolf Hitler had urged President Hindenburg to appoint him chancellor. For months he had been arguing that his popular following was sufficiently large to justify such an appointment. However, Hindenburg had repeatedly refused to sanction such a move, arguing that he could not 'transfer the whole authority of government to a single party'.

Since that exchange, the political crisis had intensified. Although Hindenburg remained adamantly opposed to Hitler's appointment, when his most trusted confidants argued in Hitler's favour – among them the former chancellor Franz von Papen – Hindenburg reluctantly relented. On Monday, 30 January, he summoned the leader of the Nazi Party to an audience. When Hitler emerged from this meeting, he was chancellor of Germany.

Whilst many politicians feared that Hitler would now attempt to establish a dictatorship, Franz von Papen shrugged off their concerns with a joke. 'You are wrong,' he told them. 'We've engaged him for ourselves.' He reminded them that the Nazis had been granted just two ministerial posts in the new government. 'Within two months, we will have pushed Hitler so far into a corner that he'll squeak.'

Wolfram's father did not share Franz von Papen's optimism. He was appalled by the news from Berlin: it was what he had feared all along. He remained convinced that Hitler was a troublemaker who would lead Germany back to the abyss of war.

In the first few hours of Hitler's chancellorship, all eyes were focused on Berlin. It quickly became apparent that Hitler intended to govern Germany in a radically different fashion from his predecessors. On the very evening of his appointment, his political comrade, Joseph Goebbels, organised a spectacular torchlit parade of brownshirts and

SS men. They marched with crashing feet and swastika flags – a precursor to the triumphant rallies that were to become a hallmark of the Nazi regime.

In these days before television, Goebbels recognised the propaganda value of such torchlit parades and he ordered them to be held in towns and cities across Germany. In Pforzheim, the local office of the Nazi Party attempted to emulate the Berlin extravaganza by organising their very own nocturnal fanfare.

Many of Wolfram's childhood friends and contemporaries stood in the streets that night, watching in awe as uniformed men carrying flaming torches marched through the town in celebration of Hitler's triumph. Suddenly, everyone seemed to be wearing uniform. And although the children were still too young to understand what was taking place, they could feel the renewed sense of hope and joy. People were saying that from now on things would look up.

For many German youngsters, joining the celebrations felt like signing up for a new religion. The Nazi leadership had great expectations of them; they were being implored to join forces with the new political elite and throw their youthful energies into building a great future for Germany.

On the morning after the election parade, a young Pforzheim schoolgirl, Hannelore Schottgen, was still drunk with enthusiasm. She and her friends greeted their teacher with 'Heil Hitler' when he entered the classroom. The teacher was not amused and reprimanded them. They should stop such nonsense, he said. What was taking place in Germany was not a joke.

For those who did not support the Nazis, there was a sudden feeling of ostracism from the mainstream. The

Aïchele family took no part in the Pforzheim celebrations
on the evening that Hitler became chancellor; Wolfram's
parents had no desire to witness the public euphoria.
Wolfram spent the hour before dinner feeding his father's
deer, as he did each day, and he also helped to carry buckets
of putrid meat to the workshop in the garden, where it
would be chopped into chunks, then tossed to the falcons
and other birds of prey.

In the evening breeze, a few snatches of martial music
could be heard drifting towards Eutingen from the Nazi
parade in the valley far below. Erwin, who did not want to
listen to it, chose a Beethoven symphony from his small
record collection and asked the young Wolfram to wind up
the gramophone.

For the first few weeks after the change of political leadership in Berlin, life in the Aïchele household was seemingly
unaffected. Friends continued to visit the family at their
Eutingen villa and the cycle of rural life remained
unchanged. This was still a time when itinerant shepherds
spent the chill winters wandering from farm to farm with
their flocks of sheep.

With the tentative arrival of spring, Marie Charlotte
started to take Wolfram on long country walks to show him
the many jewels in the countryside beyond Eutingen. One
day she led him on a four-hour hike across rolling farmland
to visit one of the greatest gems of medieval Swabia.

It was close to midday when they caught a glimpse of the
village of Tiefenbronn, which straddled a steep hump-
backed hill, its gabled farmhouses set into the contours like
a row of wonky teeth. On the crest of the hill, its

spire pointing sharply to the heavens, was the goal of their artistic pilgrimage: the gothic church of St Maria Magdalena. Its unassuming exterior betrayed no inkling of the rare treasures that lay inside.

The door opened with a clunk; mother and son stepped into the gloom. In those days there was no guardian and no entrance fee, no opening hours and no postcard stands. Tiefenbronn's marvels had yet to be revealed to the outside world. As Wolfram's eyes grew accustomed to the darkness, a spectacular array of wonders began to glitter through the shadows. Suspended at the far end of the nave was a medieval high altar of such scale and magnificence that it completely outshone the workaday architecture of the church.

In the hands of the master carpenter, whose identity had been lost to the centuries, the carved representation of Christ's crucifixion had been transformed into a veritable microcosm of medieval Swabian life. Peasants in coifs, maidens in homespun kirtles and impudent young shepherd lads: all had been tenderly carved from the unyielding oak. The ruddy cheeks and piercing blue eyes of John the Evangelist spoke of a Teutonic lineage; John the Baptist had the rugged air of a Swabian farmhand. The newborn lamb he was clutching might well have been born in the next-door farmyard.

And which local maiden had inspired the figure of Mary Magdalene? Her golden tresses and carnation-pink cheeks hinted at a playful coquette; her neat wimple, at a respectable piety.

There were other marvels to behold in the church of Tiefenbronn. Marie Charlotte led her small son over to a side altar painted by Lucas Moser, perhaps the most talented master craftsmen working in the late Middle Ages.

Moser's scenes from the life of Mary Magdalene represented one of the earliest and boldest adventures into perspective. Receding hills, silhouetted trees and a faraway shoreline: all were caught in the fading golden twilight.

Marie Charlotte watched Wolfram's reaction to the treasures of the church and was intrigued. No other eight-year-old boy would have spent the days that followed making faithful drawings of the gothic diptychs and polyptychs. It confirmed what she already suspected: that Wolfram was of a very different temperament to his contemporaries. He spent half his time living in another world.

Wolfram was indeed spellbound by his visit to Tiefenbronn; he had never imagined that such extraordinary artworks existed on his doorstep. No sooner had he returned home than he equipped himself with a block of wood, some chisels and an adze. Already harbouring vague dreams of one day becoming a master craftsman, he spent all his spare time trying to reproduce the exquisite visions he had seen in Tiefenbronn.

Wolfram and his siblings were too young to have realised that a political revolution had taken place in Berlin. The village school in Eutingen was unaffected by the change in leadership and the only time that Wolfram encountered Nazi brownshirts was when he accompanied his mother on shopping expeditions to Pforzheim.

Nevertheless, Hitler's inner circle was now hoping to capitalise on the general optimism that surrounded his appointment to the chancellorship. 'Wild frenzy of enthusiasm,' wrote Joseph Goebbels in his diary on the night of the Berlin parade. 'Prepare the election campaign.'

A national election had indeed been one of Hitler's preconditions for accepting the post of chancellor. Now, the date was set for 5 March. In the Aïchele household, there was a sudden flurry of excitement. Their cleaning lady, Frau Lehman, was a hardline Communist who had long expressed her desire to emigrate to Soviet Russia. Lacking money and resources, she had resigned herself to another year or two in rural Eutingen. Her great hope was that the German Communist Party, led by Ernst Thälmann, would win scores of seats in the forthcoming election.

She was passionately devoted to the cause. 'Vote Thälmann, Herr Aïchele,' she would say to Wolfram's father. 'All artists vote for Thälmann.'

There was some truth in this: many artists did indeed favour the Communists, but in this particular election, all who supported Thälmann were to find themselves unexpectedly deprived of the vote.

Hitler had never hidden his deep aversion to the Communists. 'Never, never will I stray from the task of stamping out Marxism,' he told supporters at an election rally. 'There can be only one victor: either Marxism or the German people.'

He soon found the pretext for crushing the rival ideology in quite spectacular fashion. On 27 February 1933, the Dutch Communist, Marinus van der Lubbe, set fire to the parliament building in Berlin. It was a lone act but a particularly destructive one. 'The Reichstag in Flames' was the headline in Erwin's Pforzheim newspaper on the following morning.

Hitler had rushed to the scene, forced his way into the burning building and stared into the sea of flames, seemingly mesmerised by the blaze. 'There will be no more mercy now,' he shouted to those who were with him. 'Anyone who stands in our way will be butchered. The German people won't have any understanding for leniency. Every Communist functionary will be shot where he is found . . .'

Four thousand Communists were indeed arrested, including most of the Reichstag deputies. Hitler then introduced a decree that suspended civil liberties and prevented any Communist candidate from standing in any future election. Overnight, the Aïcheles' cleaning lady was disenfranchised.

In putting his signature to the Decree of the Reich President for the Protection of People and State, Hitler was signing the death warrant of the old republic. It placed potentially draconian restrictions on personal liberty and the right of free assembly. It also permitted the state's intrusion into all postal and telephonic communications.

Although Hitler had produced no evidence of a Communist revolution, in one bold stroke he had taken control of the state. In a radio address on the morning after the Reichstag fire, Goering appealed to the entire German nation to vote in the election that was now only four days away.

They did so in their millions: at 88 per cent, voter turnout was unprecedented. Yet even in an atmosphere of violence and intimidation, the Nazis still failed to win an overall majority.

In the last election for many years to come, almost six out of every ten Germans voted against Hitler.

Wolfram's ninth birthday fell just a few weeks after the election. When he was given money by his parents, he knew exactly how he was going to spend it. In his first moment of free time, he cycled down into Pforzheim and went to the Bögel bookshop, which specialised in art books.

He had first visited the shop when he was six, dragging his mother inside so that he could look at the titles on display in the window. Two volumes had particularly caught his young eye. One had on the cover a reproduction of Andrei Rublev's famous icon of the Holy Trinity. The other displayed a Van Gogh painting of a man leading a donkey.

The bookshop's owner had been bemused and somewhat startled when the young Wolfram asked whether he could look at these books, but ever since, the boy had been one of the shop's most loyal customers. Each fortnight, he would cycle into town in order to plan his next purchase, paid for with his pocket money.

He usually headed straight to the shelves containing books on gothic art, but on the occasion of his ninth birthday his eye had been drawn to a more enticing prize. It was a large and expensive hardback about Pieter Bruegel and as Wolfram flicked through the pages he knew that this was what he wanted to buy.

Nervously he took it to the counter and asked the price. The shop's owner smiled sadly: it was 35 Reichsmarks – far beyond the budget of a small boy, even one with birthday money. Wolfram reluctantly put it back on the shelf, vowing to himself that one day, when he was rich, he would buy it. (Another twenty-five years would pass before he finally bought the book in a second-hand bookshop in Paris.)

He returned home to Eutingen wiser about the value of money but nonetheless disappointed. He was consoled by his father, who contacted all his artist friends and found that one of them, Professor Hillenbrandt, owned a copy of that very edition. He then arranged for Wolfram to visit the doctor's house in order to study the pictures.

That spring was warm and sunny and the villa in Eutingen was looking at its best. The newly planted wisteria flowered for the first time, its mauve blooms hanging down in clusters like scented pendulums, and on the trellised ironwork, miniature buds of unripe grapes dangled in jewel-like bunches.

Marie Charlotte prided herself on the riotous patchwork of pinks, reds and violets that spilled from the beds and borders. Each morning she would cut a dozen or more stems and arrange them into artful bunches for display in the entrance hall. She had studied botany and knew the names of all the flowers – both their common monikers and their Latin titles: *hyacinthus* and *xeranthemum* and all the different varieties of *tulipia*.

The somnolent pace of life in Eutingen belied the dramatic transformation that was taking place in provincial towns across the state of Baden. At dawn on 6 March 1933, just hours after the votes had been counted in the national election, local Nazi leaders raised the swastika on scores of public buildings in Pforzheim. Twenty-four hours later came the announcement that Robert Heinrich Wagner, a fanatical anti-Semite, had been appointed Reich commissar for Baden.

Politicians of the left and centre parties were horrified by Wagner's appointment and immediately lodged a complaint with the German Supreme Court in Berlin, but the court deemed itself powerless to overrule Hitler's choice.

Wagner travelled by train to the large industrial town of Karlsruhe, some twenty miles to the north-west of Pforzheim, to make a public address to a crowd of 3,000 enthusiastic SA and SS men. They roared their approval when Wagner, with great fanfare, unfurled an enormous swastika from the windows of his new ministry building. He then assumed full police powers over his new fiefdom and began an immediate purge of all the officers who were not sympathetic to the Nazi cause.

The Baden state government reacted by resigning en masse – a calculated political manoeuvre that would force the election of a new government. Ministers confidently predicted that they would increase their authority at the expense of the Nazis.

Their plan spectacularly backfired. Wagner used the crisis to seize control of the regional government, claiming key ministerial posts. Less than seventy-two hours after the election results had been announced, he was master of both Baden's government and police force.

With his piercing eyes and blond hair, Wagner looked the very epitome of a loyal Nazi. He had, indeed, been an early and fanatical convert to Nazism. In the spring of 1925, he had secured Hitler's permission to establish the Nazi Party in Baden; by the autumn of that year, he was already touring towns and villages, giving virulently racist speeches about the Jews. He saw Judaism as a disease – 'the source of all ills of its host nation' – and argued that serious diseases required radical cures.

Now that he was in a position of authority, his ruthlessness came to the fore. Socialist and Communist deputies were arrested, left-leaning newspapers were banned, and three penal camps were established. Pforzheim felt the full brunt of his ire: two of the town's papers, the *Freie Presse* and the *Pforzheimer Morgenblatt*, were shut down. The local mayor and other councillors were sacked. Two of the prominent Jewish members of the Chamber of Commerce were forced to resign.

Wagner also ordered a boycott of Jewish shops and encouraged demonstrations outside the homes and businesses of prominent Jews. These were small-minded and often unpleasant. On the evening of 1 April 1933, uniformed members of the SA pushed their way into the large Pforzheim department store, Schocken, and told shoppers to leave. Later that evening, they stuck posters on to the windows of the town's larger stores. 'Closed! Gone to Palestine!'

On the following morning, those same SA men reappeared and formed ranks outside the other big Jewish stores – the shoe shop, Edox, and the clothes shops Globus and Dreifus. In the Marktplatz, or main square, they also blocked access to Knopf, Kruger and Wolff & Kahn. Their placards declared, 'Those who still buy Jewish goods are good-for-nothings and traitors!'

Wagner announced with considerable relish that the state would soon pass laws to punish the Jews: 'Jewish influence in business and public life will be relentlessly cut back.'

He quickly put this into effect in his own fiefdom. All Jewish doctors and dentists were excluded from Baden's social security system, which meant that their patients were no longer entitled to reimbursement for prescription drugs. Jewish lawyers were prohibited from even entering the courthouse – a fast track to financial ruin.

The momentous political transformation of Baden – and of Germany – had its first direct effect on the Aïchele household within a few weeks of Hitler becoming chancellor. Wolfram's father was brought news that Pforzheim's free-masonry lodge, of which he had been a member for many years, was to be closed. Its membership was forbidden from gathering and the lodge itself was to cease functioning.

The regime further announced that all masons who had not left their lodges in January 1933 were to banned from ever joining the Nazi Party – a stricture that Wolfram's father exploited to the full. Over the coming years, whenever he was quizzed as to why he, a state employee, had not joined the party, he answered that had failed to leave his Masonic lodge in time and was therefore not eligible to become a member.

Such an argument was not without danger. Former free-masons found themselves increasingly targeted by the Nazi regime; by 1935, Reinhard Heydrich, chief of the Security Police, was calling them 'the most implacable enemies of the German race'.

The changes to the political situation in Baden had another direct effect on Erwin. For years, he had made a steady income from his illustrations for a well-known hunt-ing magazine. Now, without any warning, his contract with the magazine was abruptly terminated. Within days, the publication had disappeared from the news-stands.

Erwin did not have to wait long to discover the reason why the magazine had been banned. The publisher was a prominent Jewish businessman and Goering had ordered its publication to be suspended.

This only served to increase Erwin's hatred of all Nazi politicians. He started referring to them as a disgusting bunch who meddled in other people's lives.

In the new Germany there was no possibility for redress and no avenue for complaint. The regime had already warned that anyone who challenged its decisions would be severely, ruthlessly punished.

CHAPTER THREE

A VISIT FROM THE FÜHRER

'So many people . . . his car could advance
only at walking pace.'

T he young Wolfram was fidgeting in his seat in Pforzheim's picture house. It was spring 1934, and an exciting new film was about to be screened.

The audience in the auditorium was small, for the movie was not to everyone's taste. Wolfram, however, was desperate to see it and had spent the previous two days begging his parents to accompany him.

At long last the curtains went up and the title flickered on to the screen: *Man of Aran* by Robert Flaherty. It was a documentary chronicling the hardships of daily life in the remote Aran Islands.

Wolfram was fascinated from the opening scene. The seascapes of western Ireland and the rich local folk traditions left a deep impression on him. The lives of these people seemed so strange and exotic: it was as if they hailed from another planet. Wolfram stored the images in his mind to use them in his pictures.

A short time after watching the film, he found his own

home playing host to a colourful stranger. One morning, his father and an artist friend named Herr Siebert were wandering through Pforzheim when they were struck by an odd-looking tramp slouched on a bench. He had a most quixotic face, craggy and angular, and Herr Siebert expressed a desire to paint him. When the tramp agreed to pose as a model, Erwin suggested that he come and stay in Eutingen for a few days.

Wolfram was a little surprised when his father arrived home with the tramp and even more taken aback when he was given the guest room. He suspected that such a thing would never have happened, were it not for the fact that his mother was away at the time.

Yet it was a gesture typical of Erwin. He cared little for what friends and neighbours might think, nor, for that matter, was he in the slightest bit bothered about other people's opinions, political or otherwise. What mattered for him, above and beyond everything else, was whether individuals looked interesting; whether their unusual faces or unexpected expressions appealed to his artistic eye. The racial conformity of Nazism left him completely cold – indeed, it was a complete anathema to his artistic sensibilities.

Adolf Hitler had been chancellor for less than five months when a dramatic event occurred in central Pforzheim. Throughout the morning and afternoon of 17 June, adolescent members of the Hitler Youth had been combing libraries, bookshops and houses, including those of their own parents, in search of literature deemed unsuitable by the Nazi regime. Now, as darkness fell, the mountain of books was to be ceremoniously burned in the Marktplatz.

The exercise had, according to the local newspaper, been a triumph. 'The collection of "dirt and shame" was such a huge success,' said the *Pforzheimer Anzeiger*, 'that the Hitler Youth had to use lorries belonging to the municipal authorities [to transport all the books].'

Not for the first time, the Nazis had turned to the German youth in order to implement their policies. 'Our young people have been given a mission,' continued the newspaper, 'and they have showed themselves worthy of the task . . . now, the whole nation must be convinced of the necessity of the fight against un-German writing.'

Wolfram did not see the book burning, nor, indeed, did his parents. They certainly would have had no desire to witness such an act. Ever since the introduction of the Decree of the Reich President for the Protection of People and State in early 1933, many of Marie Charlotte's favourite authors, including Thomas Mann, had been condemned. The new legislation placed strict controls over the publishing industry and gave the Gestapo virtually unlimited powers to confiscate literature considered undesirable. 'Printed matter whose content is calculated to endanger public order,' read the decree, 'can be confiscated by the police.'

The great pyre was to be lit at exactly nine o'clock in the evening on Saturday, 17 June. Although it started pouring with rain just as the crowds began to assemble, this did nothing to diminish the pageantry of the occasion. The youth leaders marched into the Marktplatz in military formation and were met by city officials, including the head of the town's police force. A local brigade leader named Schenkel then made a speech in which he heaped praise upon Pforzheim's youth.

'Their mission,' he told the crowd, 'was full of honour and proved that the National Socialist Party was right in putting its trust in the young generation.' As his address came to an end, one of the Nazi dignitaries ceremoniously placed Erich Remarque's novel, *All Quiet on the Western Front*, on the very top of the pyre.

'The flames ate deep into the pile of books . . . the buildings around the Marktplatz were lit in a ghostly way and the onlookers were bathed in a red glow.' And then – hesitant at first, but then much louder – a cry went up from the crowd.

'A chorus of voices began chanting an incantation – *"undeutsche schrift verbrenne!* – Burn, un-German writing, burn!"' As the mob continued to shout, a Communist flag was thrown on to the top of the pyre.

'The difficult times went up with the flames,' wrote the journalist covering the story. 'New life, new writing, new faith will blossom from the ashes.'

Wolfram's parents became aware that Hitler had introduced an element of fear into every aspect of daily life within weeks of his becoming chancellor. Just a short time earlier, Erwin had spoken quite openly of his contempt for the Nazis, especially when in the company of Herr Becher, the urbane clergyman from the family's parish. Now, however, whenever the two men spoke of the dangers that Hitler posed, Becher would get up from his chair and close the dining-room door so that Clara, the Aïcheles' new maid, could not eavesdrop.

Clara was indeed nosy and was forever listening in on their conversations. Believing Hitler to be a godsend for

Germany, she was particularly infuriated by Becher's strident opinions. 'Frau Aïchele,' she said one day to Wolfram's mother, 'if Herr Becher says such nasty things about Hitler one more time, I'll leave and won't come back.'

There were many other subtle but disquieting changes. Goebbels had declared that the new government 'no longer intends to leave people to their own devices'. True to his word, Nazi ideology was brought to the fore in every sphere of personal activity. The regime banned the traditional Swabish greeting, '*Grussgott*' or 'God be with you', which had been used in southern Germany for centuries. Henceforth, everyone was obliged to say 'Heil Hitler' when they met with acquaintances in the street.

Wolfram's parents avoided greeting close friends in such a fashion, but it was a different matter when Erwin went to work. All state employees were obliged to used the new form of address, 'raising their right arm . . . while at the same time saying out loud: Heil Hitler'.

It became apparent that the regime intended to impose itself on the calendar too. Hitler's appointment as Reich Chancellor (30 January) became a holiday; the refounding of the Nazi Party (24 February) was a day of festivity; and Hitler's birthday (20 April) was to become a time of national rejoicing.

Particularly upsetting to Wolfram's parents was the discovery that names of streets were being constantly changed. The principal thoroughfare in the north of Pforzheim was renamed Adolf Hitler Avenue and one of the larger high schools in the town was also named after the Führer. There was Avenue Hermann Göring (along with a Göring High School), as well as a newly renamed Goebbels School and a

Horst Wessel School – the latter named in honour of the Nazi activist murdered three years earlier.

The regime also began replacing the old religious festivals with their pagan equivalents. Just five days after the book burning, in the summer of 1933, the authorities in Pforzheim organised a big festival to celebrate the solstice. Many young lads dressed up in uniform for the occasion and prepared to join in the celebrations. So, too, did the young girls of Pforzheim. Among them was Hannelore Schottgen, who was deeply impressed by the flags, the burning torches and the military music. She was no less impressed by a dynamic young fanatic who explained to the crowd that the Führer was awakening old Germanic traditions. He added that the Nazi Party wanted to encourage people to learn about the roots of the Aryan race and the blood of their ancestors.

A huge bonfire was then lit. The assembled youths held hands in the growing darkness and sang haunting songs about the old Germany. Young Hannelore found herself profoundly moved by the thought that at that very moment, all over Germany, young boys and girls were gathered together to celebrate their country's rich Germanic past.

Wolfram and his brother were not among the celebrants of the solstice. Wolfram, who detested uniforms, thought the mustard-brown colour offensive. His refusal to have anything to do with the festivities greatly pleased his parents, but his non-attendance was the exception to the rule. All the rest of the Pforzheim youth – along with boys and girls from the surrounding villages – turned out for the pagan festival.

The newly awakened interest in Germanic traditions was

matched by a corresponding adulation for Adolf Hitler. The cult of the Führer had been an integral part of Goebbels' propaganda machine from the very beginning. By the summer of 1933, portraits of Hitler began appearing in every shop in Pforzheim: looking strict, thoughtful, smiling with children or playing with his dogs. To young Hannelore's eyes, it was as if you could no longer walk down a street without seeing a dozen or more images of their leader.

On Wednesday, 13 September, Hitler appeared in person in Pforzheim. The occasion for his visit was a devastating fire that had swept through the village of Oeschelbronn, just a few miles away. Hundreds of timbered houses had been consumed by the conflagration, leaving families homeless and destitute.

Hitler arrived by plane in Karlsruhe and was met by a phalanx of local Nazi dignitaries. Among them was Robert Wagner, who led the Führer through the city to the accompanying music of a martial band. Once Hitler had greeted the adulatory crowd, his entourage set off for Pforzheim.

'Thousands of schoolchildren lined his route and next to them were tens of thousands of people, all cheering the Führer and waving at him,' recorded Karlsruhe's local newspaper. 'There were so many people that his car could advance only at walking pace.'

Among the villages that Hitler passed through was Eutingen, home to the Aïcheles. All their neighbours had turned out to watch, their numbers swelled by the inhabitants of nearby villages. Soon, the hedgerows and embankments were packed with supporters, enthusiasts and the merely curious. 'The National Socialist divisions and schoolchildren were standing in all the villages,' reported the newspaper, 'even though it was stormy and there had been a lot of rain.'

There was a huge propaganda effort on the part of the local Nazi Party in Eutingen. All the schools were closed for the day and the Aïcheles, like everyone else in the village, were given details of Hitler's schedule so that they could be outside to cheer him on.

Wolfram was delighted to discover that there was no school; it gave him the whole day to draw and paint. Neither he nor his parents had any interest in seeing Hitler. Erwin spent the day in his workshop and Wolfram embarked on another pencil study of a medieval market town.

Only later that evening did Erwin and Marie Charlotte learn that their absence from the cheering crowds had been noted by many people. A number of their neighbours thought their behaviour egotistical and unpatriotic.

Erwin dismissed such nonsense with a shake of his head, taking the opportunity to remind Wolfram not to follow others like sheep.

Christmas Eve, 1933, was a sombre affair. Wolfram and his siblings spent the morning in the garden, decorating all the tombs of the family dogs with miniature Christmas trees. Then, as evening fell, Wolfram's mother trudged through the snow to the festive service at their church in Pforzheim.

The parish pastor, Otto Becher, celebrated the service with as much joy as he could muster, but the little congregation was deeply troubled by subtle changes that the Nazi regime was introducing to the festive season.

The traditional *weihnacht* or holy night of Christmas had

been renamed *rauhnacht* or rough night, emphasising the pagan festival of the winter solstice. The popular devotion of St Nikolaus had also been paganised. The bishop-saint was stripped of his white-and-gold vestments and deprived of his crook. Now, he became a secular Father Christmas, a bearded man dressed in red.

Wolfram's parents zealously guarded their family traditions and, in the privacy of their own home, refused to change the way in which they celebrated the festive season. So, too, did their church friends, the Rodis. However, some families in Pforzheim did their best to conform to the strictures imposed by the Nazis.

Hannelore Schottgen found Christmas that year very different from previous ones. Although houses and community halls were still decorated with Christmas tree branches, as in previous years, instead of singing carols, people listened to Beethoven and sang old songs about the solstice, along with other Germanic winter songs that had no reference to Christmas.

Everyone was describing Hitler as a unique and very special person and there was universal agreement that God was wise indeed for having given the beloved Führer to Germany. A new phrase was on every lip that year: '*Ein Volk, ein Reich, ein Führer*'.

The Christian Community of Pforzheim was an early target of the Nazi regime. What particularly shocked parishioners was the coarse manner in which it occurred. For years, the town's daily paper, *Pforzheimer Anzeiger*, had been a reliable source of news. Conservative in outlook, it was the favoured choice of the town's bourgeoisie.

No sooner was Hitler in power than the editor threw in

his lot with the Nazi Party and the newspaper became a mouthpiece of the new order.

One morning, the Aïcheles and the Rodis opened their morning paper and were appalled to read a vitriolic article attacking Rudolf Steiner, upon whose philosophy their church was founded. It said that Steiner was a Jew – which was untrue – and added that he was a liar like none other. It was a decisive moment for the Rodi parents. They never again bought the *Pforzheimer Anzeiger*.

The article marked the beginning of a sustained assault on traditional Christian teaching that would culminate in Hitler's decree that teachers change the text of the Bible. The sentence, 'Salvation comes from the Jews', which Jesus says to the Samaritan woman, was unacceptable in the eyes of the Nazis. Schools across Germany were instructed to delete this line from the Bible, as well as from all books of biblical history.

Young Frithjof Rodi was a pupil in his father's class on the day that this was put into effect. Max Rodi had to instruct his pupils to bring their copies of the Bible to the front of the class. Then, with his own fountain pen, he had to put a line through the offending sentence.

Max, however, could not bring himself to do this without passing comment. He got the whole class to read aloud the offending passage; this was followed by a long discussion as to what Christ meant by it. Then, when the discussion was finally over, he told the children that he had been ordered to delete it from their copies.

In Wolfram's class, the new ideology was also beginning to bite. One afternoon, there was a visit to his school by a German émigré newly arrived from the Volga. Like so many ethnic Germans, the man's family had lived there for more than two centuries. Now, in the wake of Stalin's persecution, they were flooding back to Germany.

The man brought pictures of starving and malnourished children, and told Wolfram and his classmates that the Russians were deliberately denying them food. There were endless images of corpses – entire cartloads of them – and he recounted harrowing stories of cannibalism. The photographs were so vivid that Wolfram had nightmares for weeks afterwards.

The Nazis wanted children to grow up with an intrinsic fear of Communism, but exhibiting these gruesome photographs to the pupils at the school angered many of their parents.

Wolfram's mother and grandmother were horrified when Wolfram told them what he had been shown at school that day. Both of them were already very anti-Nazi. This only served to intensify their hostility.

In the summer of 1934, Wolfram's father decided to take his two sons to the North Sea coast for three weeks' holiday. It was a spot that Erwin loved – the windswept island of Hallig, close to the Danish coast. The three of them lodged with a family of farmers who lived in a quirky hilltop house. The boys played at being Robinson Crusoe while Erwin spent his time painting.

No sooner were they back in Eutingen than Wolfram's favourite uncle, Walter, brought news that daily life had taken a turn for the worse in the time they had been away. Pforzheim's Jews had come under attack from the Nazi regime and were in a state of despair. Their shops were boycotted, their livelihoods put at risk. The head of the Baden Synagogue Council, a certain Dr Moses, stated that living under the new Nazi dictatorship made one feel 'as if one is in front of a state of rubble'.

It was almost a year before the introduction of the notorious Reich Citizenship Law, yet one respectable Pforzheim family had already fallen foul of the regime. Werner Becker – son of one of the town's Protestant vicars and well known to both the Aïchele and Rodi families – had fallen in love with Margot Bloch, the Jewish daughter of a local lawyer.

The banns were published on 13 May 1935, an event that signalled an escalation in their problems. A few days later the young Becker read in a Berlin newspaper that a state functionary in Pforzheim had, for the first time since Hitler came to power, refused permission for an Aryan to marry a Jew. To his horror, Becker realised that the article was referring to him.

A couple of days later, the local Pforzheim newspaper picked up the story. Under the headline, *'Rassenschande'*, or 'Race Shame', it described Becker as 'an enemy of the state and a disgusting adversary to the Nazi Party' who had sold himself to an alien race.

Each subsequent day, the newspaper carried articles that condemned him for his choice of bride while praising the state functionary who had put a stop to the marriage. That same functionary received official congratulations from the Reich Minister of Justice.

The young couple's love was only strengthened by the abuse that was daily heaped upon them. Determined to marry, and revolted by the new Germany, they fled first to Switzerland and then to Argentina.

Wolfram's parents followed the story with heavy hearts, yet this was by no means an isolated case. Indeed, it marked the beginning of a dramatic increase in state-sponsored activity against the town's Jewish population.

One day, Hannelore Schottgen accompanied her mother, Frau Haas, into the centre of town for groceries. Large groups of SA men were standing at the entrance to one of the Jewish-owned supermarkets with big posters that read: 'Germans be careful: Don't buy in Jewish shops: The Jews bring bad luck.'

Frau Haas turned to her young daughter and said: 'Well, don't look at them. I'm going to go shopping where I want. They can't forbid me.'

What she had not realised was that two of the men standing outside the store were taking photographs of everyone going inside. She returned home with her shopping and quite forgot the incident, but she was soon in for a rude awakening. At the cinema that evening, the main film was preceded by pictures of all the people who had shopped at the town's Jewish-owned department stores.

The photographs were shown with captions such as 'This lady shows no shame: she still buys her provisions in Jewish-run stores,' or 'This man is a slave to the Jews – he still shops there.'

Now it was Frau Haas's turn to be shamed. Her husband's employer phoned that very evening to tell them about the film. Although the photo was a little blurred, he said that it looked very much like Frau Haas, and warned her to be more careful in future. 'The wife of a German educator,' he said, 'does not buy in Jewish shops.'

From this point on, young Hannelore was sent to do the shopping on her own as the Gestapo were forbidden from taking pictures of children.

Among the well-known figures in the Jewish community was Wolfram's uncle, Walter, a supporter of the now-banned Communist Party. Eccentric and uncommonly erudite, he had studied theology at university with the vague thought of becoming a priest. As his fascination increased with the languages of the Middle East – Arabic and Hebrew – he changed his mind and became a specialist in the latter.

He often went to the synagogue in those early years of the 1930s, not because he was particularly religious but because he loved the ceremonies surrounding Judaism. He also had great respect for those who were earnest about their faith and practised it with conviction.

Although it was not the most auspicious of times to develop a passion for Judaism, Uncle Walter became greatly sought after in the Jewish milieu. Jews across Germany had seen the way the political wind was blowing and had decided to sell their properties, quit the country and rebuild their lives in British-controlled Palestine. Herein lay a problem. The British required potential settlers to speak Hebrew, something that was beyond the capabilities of most bourgeois Jews. Walter suddenly found himself much in demand as teacher of classical Hebrew.

One family who had taken the decision to leave was the Guggenheims, who ran an elegant hat shop in central Pforzheim. Young Hannelore Schottgen bumped into them one evening as she and her father walked past the local synagogue.

Herr Guggenheim came over and greeted them cordially, but he did not make his usual little jokes. Indeed, he was very grave as he broke the news that his family had opted to emigrate to Palestine.

Hannelore's father went very quiet. 'But that's not possible,' he said to Herr Guggenheim. 'You can't leave everything behind and quit your homeland because of stupid propaganda.'

Herr Guggenheim shook his head, confessing that he was scared for his family. 'Read the newspapers,' he said.

The departure of the Guggenheims was shortly followed by an exodus of other Jewish families. The Salamons, owners of a luxury lingerie store, were the next to go. Then Doctor Weill, a well-respected Pforzheim lawyer, announced that he, too, was emigrating. This proved the last straw for Hannelore's father.

'I can't believe that Weill also wants to leave,' he said when he heard the news. 'I can't understand why they're all leaving.'

The Aïcheles' Jewish friends – or those with Jewish origins – were also getting out of Germany. Herr Gradenwitz, one of the pastors at their church, moved to Holland. Dr Schnurmann prepared to go after being jailed for several days in Mannheim prison. His crime was to have been spotted (and promptly denounced for) reading a book of jokes about Hitler that he had bought in Basle.

The number of Jews wishing to emigrate to Palestine was still small in 1934 but it was to increase dramatically in the following year, after the introduction of the Reich Citizenship Law, which was designed to safeguard the purity of German blood.

'Marriages between Jews and citizens of Germany or kindred blood are forbidden,' declared Hitler in a landmark speech to the Reichstag. In one short sentence, Jews had become outsiders in German society.

Hitler claimed the law was necessary for the restoration of blood purity. Other clauses prohibited Jews from employing German-born domestic servants and from flying the national flag from their houses.

The legislation divided Jews into different categories: among them were full Jews; *mischlinge* or part Jews of the first degree (those with two Jewish grandparents); and part Jews of the second degree, who had one Jewish grandparent.

The reaction of Pforzheim's Jewish community to such events ranged from despair to outrage. Their difficult situation was made even worse by Gauleiter Robert Wagner, who allowed the courts to start tampering with the legal rights of Jews. The court of appeal in Karlsruhe won the dubious distinction of being the first German court to grant a divorce on racial grounds. A Heidelberg man had filed for divorce from his Jewish wife because, he said, he 'had not known about the full concept of this race' when they were married.

Soon after this infamous case, Wagner allowed state courts to ask 'racial experts' like Professor von Verschuer of Frankfurt's Institute of Heredity and Racial Hygiene whether or not someone was Jewish. In one notorious case, the Karlsruhe court ruled that a boy was a Jew 'because he looked like a Jew'.

A new law required all families to fill out a *stammbuch* or family record book with the names, dates and religion of their ancestors stretching back several generations. As people flocked to Pforzheim's archives to check birth certificates and baptismal records, some people learned to their surprise – and often dismay – that they had Jewish antecedents.

One of Wolfram's distant cousins was married to a Jewish man, albeit a non-practising one with so little interest in his faith that he had never even told his wife about his erstwhile religion. It was only when she accompanied him to a family funeral in Vienna that she realised that he – and, by extension, her young daughter – had Jewish blood flowing through his veins. In danger of falling foul of the regime's anti-Semitism, the family took great pains to conceal their Jewish origins.

In this they were successful: their daughter's blonde hair and classic Germanic features would later see her celebrated by the Hitler Youth as an outstanding example of Aryan purity, an irony that was lost on everyone except her parents.

CHAPTER FOUR

FLYING THE NAZI FLAG

'Be careful or you'll be sent to Dachau.'

I n the winter of 1934, Wolfram's maternal grandfather died. Two weeks later, his maternal grandmother also passed away, ostensibly of a broken heart. Yet there is a sense in which both of them had chosen the time of their passing, no longer feeling at ease in the new Germany. Marie Charlotte's father had, in the late 1920s, been supportive of Adolf Hitler's appointment as chancellor. As a general in the army, although a retired one, he saw the need for a strong leader, but the Rohm putsch and the brutal violence that followed had repelled him. Nazi Germany was no longer a country in which he could take any pride.

The death of Wolfram's grandmother, Johanna, came as a particular blow. She had nourished Wolfram's passion for gothic art, whisking him off to Freiburg to see the sculpted masterpieces of Germany's medieval heritage. She had also encouraged him in his drawing, aware that he had a precocious talent for draughtsmanship.

Wolfram's grandparents had lived in a substantial property in the village of Uffhausen, near Freiburg. Its salons and parlours were filled with an eclectic gallimaufry of antiques: high-backed Louis XIV dining chairs, rustic farmstead trunks, settles and Palatine sideboards, samovars and posnets, pitchers and goblets, and homespun folk art that dated back to the eighteenth century. Now, many of these precious heirlooms were brought to Eutingen where they lent a further splendour to the villa. In difficult times and in increasingly desperate circumstances, Marie Charlotte clung to such objects of beauty. Antiques, freshly cut flowers and classical music brought her solace in these troubled years.

Wolfram shared his mother's love of old things; indeed, his interest in heirlooms and antiques would develop into a passion. It had been sparked by a stay with cousins in Brunswick who owned a rambling villa. Its darkened salons were full of old oak and polished mahogany, every cabinet and bench steeped in history. Wolfram returned to Eutingen clutching at the shadows of his medieval forbears.

When he learned that neighbours in Eutingen also had a house stuffed with rare antiques, he begged his parents to ask if he could be shown around. The two elderly ladies who lived there were a little taken aback when Wolfram's mother enquired as to whether her eleven-year-old son could be given a guided tour. They were no less perplexed when Wolfram began examining every object with the greatest scrutiny, trying to work out when it had been made and from which part of Germany it originated.

They assumed that their young visitor would soon tire of their inlaid tables and marquetry chests. However, Wolfram spent the better part of the afternoon in the house and later told his mother that he had scrutinised every item of furniture – and seen every room – except the toilet. When Marie

Charlotte repeated this to the ladies, they invited Wolfram back for a second visit and made good the deficit.

That summer, the summer of 1935, Wolfram's father decided to escape the oppressive atmosphere of Pforzheim and take his two sons, together with the family's French lodger, on a hike along the banks of the River Neckar. His daughter, Gunhild, just seven years old, was considered too young for such a trip. Erwin wanted to show the boys the castellated citadel of Bad Wimpfen, one of the most arresting sights in the whole of Baden.

Perched atop a thundering bluff of rock, Bad Wimpfen had once been the summer pleasure palace of the mighty Hohenstaufen dynasty. Eight centuries earlier, Emperor Frederick Barbarossa had chosen this neglected backwater as his country retreat – a place for hunting and carousing with vassals from across the Holy Roman Empire.

Wolfram was spellbound by the remnants of the citadel with its vertiginous ramparts, machicolated battlements and lofty pinnacles. No sooner had he and his brother returned home than they began re-creating Bad Wimpfen in miniature. Diminutive farmsteads and peasant hovels, held together by stone and cement, began to encroach on the lawn of the lower garden in Eutingen.

When the weather closed in, they continued their model-making indoors, creating an entire medieval burgh out of matchboxes, cartons and old scraps of wood. As Wolfram worked on his village in the downstairs salon, he peopled it with the peasants and pilgrims whose stunted frames and bearded jowls he had glimpsed in the candlelit retables of the local churches. Tonsured abbots and buskined farm-hands, franklins, pedlars and wizened apothecaries: all were conjured to life in Wolfram's miniature Nibelungen world.

'*Wolfram! Mittagessen! Lunch!*' A shout from Clara the maid ought to have broken the spell, but Wolfram was still in a trance, absorbed in his handiwork. When her call failed to summon him and his brother to the dining room, she went to fetch them and later eulogised Wolfram's work to Herr Becher, who had come to Eutingen that very day for his luncheon with the family.

'Oh, just look at those model houses! What a wonderful thing the boys have created!

'Wolfram, your model village is fantastic! And so well crafted. You really *must* give it to the Führer for his birthday. Don't you think so, Herr Becher?'

Hitler was riding high in popularity by the mid-1930s. The economy was stirring at last and unemployment was steadily falling. There was a feeling among many in Pforzheim that Germany was regaining its standing in the world.

However, not all was quite as it seemed. Propaganda and media manipulation had put a highly attractive gloss to what was actually a very modest economic recovery. Nor was the reduction in unemployment anything like as dramatic as the official figures suggested. The ostensible fall in the number of people out of work, from 6 million in 1933 to 2.5 million in 1935, belied a more complex picture.

Short-term contracts, the exportation of the young unemployed to the countryside (part of the so-called Voluntary Labour Service) and massive financial incentives to put women back in the home all helped to distort the figures.

Prestige projects, such as the building of autobahns, featured heavily in Nazi propaganda and gave the impression of a government working tirelessly to create new jobs. Yet the much vaunted road-building programme involved at its peak a mere 84,000 people.

Hitler had also won many plaudits for bringing an end to the street violence of previous years. In the last days of June 1934, he had moved to crush the power of the increasingly wayward SA. Its leader, Ernst Röhm, was shot, along with his closest advisors during the Night of the Long Knives, which provided the Nazis with an opportunity to get rid of many of their chief critics. Kurt von Schleicher, Hitler's predecessor as chancellor, was shot dead by the SS, as were others considered enemies of Nazism. 'Shoot them down . . . shoot . . . shoot at once,' screamed Goering as he studied a list of names. Eighty-five people were executed without trial, including twelve Reichstag deputies.

Hitler took full responsibility for the killings, arguing that they were necessary for preserving internal security. 'I gave the order to shoot those parties mainly responsible for this treason . . .' he said. 'Every person should know for all time that if he raises his hand to strike out at the State, certain death will be his lot.'

Many in Pforzheim were willing to excuse Hitler for the night of reckoning, but not everyone was convinced that he was putting the country on the right track. Among the dissenters were all of the parishioners worshipping at the Aïchele's local church – and with good reason. In November 1935, Reinhard Heydrich, director of *Third Reich* security, issued a decree that banned Rudolf Steiner's anthroposophical movement. All property belonging to the society was confiscated and the founding of any organisation to replace it was strictly forbidden. Heydrich had acted, he said, because the Steiner movement had 'an international outlook and has links with foreign freemasons, Jews and pacifists'.

He criticised Steiner for promoting the individual over society, something that ran counter to the basic premise of Nazi ideology, adding: 'It has nothing whatsoever to do with the National Socialist rules on education.' Heydrich considered the entire network to be 'an enemy to the state'. By implication, all former members, including Wolfram's parents, were enemies too.

In the early years of the Third Reich, Erwin and Marie Charlotte were able to avoid the impact of many of the regime's harshest strictures, largely because their house stood apart from its neighbours and was surrounded by an enclosed garden. It was a very different story for their church friends, the Rodis. Still living in an apartment in the heart of Pforzheim, they came under increasing surveillance.

For young Frithjof Rodi, the *blockleiter* or block leader was the worst daily irritant. He was the lowest in the Nazi hierarchy in Pforzheim but the most invidious of them all, preying on every detail of people's lives.

Most block leaders had about fifty households under their supervision. Their task was to provide a link between the national party and the population at large. They were also charged with promoting party ideology while spying on those living in their patch.

To Frithjof's eyes, they represented a constant danger, capable of denouncing people for any number of minor misdemeanours, such as not having a picture of Hitler in the house or not hanging out the swastika on appointed days.

Those who contravened party strictures risked internment in a concentration camp, the nearest one to Pforzheim being Dachau. The threat of Dachau hung over everyone in the area as a permanent menace. Unlike the extermination camps of later years, which were kept a strict secret, the concentration camps were frequently mentioned in the press. The regime wanted the populace to know that they would be severely punished if they did not conform.

The young Rodi children used to taunt each other with: 'You'd better be careful or you'll be sent to Dachau.' They never found out what went on there, for the few inmates who were released never spoke of what had happened to them. It was too perilous to talk of such things.

The block leader who oversaw the Rodi tenement had noticed that the family attended the Christian Community each Sunday morning. He had also discovered that Frithjof's parents were active members of the maligned Rudolf Steiner movement. When he learned that they held weekly meetings at their apartment with local activists, he informed the Gestapo.

The Gestapo acted immediately, approaching the owner of the flat directly below to ask whether they could plant listening devices in his ceiling. However, the tenant was an old-fashioned high-school teacher with a strict sense of moral propriety. Although not on particularly friendly terms with the Rodis, he refused to grant access to the Gestapo out of indignation at their tactics. He also warned Max Rodi of what had taken place.

Wolfram's parents were as hostile to the Nazi regime as

Max and Martha Luise. They also shared a determination to muddle through day by day, remaining as true to their principles as they could without putting their loved ones at risk. They were fortunate to be shielded from the worst excesses of Nazism by their former Pforzheim neighbour, Herbert Kraft. He had climbed the local party hierarchy over the previous few years and now held a senior position in Karlsruhe's Organisation I, a body charged with converting people to Nazi ideology.

He could – indeed, *should* – have denounced Wolfram's father for his continual refusal to join the party, but he retained a great affection for Erwin and went out of his way to help his old friend. When a part-time post became available at the Fine Art School in Karlsruhe, he ensured that Erwin got the job. This made Erwin extremely unpopular with some of the teachers, who complained that he had gained promotion without even being a member of the Nazi Party. Kraft silenced the critics and Erwin remained in his post.

Kraft was a regular visitor to the Eutingen villa, in part because he had taken a fancy to Clara, the family's maid. Wolfram used to snigger as he watched Kraft go into the kitchen and pinch her bottom. Clara loved the attention – especially as it came from a senior Nazi official – and would smile with smug satisfaction.

Herbert Kraft's protection brought Erwin many benefits and enabled him to retain his position as a state-employed teacher throughout the long years of the Third Reich. Kraft also shielded Erwin from overzealous block leaders. His catchphrase, repeated like a mantra to his junior staff, was: 'If you touch Aïchele, then you'll have big trouble from me.'

*   *   *

Wolfram's mother, in common with so many of her contemporaries, could see a side to Hitler's Germany that was compellingly attractive. Not only had the Fatherland apparently regained some of the pride it lost in 1918 but it had a leader who seemed determined to restore the country to greatness. Whilst Marie Charlotte would never take the step that would usher her into the party fold, she nevertheless had moments of hesitation about Nazism and needed to be brought back to earth with a bump, either by her husband or by one of his friends.

One particular such moment came in the spring of 1936, prompted by the visit to Pforzheim of a senior Nazi minister. Dr Bernhard Rust was the Minister of Science, Education and National Culture – an influential politician who had become part of Hitler's inner circle. Marie Charlotte had read an article advertising his visit in the local paper. He was to stay at the Hotel Ruf, close to the train station, and had extended an invitation to anyone in Pforzheim who might wish to meet him.

Marie Charlotte decided to go. She had been at school with Dr Rust's wife and was keen to have news of her. However, there was another reason too. She was tickled at the idea of knowing someone so senior in the government and liked the thought of being one step away from a close associate of Hitler.

Marie Charlotte asked her husband to accompany her but was met with a gruff refusal. 'You go if you want,' he told her, 'but I don't want to know anything about it.'

Erwin had good reason for his reticence. It was Bernhard Rust who had ruled that teachers and students must henceforth greet each other with the Nazi salute, describing such a greeting as a visible symbol of the new Germany and adding that 'the whole function of education is to create Nazis'.

Having been unsuccessful in persuading her husband, Marie Charlotte asked her two sons whether they would like to go. Wolfram was tempted, but only because he would miss three hours of school. However, he so hated the idea of putting on a uniform just to meet Dr Rust that he eventually declined, leaving his reluctant older brother, Reiner, to accompany his mother.

Mother and son were eventually introduced to the great man and allowed to ask a few carefully vetted questions. Marie Charlotte explained to Dr Rust that she had been at school with his wife and asked whether she was well. The Nazi politician mumbled a few pleasantries but was clearly not interested. 'She'll be pleased that you remember her,' he told her with a feigned smile, then stood up, signalling that the audience was over. Marie Charlotte was left wondering if it had been worth the effort.

It was Herr Becher, the pastor at their church, who later informed her about the various lunacies that Rust wished to inflict on Germany. His most eccentric idea was the rolling eight-day week with six days of study, one day of youth activities and then a rest day. It meant that the calendar was forever catching up with itself – an unworkable system that was abandoned shortly after being instituted.

As time wore on, Rust's ideas became increasingly disturbing. He purged most educational institutions of their Jewish teachers and also directed the sinister research centre that used prisoners for medical experiments. There were many, even among the Nazi elite, who considered Rust to be mentally unstable.

How much Herr Becher knew about the detail of Rust's policies is unclear, but one thing is certain. By the end of an evening in Becher's company, Wolfram's mother had lost her enthusiasm for knowing senior members of the Nazi hierarchy.

The long summer of 1936 was gloriously warm. *Schönes wetter* were the words on everyone's lips that year. In the fields around Eutingen, the wheat had been bleached to the colour of straw and harvest time looked set to be weeks in advance of normal years.

This was an event that Wolfram looked forward to enormously. Ever since the Nazis had come to power, harvest festivals across Germany had become magnificent spectacles, in homage to the days of yore. Party officials instructed farmers to make floats pulled by oxen and each one would demonstrate an element of the farmer's skill – whether threshing, winnowing, or pressing juice-filled fruit.

Everyone was encouraged to wear national costume. The party urged citizens to look into their wardrobes and dig out clothes that had not been worn for a generation or more. It all made for a wonderfully colourful spectacle.

Wolfram, who loved the costumes of old Germany, spent many hours poring over pictures of jackets and lederhosen from Bavaria, comparing them with clothes from Swabia, the Palatinate and elsewhere. He quickly became an expert on such costumes and could identify different folk styles from every corner of Germany.

When he learned of a competition in which entrants had to match traditional costumes with traditional houses, he rose to the challenge. Many thousands entered the competition but he managed to clinch first prize: a lovely, hand-embroidered tablecloth. Having expected the entrants to be housewives, the organisers had not entertained the possibility of the winner being a twelve-year-old schoolboy.

There were other distractions that summer. In distant Berlin, the Olympic Games had opened to wild acclaim. Most foreign visitors were unaware that all the anti-Jewish signs had been temporarily removed from the city streets. Nor did they know of the arrest and internment of gypsies living in the environs of Berlin. Yet there were numerous tell-tale signs to suggest that this was to be an Olympiad unlike any other. Hitler was determined to demonstrate the superiority of the Germanic race: in the German national team, only Aryans were allowed to compete.

The Olympic Games received scant attention from the Aïchele family. Wolfram cared little for sport, preferring, instead, to go on long walks with Uncle Walter, traipsing along dusty paths and swigging home-pressed apple juice. Their walks took them far from Eutingen: to the village of Kieselbronn and the forbidding Cistercian abbey of Maulbronn.

On one of these country walks, Walter and Wolfram paused for a jug of apple juice in a wayside tavern. A local farmer greeted Walter and asked him what he thought of Hitler's speech on the previous evening. It was a leading question: the farmer clearly expected him to praise it. As Walter could not bring himself to do so, playing the fool, he used his idiosyncratic humour to dodge the question.

'*Whose speech?*' he said. '*Hitler's?* No, sorry, I don't know him.'

The man was thunderstruck. 'Hitler!' he exclaimed. 'Surely you must know Hitler?'

'No,' replied Walter. 'Can't say I do. No one called Hitler has ever come round to my house.'

The man persisted. 'But you are German?'

'I guess I must be,' said Walter. 'That's what it says in my passport.'

The man looked away in bewilderment, not wishing to pursue a conversation with someone so obviously deranged. Walter let out a sigh of relief: he had once more managed not to compromise his values and opinions. But the incident served as a stark warning that he lived in a land where freedom of expression was increasingly a thing of the past.

As the Nazi grip over daily life tightened, it became ever more difficult to avoid the strong arm of the state. The Hitler Youth was one of the most unwelcome intrusions into the lives of both the Aïchele and the Rodi families.

At the time of Hitler's appointment as chancellor, the Hitler Youth was just one among scores of organisations, with a membership of a mere 55,000. Within twelve months, virtually all other youth groups had been 'co-ordinated' as children across Germany were automatically co-opted into the Hitler Youth.

There were still many who did not join and Wolfram was one of them. However, it soon became clear that the nonconformists would be dragged forcibly into line. Shortly before Christmas 1936, Hitler signed a decree that made the Hitler Youth an official educational institution. 'All German young people,' he declared, 'apart from being educated at home and at school, will be educated in the Hitler Youth, physically, intellectually and morally, in the spirit of National Socialism to serve the nation and the community.'

Wolfram was dreading his first Saturday morning at the Hitler Youth, for he loathed being told what to do. To his great surprise, the experience proved far more enjoyable than he had expected. His age group was led by a sympathetic young theology student who got the children building camps in the woods and cooking around open fires.

That first outing was also the last that he led. On the following week he was replaced by an enthusiastic apparatchik of the Nazi Party who dutifully implemented all the new directives issued by his seniors. Henceforth, Wolfram and his friends would spend their time marching, drilling and learning how to pitch and strike tents.

What particularly upset Wolfram was the fact that he no longer had time to head into the countryside on his bicycle in order to draw and paint. He complained to his father, who was so angered by these impositions that he asked his friend Dr Vögtle to write a letter excusing Wolfram from attendance on grounds of ill health.

The doctor was more than willing to oblige. Considered a crank by some in the local community, he, like Wolfram's parents, had designed his own house. He had built it with a flat roof, for which he was roundly condemned by his neighbours, who claimed that true Germanic houses never had flat roofs and attacked him for his 'un-German' behaviour.

Dr Vögtle had a soft spot for Wolfram and celebrated the fact that he was so different from his peers. He duly wrote a letter excusing both Wolfram and his brother from the Hitler Youth on the grounds that they had weak constitutions. For the next thirty-six months, Wolfram managed to avoid going to a single meeting.

His case was far from usual. For most youngsters, opting out was not so easy. Peter Rodi, two years younger than Wolfram, was forced to join in 1936, when he was ten years old. He went twice a week, on Wednesdays and Saturdays, and found it a complete waste of time. He disliked the war games and sporting activities, as well as the fact that he had to wear a uniform.

From an early age Peter had displayed a defiant streak that now developed into outright adolescent rebellion. On one occasion he helped himself to a rifle from the Hitler Youth, took it home with him and shot out all the windows of a nearby water tower, one by one. It could have landed him in serious trouble, but no one ever discovered that he was the culprit.

It was fortunate that Peter and his siblings were extremely musical. They were soon co-opted into the orchestra of the local Hitler Youth, along with their church friends and the children of other cultured people from Pforzheim. This was in fact a useful escape route for those who abhorred Nazism, shielding them from the more militaristic elements of the organisation whilst allowing them to indulge their favourite pastime.

On one occasion, the children were asked to give a concert to an assembled crowd of local Nazis, performing Haydn's 'Emperor' Quartet – Opus 76. When they reached the famous adagio, whose music had been the setting for the German anthem 'Deutschland über alles', there was sudden pandemonium. All the Nazis rose to their feet, clipped their heels together and stood to attention for the duration of the adagio, leaving the young musicians perplexed and not a little amused.

Although the Aïchele and Rodi children despised most elements of the Hitler Youth, many of Pforzheim's youngsters thought it was terrific fun. Hannelore Schottgen had voluntarily joined her local branch of the League of German Girls and liked the feeling of belonging to a group. The leaders told the girls not to listen to their parents or even to let the old people have any say in their lives. 'The future,' they would say, 'is yours.'

Hannelore's mother had initially resisted her daughter joining the League because she thought it unseemly for young girls to be marching through the streets, but eventually relented. The impressionable young Hannelore was taught that girls were to be involved in building the new Germany and should show their gratitude and love for the Führer.

On one occasion, a group of Pforzheim children was chosen to go to Nuremberg in order to see Hitler addressing a mass rally. Hannelore was desperate to be selected because she had been told that when women met Hitler they often collapsed with joy. Her neighbour's husband had been deeply moved by his own experience. He had shaken hands with the Führer and had not washed his right hand for weeks afterwards.

Hannelore was to be disappointed. When the time came for the selection process, she was told that she was not tall enough to represent the typical German youth.

By the summer of 1937, even a little backwater like Eutingen had fallen prey to the Nazi revolution. One of the local functionaries, an enthusiastic Nazi named August Issel,

was determined to impose discipline on his diminutive fiefdom. His tenure brought changes both great and small to
the daily routine of village life, and it was often the small
ones that caused the greatest annoyance.

The rules on flags were among the more tiresome
instances of state interference. On every public holiday and
Nazi-inspired festivity, everyone in the country was required
to hang out a swastika.

It soon came to the attention of Herr Issel that there was
one family in Eutingen who never displayed a flag. Wolfram's
parents had no desire to hoist one above their property;
they had managed to flout the rules for several years by
virtue of the fact that their villa lay at some distance from
the centre of the village. Herr Issel was unimpressed by
their lack of enthusiasm for the Nazi cause and ordered
them to hang out a swastika flag like everyone else.

Although extremely unhappy about this, Wolfram's
mother and father had little option but to comply. They
erected an enormous wooden flagpole in the garden in
order to show their goodwill, then painted it with tar to
preserve the woodwork.

As they suspected, the tar remained sticky for weeks,
preventing them from hoisting any flags. When the Gestapo
came to check on the family and found that the swastika
was still not being flown from the house, Erwin feigned
indignation. Pointing proudly to the flagpole that he had
erected, he declared that he could not possibly fly the flag
until the tar was completely dry.

The Gestapo were not amused by his delaying tactic and
ordered him to hoist the swastika immediately, even though
the tar was still wet. Erwin did as he was told. It was a

blustery day and the flag started flapping against the pole. Within seconds, to Erwin's great delight, the Nazi flag had become a sticky black mess of material. It remained firmly stuck to the pole from then on.

Provocative acts like this had still been possible in the early years of Nazi rule, but by 1937 they were becoming extremely dangerous. The judgment in a lawsuit in Karlsruhe's Labour Court had made it clear that such behaviour would no longer be tolerated. A man had refused to sing the anti-Semitic Horst Wessel song while at work and had been denounced by his erstwhile colleagues. Found guilty of having an 'anti-state' attitude, he was duly convicted and immediately dismissed from his job.

The verdict – and sentence – had far reaching implications for everyone in Nazi Germany. 'By the failure to participate in parades, celebrations and other events,' declared the court, 'an employee intentionally places himself outside the national community.'

These words constituted a warning shot to families like the Aïcheles. Non-participation had become a criminal act that would result in punishment. Opting out was no longer an alternative: the Nazi state required everyone to be active participants in the new ideology.

Everyone opposed to the Nazis still had their own little way of protesting. The Rodi family, like the Aïcheles, had also managed to avoid hanging out a swastika. When one of their neighbours warned them that they would find themselves in serious trouble if they did not do so in future, they bought the smallest one possible – so tiny that it was scarcely visible.

The Gestapo was by now acting increasingly intrusively,

with frequent house-to-house visits by officers intent on enforcing the new rules, as they had been doing ever since Heinrich Himmler had become the organisation's head in 1934. In the three years since then, the scale of its network and the level of its efficiency had expanded enormously. So had the budget of its Berlin headquarters – rising from 1 million Reichsmarks in the early years of Nazi rule to 40 million by 1937.

The expansion was necessary if the Gestapo was to have any hope of enforcing the draconian new laws that tightened the Nazis' grip over the lives of ordinary Germans. The Malicious Gossip Law was one of the most notorious. It stated that 'malicious rabble-rousing remarks or those indicating a base mentality' about the Nazi Party or any of its leaders would swiftly lead to imprisonment. The law enabled the Gestapo to arrest people on suspicion of having uttered even the vaguest mutterings of dissatisfaction with the regime. Letters were opened and phones tapped; denunciations by informers and block leaders led to speedy arrests.

For four years, Wolfram's parents had managed to retain considerable privacy in the confines of their own home, but this was starting to change. The incident with the flag had been the first indication that the authorities now meant business. Soon afterwards, the Gestapo paid a second visit to the house. Wolfram's mother happened to glance out of the kitchen window one morning to see two uniformed officers standing at the garden gate.

Their visit, although unwelcome, did not come as a total surprise. Marie Charlotte had been warned by friends in the village that the local authorities were intending to redouble their efforts to destroy unsuitable literature. The Pforzheim book burning in 1933 had been merely the opening salvo in a sustained campaign against 'dirt and shame' books. The list now included works by Heinrich and Thomas Mann, Sigmund Freud, Bertholt Brecht, Stefan Zweig and Ernest Hemingway, along with many others.

Marie Charlotte greeted the officers politely and told them that she had already cleansed her shelves of 'dirt and shame'. She proudly pointed to a little box full of books that she was intending to destroy and even invited the men inside to look through her bookshelves, just in case there were any titles that she might have missed. What the officers did not know – although they might have guessed – was that Marie Charlotte had already removed all her favourites and hidden them from prying eyes.

She had packed them all into special crates and tucked them into a tiny underfloor space beneath the dining-room table. There was no way she was going to hand over books by writers such as her beloved Thomas Mann.

She was nevertheless depressed at the thought that her most esteemed authors had been condemned to a secret hideaway under the floorboards. It suddenly dawned on her that the family's private life was rapidly becoming a secret one. It would not be long before even secret lives were to be forbidden by the state.

CHAPTER FIVE

WAR OF WORDS

'We want to work on people until they have capitulated to us.'

Wolfram remained a source of intrigue to his parents' friends. He was at ease in the company of adults, who would chat with him as if he were a grown-up rather than a boy of thirteen. Among those who found him engaging company was Dr Hillenbrandt, a physician friend of Wolfram's father. Hillenbrandt had previously travelled in Africa, where he had assembled an extraordinary collection of oddities and objets d'art, including hundreds of old and rare African masks. Now that he was back in Swabia, he became a self-taught expert on the local folk art.

In Wolfram, he found a fellow enthusiast. On Saturday afternoons, the two of them would drive through the countryside around Pforzheim, visiting farmsteads in search of homespun *volkskunst* or folk art. They would knock on doors of old farmsteads and manors – anywhere, indeed, that held the promise of treasures within.

They would frequently be invited into these rambling homesteads for a draught of cider or a pitcher of fresh milk. It was perennially dark inside, for the only light came from the undersized windows whose hand-blown glass distorted trees into monsters and turned faces to jelly. In the corner of the kitchen, under a carved crucifix, a tallow candle would send out a dim flicker.

Stout oak trestles, Renaissance trunks and iron-bound strongboxes represented the inherited possessions that spanned a score of generations or more. Handed down from father to son since the chaotic time of the Thirty Years War, they seemed in the imagination of the young Wolfram like precious relics.

A few of the richer farms housed veritable masterpieces of folk art. There would be a principal room – used only on high days and holidays – in which every inch of wall, from wainscot to ceiling, was painted with picaresque murals dating from the seventeenth or eighteenth centuries. Such hidden wonders opened a tantalising window on to peasant life more than 300 years earlier. In a mural in one house, a Swabian burgher swaggered around in stiff, buttoned doublet and lace-fringed pantaloons; in another, a cheery huntsman chased a stag through a bucolic forest clearing.

When Dr Hillenbrandt found particularly choice pieces he would offer to buy them. They were not for his personal collection: he was involved in the establishment of a folk museum in Stuttgart. Furniture that he acquired was carefully dismantled and transported to this new museum where it was restored and exhibited.

These tours into the countryside provided a rich artistic education for Wolfram – and a timely one at that. They also represented a voyage into a Germanic past that was to be swept away for ever in the aftermath of the Third

The young Wolfram, here in 1934 aged 10, spent all his spare time drawing and painting. During the Third Reich, he tried to avoid the Hitler Youth in order that he could pursue his passion for art.

Wolfram's father, Erwin, in the garden of the family's magnificent villa. He was a celebrated wildlife artist and he kept a large menagerie of animals.

The Aïchele family circa 1925. Marie Charlotte, Wolfram, Reiner and Erwin. Wolfram's sister, Gunhild, was not yet born. The years before the Third Reich were happy, despite economic hardship.

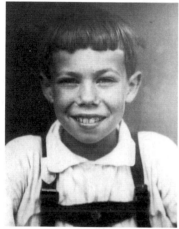

Wolfram, aged 11. He was a curious young lad with a passion for Gothic art and medieval sculptures.

Wolfram and his brother, Reiner, built a miniature medieval hamlet in the lower garden. Each cottage was about three feet high; the accuracy of the construction astonished adult visitors.

The young Wolfram had a lively sense of humour. He would later amuse his comrades – and unknowingly risk severe punishment – with his impersonations of a ranting Hitler.

Eine lustige, bunte Phantasiezeichnung von Wolfram Aichele, 11 Jahre, Eutingen.

Wolfram loved to sketch the medieval villages of his native Baden.
This drawing was published when he was just 11 years old.

Wolfram loved to play with his father's animals. Here he is, aged 15, with Peter the cat.

Marie Charlotte with Hansi and Thora.

Erwin produced animal sketches for a hunting magazine. It was banned by the Nazis because the owner was Jewish.

When local farmers found injured animals in their fields, such as this deer, they brought them to Erwin because they knew he would look after them.

The family's Italianate villa in Eutingen was very different from most houses in rural Swabia. The Aïcheles' private world, it was an island of culture that remained isolated from the worst realities of the Third Reich.

Reiner, Gunhild, Erwin and Marie Charlotte in the dining room. The house in Eutingen was filled with beautiful furniture.

Pforzheim's reformed synagogue was the principal meeting place for the town's large Jewish population. It was attacked and seriously damaged in November 1938.

The Marktplatz (or market square) in central Pforzheim. It was here, in 1933, that the town's Nazi authorities staged a public burning of books deemed un-German.

Wolfram's wood-sculpting tutor in Oberammergau, Johann Georg Lang. Wolfram became good friends with Lang's nephew, Werner, when they served together in a communications team in Normandy.

Wolfram, on the right of the picture, greatly enjoyed his time in Oberammergau. He was infuriated when he was conscripted into the Reich Labour Service.

The studio in Oberammergau. Wolfram excelled at his studies and was one of the best students in his year. He returned there after the war; it was the beginning of a lifetime's creativity.

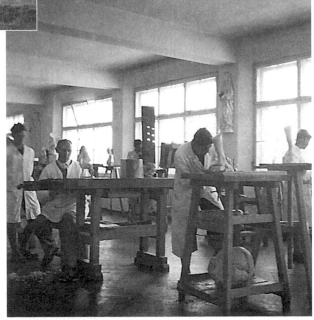

A youthful Peter Rodi says farewell to his sister, Ev-Marie, as he begins his obligatory service in the *heimatflak*, or home defence, the first inevitable step towards military conscription.

Wolfram on leave in February 1944, his final holiday before *invasionstag* (or D-Day). It was the last time his parents saw him for more than two years.

Reich. In the late 1940s and early 1950s, people enthusiastically jettisoned everything that was associated with
the days of old.

Wolfram's father was making his way to the little train
station in Eutingen on Monday, 9 July 1937, when he caught
sight of an unsettling headline in Pforzheim's newspaper.
'The New Way for German Art,' it said. 'The Führer
Inaugurates the House of German Art as a Place for True
Creative Action.'

Erwin bought the paper and read it during the short ride
into Pforzheim. The article described how German art was
to be given a radical new makeover by the Nazi regime.
The 'degenerate' art of old was to be replaced by one that
celebrated the triumphant greatness of the German spirit.
There were to be two exhibitions held concurrently in
Munich. One was to showcase all the finest examples of the
new 'Nazi' art. The other was to display the outcasts and
degenerates of the contemporary art scene.

Erwin was not only appalled by what he read but deeply
disturbed by the idea that the state should decide on what
constituted acceptable art. At a stroke, all of the pencil
sketches he had made during the First World War – depict-
ing shattered landscapes and ruined villages – had become
defeatist in the eyes of the Nazis. His more recent paintings,
of songbirds and barn owls, were less contentious. Yet it
seemed extraordinary that neither he nor his friends were
any longer at liberty to choose the subject matter, the style or
even the colours that they wished to use for their paintings.

Hitler held inflexible opinions on degenerate art, giving
them public expression in an address to the House of

German Art in Munich, some ten days after the Pforzheim article was published.

He expressed his contempt for art that was filled with 'misformed cripples and cretins, women who inspire only disgust, men who are more like wild beasts, [and] children who, were they alive, must be regarded as under God's curse'. Mocking the paintings of both Impressionists and Expressionists, he continued: 'There are men who on principle feel meadows to be blue, the heavens green, clouds sulphur-yellow.'

This, he declared, was degenerate art, which, he claimed, was so damaging to the national character that those who produced such paintings should be arrested, tried and jailed.

The dictatorship expected more than mere conformity from German artists. Joseph Goebbels, in his capacity of Minister of Popular Enlightenment and Propaganda, had set out his vision for the arts within days of the Nazis coming to power.

'It is not enough for people to be more or less reconciled to our regime [or] to be persuaded to adopt a neutral attitude towards us,' he said. 'Rather, we want to work on people until they have capitulated to us, until they grasp ideologically what is happening in Germany today.'

Among the group of locally based artists who would be persecuted by the new order was a sculptor named Otto Baum – a future tutor to Wolfram. Baum was Professor of Art at the Stuttgart Academy and much fêted as a sculptor in the years before Hitler became chancellor.

His fortunes were to change dramatically once the Nazis seized power. His works did not find favour with them and he was sacked from his post at the Stuttgart Academy.

There was worse to come. Baum's works were selected for inclusion in the Munich exhibition of degenerate art, turning him in an instant from celebrated sculptor into artistic pariah. His sole consolation was the fact that his sculptures were exhibited alongside more famous 'degenerates' such as Otto Dix and Max Beckmann.

By this point, he was struggling to make ends meet. He managed to earn a little money by making locks, a skill he had learned from his father. Not only was it scarcely enough to pay the bills but it left him with plenty of spare time in which to reflect on the swiftness of his fall from grace. Within a few short years of Nazi rule, he had been flung on to the breadline. He survived financially only because he was given a helping hand by loyal artist friends in the local community.

Baum still produced his abstract sculptures but he did so in absolute secrecy, aware that he faced several years in a concentration camp if caught. Having made them in the dead of night he would bury them in the garden, hoping that the day would dawn when he could dig them up.

There were times when it seemed that the only news was bad news. *'An alle Parteigenossen!'* was the decree issued on Monday, 4 April 1938. *'Der Führer hat das deutsche Volk aufgerufen.'* ('To all party members . . . the Führer has summoned the German people.') It was issued by Arthur Barth, leader of Pforzheim's Nazi Party, and it affected everyone who lived in Pforzheim and its environs. In six days, there was to be a plebiscite on whether or not Austria should be unified with the German Reich.

'Hitler wants this to be the biggest success in the history of voting,' declared Herr Barth's decree. He insisted that everyone, young and old, go to the ballot booth and cast their vote in favour of unification.

Hitler had sent his troops into Austria some three weeks earlier to enforce his demand that political power be handed over to the Austrian Nazi Party – as it had been. Now, there was to be a plebiscite to confirm the political revolution that had already taken place.

Hitler was determined to win with an overwhelming majority. To help ensure victory on the Austrian side of the border, he despatched the SS into the country and ordered them to round up Communists, Social Democrats and Jews – anyone, in fact, who might organise opposition.

It was a similar story inside the frontiers of the German Reich. On the day of the vote, brownshirts paraded through the streets of Pforzheim, knocking on doors and forcing people to go to the polling stations. Those who refused to vote were beaten or arrested.

The vote was not just about union with Austria; it was also coupled to a vote of confidence in Adolf Hitler. This was a most devious ploy on the part of the Nazi Party since it meant that anyone voting 'no' in the plebiscite would be doing so in defiance of Hitler and would therefore expose themselves to the risk of prosecution for treason. With rumours about ballot papers being marked so that voters could be identified, there was incentive enough to vote 'yes'.

Knowing he was set to win a resounding victory, Hitler intended it to be celebrated in towns and villages across Germany. The inhabitants of Pforzheim were given little choice in the matter. Arthur Barth laid down exactly what was expected:

1. All houses and windows to be decorated with fir branches, flags and posters acquired from specific shops by Friday.

2. By 9 April, all windows to be illuminated with little red lamps bought from the same shops.
3. From Saturday, all radio sets are to be placed on windowsills so that everything can be heard in the streets.
4. In all inns and restaurants . . . all portraits of the Führer are to be decorated with greenery.

Such a decree was an extraordinary intrusion into individual lives, yet it was by no means unusual. Wolfram's parents were growing used to being told how to behave. On this occasion, as in the past, they greeted such strictures with complete indifference and were fortunate that no Gestapo officer happened to notice their passive hilltop protest. However, in Pforzheim itself, the news provoked far stronger reactions.

Hannelore Schottgen's mother was outraged about this manipulation of the populace instigated by Hitler. 'Of course, he's got his fingers in it again,' she said to her teenage daughter. 'On their own, the Austrians don't want to join us. Is this guy never going to leave people alone?'

Hers was a lone voice. When the result of the plebiscite was announced – and people were told that 99 per cent of the electorate had voted yes – there was an outbreak of patriotic fervour in Pforzheim, as elsewhere. There were parties, singing and dancing in the streets, with everyone shouting: '*Ein Volk, ein Reich, ein Führer!*'

When Wolfram's sister, Gunhild, took a trip into town that afternoon, she noticed many of the older women wearing dirndls, the Austrian national costume, in honour of the occasion.

Those with cars headed for the Austrian border in order to join the excitement. In young Hannelore's eyes, it seemed as if there was an extraordinary outburst of support for the Führer. Whatever people's views, there was overwhelming praise for him.

The incorporation of Austria into the German Reich was indeed a personal triumph for Hitler. When, shortly afterwards, Hannelore's parents organised a social evening, her father said to his friends: 'You see, we are now one big nation – and without any war. Now Hitler's going to solve all other problems as well.'

One of those present at the soirée responded: 'I hope you're right, Eugen. I've got two boys and war would be terrible.'

The autumn of that year brought leaden skies and heavy rain to Pforzheim. It also brought a major change to Wolfram's life. Just a few months earlier he had turned fourteen, the age at which he could leave school. He jumped at the opportunity to quit full-time education, begging his parents to allow him to leave behind the travails of the classroom.

When Erwin asked him what he wanted to do with his life, he heard the answer he was expecting. Over the last few years, Wolfram had developed a deepening passion for gothic woodcarving. He drew particular inspiration from the work of the medieval master craftsman, Tilman Riemenschneider, who could capture human emotions with absolute precision, wielding his chisel like an artist's paintbrush. In the elongated fingers of his apostles, the aquiline noses of his saints and the long tresses of his prophets and bishops, Wolfram found a tender expression of piety and finesse.

Wolfram had carved his first sculpture at the age of six. Now, he told his father that he intended to make sculpting his profession. Erwin scoffed at the notion, not because he thought it ridiculous but because he feared that Wolfram would be unable to make a living. He suggested that he should first learn a trade, to have something to fall back on.

Wolfram was sent to lodge with an eccentric aunt in Stuttgart, where a position had become available for an apprentice carpenter. The hours were long and Wolfram had nothing in common with the rough types with whom he was working. Homesick, he soon returned to Pforzheim where he found employment in the workshop of a wood manufacturer.

That autumn, it seemed to Wolfram's parents as if Germany was tipping inexorably towards war. In October, Hitler had deliberately provoked the Sudetenland crisis, claiming a large swathe of Czech territory that was inhabited by ethnic Germans and describing it as his last territorial ambition. Britain's prime minister, Neville Chamberlain, was by now sufficiently alarmed by Hitler's bellicose behaviour to fly to Munich and attempt to broker a deal directly with the Führer.

Hitler was contemptuous of Britain's premier with his outmoded diplomacy and rolled umbrella. 'If ever that silly old man comes interfering here again with his umbrella,' he is said to have declared, 'I'll kick him downstairs and jump on his stomach in front of the photographers.'

The ensuing Munich Agreement, which gave Hitler all of the Sudetenland, led to a flurry of anti-British propaganda in the German newspapers, expressing sentiments that were widely shared in Germany at the time.

Even friends of Wolfram's parents, who were generally open-minded and enlightened, had a stereotypical view of the British in the year prior to the outbreak of war. They laughed at the way they dressed, supposing all Englishmen to wear a top hat and carry a rolled umbrella, while clamping a newspaper under one arm.

The umbrella was the object of greatest satire. When it rained in Germany people wore long coats with hoods or simply allowed themselves to get wet. They never carried umbrellas. Wolfram's father called the English the *regenschirmbürger* – the umbrella-carrying nation, of which Chamberlain was seen as its ultimate personification.

Newspaper articles about the British changed tack in accordance with the views of the Nazi elite. So, too, did the lessons in Pforzheim's schoolrooms. For the previous four years, children had been taught that Shakespeare was a bad man who had abandoned his wife and children. Schiller, by contrast, was portrayed as loyal and ever faithful. However, when it looked as if England was growing closer to Germany, everything went into reverse and it was said that the English were really of German origin. Shakespeare was therefore almost German and it was just by chance that he happened to have lived in England and not in Germany.

As the international friction mounted – and Britain signalled her solidarity with Poland in the event of Hitler harbouring ideas of further territorial expansion – so Shakespeare once again fell out of favour. The bard had become the barometer of international diplomacy.

It was the internal politics of Germany that were about to undergo the biggest and most dramatic alteration. Tensions were evidently being deliberately stoked by Adolf Hitler and were soon to reach breaking point.

Shortly before eight on the morning on 10 November 1938, the young Peter Rodi was kicking his way through the centre of Pforzheim on route to school. As he turned into Goethestrasse, he immediately saw that something dramatic had taken place during the night. All around him lay a scene of vandalism and destruction. Shop windows were smashed and the pavements strewn with broken glass. In places it was so deep that it looked like drifts of crystal snow.

At one point, Peter stooped down, picked up one of the shards and popped it into his pocket. Although unsure what prompted him to keep it, he must surely have realised that something of great significance had taken place – something, indeed, that was to cause shock and revulsion right across the globe. Kristallnacht, the Night of Broken Glass, was a dramatic escalation in state-orchestrated violence against the Jews of Germany.

It all began shortly before noon on the previous day. Peter was sitting in his classroom at school when someone came in – a local official – and opened all the windows. A few minutes later, there was a sudden and violent explosion that rocked the ground.

The large city synagogue, which lay just a short distance from the school, had been the target. Although the structure was still standing, the fine masonry was seriously damaged and all the windows had been blown out. The man who had entered Peter's classroom clearly had advance knowledge of the explosion and had opened the school windows in order to preserve the glass.

Peter and his classmates were met by a disconcerting sight as they left school to go home. Someone high up on the dome of the synagogue was trying to hack off the Star of David. Unable to cut through the metal, he left it dangling at a precarious angle from the cusp of the roof.

Wolfram

The explosion marked the beginning of twenty-four hours of aggression directed towards Germany's Jews, sounding the alarm to all those still living in the state of Baden.

Joseph Goebbels would later present the vandalism as a spontaneous uprising of the German people against the Jews. It was no such thing. The violence was a carefully organised response to the assassination of a Nazi official in the German embassy in Paris. Local party offices across Germany were contacted by Nazi hierarchs in Berlin and ordered to prepare a wave of retaliation targeting Jewish property.

Wolfram awoke on the morning of 10 November unaware that anything untoward had occurred during the night. His sleep had not been disturbed, nor was there any visible sign of any damage having been done in Eutingen. When he arrived at his carpentry workshop, the owner was in an agitated state. In whispers, he confided to Wolfram that the sound of breaking glass had kept him awake for much of the night.

The smashing of windows and destruction of property were only a part of the story. Brownshirts had also broken into Jewish apartments in the early hours of the morning and attacked the families living there. Twenty-three Pforzheim Jews were arrested on trumped-up charges and sent to Dachau concentration camp. Many more were beaten senseless by uniformed thugs armed with batons and cudgels.

Many people in Pforzheim who had hitherto been keen supporters of Hitler were appalled by what had happened that night. Hannelore Schottgen's father could hardly look at his daughter when she asked him what he thought about it, as he was fighting back tears. Never having seen her parents so upset, she did not ask any more questions.

In Pforzheim, the ferocity had been directed primarily against property, but in surrounding towns, people themselves had been the principal target. In the nearby village of Eberstadt, the local Nazi Party leader, Adolf Frey, had acted with extreme brutality, paying a visit to one of the town's oldest Jews, a widow of eighty-one named Susanna Stern, and ordering her out of her house. When she refused to get dressed, he shot her in the head and chest. When she continued to murmur her protests, he shot her for a third time.

The case was brought to court – one of the rare cases of a Nazi activist being called to account, but Frau Stern's family were to be cheated of any justice. The elderly lady was described by the judge as a boisterous troublemaker who had provoked the attack. Frey, by contrast, aged twenty-six, was described as a 'decent solid young man' with an excellent reputation.

All charges against him were dropped.

Kristallnacht was a dramatic wake-up call for Pforzheim's Jews. Many more now saw the writing on the wall. Of the 20,000 Jews who had lived in the state of Baden in 1933, some 7,000 had already left by 1938. Of the 800 still living in Pforzheim, 231 now decided to pack their bags and flee. Doctors, lawyers, physicians: many of the educated Jews decided to get out of Nazi Germany while they still had the chance.

Among them was the Rothschild family, owners of a large jewellery business in the centre of Pforzheim. They were on particularly friendly terms with Hannelore's mother and father and often invited them for social evenings at their large suburban villa. By 1938, such visits had to be made clandestinely, after dark.

On one such occasion, the Rothschilds announced that they had taken the decision to leave; they needed to get rid of all their belongings in a short space of time since Jews were forbidden from taking anything with them when they emigrated. Their beautiful old dining-room furniture and two fine portraits were bought by Hannelore's parents.

The Rothschilds were wise to get out when they did. In the months that followed Kristallnacht, all the remaining Jews of Pforzheim were moved out of their family homes and required to live in officially designated Jewish houses. The regime had decided to confine them to a ghetto that could more easily be watched and monitored by the Gestapo. There would remain until October 1940, when their fortunes were to take a sharp and terrible turn for the worse.

Uniformed marches through the centre of Pforzheim became increasingly commonplace as Germany drifted towards war. There was scarcely a public festival that did not involve the massed ranks of party stalwarts goose-stepping their way through Pforzheim. One particular day of festivity and national rejoicing fell on 20 April 1939, Hitler's fiftieth birthday, when the Nazi hierarchy and party officials bent over backwards to organise elaborate celebrations.

Gauleiter Robert Wagner saw the event as an opportunity to demonstrate his fanatical loyalty to the Führer. There were to be marches and parades through the streets – colourful affairs with flag-bearers and Nazi pageantry. The marchers carried vast brick-red banners that were unfurled in the stiff spring breeze. 'In our unity and togetherness lies our strength,' read the motto on a thousand such banners.

For the Aïchele family, Hitler's birthday was an occasion to work in the garden and keep a low profile, but in the Rodi household, Peter, the eldest son, could not resist ridiculing the day's solemnities. He pinned up a postcard of Hitler in the entrance hall and decked it with a colourful garland. The postcard was the only image of Hitler in the house, sent to the family by a concerned cousin who feared that Max Rodi, a state employee, would get into severe trouble if he was discovered not to be in possession of an obligatory portrait.

On this festive day, that tiny picture with its garland of flowers was turned into an object of satire. Peter's dressed up in his Hitler Youth uniform and persuaded his sisters to do likewise before calling for his parents.

The children recited to them trite poems celebrating Hitler and also sang the Nazi songs they had been forced to learn in the Hitler Youth. Their mother, half bemused and half shocked, did not quite know how to react.

The long summer holidays of 1939 were overshadowed by talk of war. For weeks there had been the same daily news on the wireless. The constant refrain was that the Poles were mistreating the ethnic German minorities who lived in the border regions of Poland. Hitler, it was said, was no longer prepared to tolerate this and would soon put matters straight.

The Aïchele parents, in common with their church friends, the Rodis, were convinced that war was now only a matter of months away. Yet many people in Pforzheim continued to believe Hitler's assurance that he would avoid plunging Germany into conflict, even though the facts seemed to contradict this.

Hannelore Schottgen came down from her bedroom at the

end of August to see lots of colourful cards laid out on the table. Her father told her that they were rationing cards. 'Everyone gets the same,' he explained. 'Food, meat, bread, soap.'

Hannelore's mother was not impressed. 'You're not trying to tell me there's not going to be a war with such preparations,' she said to her husband and began to make her own, ready for the conflict that she felt certain was to come.

A very elegant bag made from pig's leather, which was discreet and could hold a great deal, now came into its own. Five times a day, she headed to the shops and bought sugar, rice, coffee, chocolate and other essentials.

She had to be extremely careful not to be caught stockpiling provisions. People who purchased more than was strictly necessary could be denounced for displaying a lack of confidence in the regime.

As the holidays came to an end, the news grew increasingly gloomy. Hitler was playing a dangerous game of brinksmanship in the international arena, convinced that he would get everything he wanted. He not only demanded the return to the Reich of German-speaking Danzig but he also wanted a road and rail link through the so-called 'Polish corridor' that separated East Prussia from the rest of Germany.

Poland had no intention of acceding to these demands. Pforzheim's morning newspaper was indignant at what it believed to be Polish intransigence. 'In the last four days, the nerves of the German people have been stretched to the limit . . . all of Germany has been waiting by the wireless in order to listen to the words of the Führer and the red heat of anger has inflamed their faces as they have listened to his numerous attempts to find a solution to the Danzig problem.'

The paper claimed that Hitler had bent over backwards to avoid conflict and that he had even pursued suggestions proposed by the British prime minister, Neville Chamberlain. 'But the Polish people simply laughed dismissively.'

Less than twenty-four hours after the appearance of this article, Germans heard the tidings they most feared. A peaceful solution to the crisis had not been found. Their country was once again at war.

Fifteen-year-old Wolfram was on a solo cycling tour in the Vorarlberg region of Austria and was sleeping in a rural barracks when the news broke.

The local farmer rushed into the barracks and announced to the soldiers that Germany was declaring the outbreak of hostilities. There was a stunned silence as everyone considered what it meant. The unwelcome intelligence came as a particular shock to the village youth, who were immediately conscripted. Most were dismayed by the very thought of another war and had no clue why Hitler wanted one anyway; several of them confided to Wolfram that they had thought the Polish corridor was the name of an English politician.

The next morning, Wolfram headed to the canteen for his usual breakfast of fried polenta and coffee, but there was one dramatic change. All the soldiers had left in the night, having been drafted back into the army.

The reaction to the gathering storm was very different in Innsbruck, which Wolfram visited on the following day. The people there were less pessimistic and more confident in Hitler's ability to succeed.

As Wolfram made his way back over the border into Germany, he witnessed scenes of mayhem in towns and villages as lads of fighting age sought to register themselves for the military.

Frithjof Rodi was in his bedroom when the announcement came over the radio. His father came in wearing full military uniform to say his goodbyes. As a former officer in the First World War, he had been recalled to service in the forces. He was sent to Brno in Czechoslovakia where he was charged with training artillery for the battles that were sure to come.

That morning, in the centre of Eutingen, young Doris Weber, a friend of the Aïchele family, leaned out of her apartment window and immediately realised that something of great significance was taking place. Hundreds of soldiers were marching through the village, in uniform and carrying flowers they had been given. Everyone was hanging out of their windows to watch the soldiers go by, shouting: 'We're going to war!'

Wolfram's parents were deeply alarmed by the news. They had two possible channels for getting more information on the morning that war broke out: the state-controlled radio or the state-controlled newspapers. Both presented a very similar version of events. Polish troops were said to have started the conflict by attacking a local transmitter on the Polish–German frontier. This, according to Hitler, was the *casus belli*. Germans had the right to defend themselves.

Unbeknown to the Aïchele family – and to almost all other Germans – the Polish attack had been an elaborate deception. One hundred and fifty inmates from a German concentration camp had been dressed in Polish military uniform and forced to stage a mock assault on the transmitter in the frontier town of Gleiwitz on the night of 31 August 1939.

This gave the German war machine the excuse to go on the offensive. Bombers and fighters screamed into action, attacking air bases, road and rail communications, and munition dumps. Dive-bombers were sent to strafe columns of Polish troops; soon after, motorised infantry and artillery launched the first blitzkrieg ground offensive of the Second World War. Speed was the operating tactic of the German army whose intention was to strike with such rapidity that the enemy would be completely overwhelmed.

On that opening day of the campaign, Hitler made a speech to the Reichstag that was broadcast on the wireless. It was listened to with nervous anticipation by both the Aïchele and Rodi families.

'My whole life has been nothing but a struggle for my people, for their revival, for Germany,' said the Führer. 'This struggle has been fought continually under the banner of faith in this nation. There is one word which I have never learned: capitulation.'

The outbreak of war came as a thunderbolt to many Pforzheimers who had hitherto supported Hitler. Hannelore Schottgen's father was speechless, having really believed that Hitler did not want military action. Hannelore herself was upset all day; war had finally arrived – the big thing that everyone had been talking about.

Yet many also felt that German pride could at long last be restored. Goebbels' propaganda machine used every possible means to whip up a sense of patriotism in those initial days. And there was a great sympathy for the army, especially after its defeat in the First World War.

In the Rodi family, there was a feeling that something

ought to be done. On the first weekend that Max Rodi had leave, he suggested that the family protect themselves in some way and got the two boys to dig a defensive trench in the garden as a protection against air raids.

Frithjof and Peter set to work with pickaxes and shovels; the trench grew longer and deeper with every hour that passed. Then it started to rain and the mud in the bottom turned into a swamp. When their father returned to his regiment on the following day, a neighbour came round to inspect the work. He told the boys it was ridiculous, so they filled it in.

Their mother, Martha Luise, also felt that the grave situation required some sort of response. She bought a large map of Poland, pinned it to the dining-room wall and then made lots of little flags – each one representing a division of troops – so that she could monitor the campaign. The family followed the battles closely and always listened to the daily news bulletins.

Crouched around the wireless, they would absorb each fresh despatch from the front line. The bulletins always began with music by Liszt, followed by interminable speeches by Hitler, riddled with references to treachery, betrayal and the ultimate victory of German arms.

Max Rodi was disgusted by the Führer's ranting monologues. In one speech, Hitler claimed to have destroyed nothing in Germany. Max exploded and shouted out: '*Nothing!* What about the synagogues?'

CHAPTER SIX

DEPORTING THE JEWS

'If we lose this war, then God help us!'

Everyone in Pforzheim was stunned by the opening days of the military campaign in Poland. Hitler's gamble had proved a spectacular success. Wolfram's mother tuned in to the state radio each evening to hear that the German army was sweeping all before it. Warsaw had been heavily bombed by a formation of forty planes and many other Polish towns were also subjected to heavy raids. The Nazi regime's bellicose policy had, it seemed, been triumphantly vindicated.

Marie Charlotte, concerned that the news on German radio might not be trustworthy, tuned in to a Swiss channel, even though it was strictly illegal, only to find that the broadcasts were remarkably similar to what was being reported on German radio. Hitler's military invasion of Poland had indeed turned into a spectacular rout. On 6 September, Krakow fell to the German army. Less than two weeks later, Hitler himself addressed a triumphant crowd in Danzig. By the end of the month, Warsaw had fallen and 140,000 Polish troops were taken into captivity.

The good news was tempered by bad. Britain's declaration of war on Germany, two days after the invasion of Poland, came as extremely unwelcome tidings to Wolfram's parents, as to all their Pforzheim friends. It even alarmed senior figures in the Nazi hierarchy. When Goering was informed of it, his initial reaction was one of panic: 'If we lose this war,' he said, 'then God help us!'

Goebbels' Propaganda Ministry was undaunted by Chamberlain's defiant stand. Fully forty-eight hours before Britain had declared war on Germany, the ministry had already issued a confidential press directive to all newspapers editors in the country, informing them how to react in the event of such an outcome.

It read: 'Britain is the true aggressor in the world . . . It is clear that the British mediation was merely hypocritical and that the British government never intended to produce a settlement.' It went on to instruct editors how they should report the news of a British declaration of war.

Pforzheim's two newspapers took Goebbels' advice to heart on the morning of 4 September. Both contained long articles about the insolence and treachery of erstwhile friends. 'England Betrays Europe,' was the headline in Marie Charlotte's paper. 'The British hypocrisy has come to a head.'

The talk was bullish and defiant: the British people, said the *Pforzheimer Rundschau*, were going to have to pay the consequences for their warmongering leaders. 'There is no way they can avoid the ring of iron and concrete in the West which is manned by stubborn German men who have been sent by the whole German nation to fight until the final victory.'

Pforzheimers were reminded that Germany had never sought conflict with the British. 'England has declared war on us. She has thrown down the gauntlet. We are now picking it up and will fight against these "holier than thou" troublemakers on the banks of the Thames.'

The local Pforzheim newspapers, in common with their counterparts across Germany, only ever covered stories that had been approved by Goebbels' ministry and were quick to publicise the military successes of the Polish campaign. What they neglected to report was the fact that Hitler had ordered three SS Death's Head regiments to follow in the wake of the army, under orders to 'incarcerate or annihilate' all enemies of Nazism, notably Poles and Jews. Reinhard Heydrich had made it quite clear what this meant: 'The nobility, the clerics and the Jews must be killed.'

The SS began its covert operation within forty-eight hours of the invasion being launched, shooting Polish and Jewish civilians in cold blood. It was the start of a murderous six years for the inhabitants of Nazi-occupied Poland. The country was carved up, with three large districts incorporated into the German Reich. The rump, which became the General Government, was handed over to the rule of Dr Hans Frank. 'Poland,' he said, 'shall be treated like a colony. The Poles will become the slaves of the Greater German Empire.'

Such sentiments were not for public consumption and were certainly never broadcast. Marie Charlotte continued to tune in to Swiss radio, in the hope of receiving news that had not been manipulated by the Ministry of Propaganda. However, it proved remarkably difficult to get reliable information from the outside world, as well as extremely dangerous to pass on such intelligence to others in the local community. Wolfram's mother and father certainly did not exchange news with their neighbours, or even with close friends. People had already learned never to ask any questions and to keep quiet about everything that was taking place.

The outbreak of war with Britain brought few changes to the daily routine. Wolfram's father continued teaching at the art school while Wolfram himself was still working as an apprentice at the local carpentry workshop. A few of the basic foodstuffs were now rationed – among them meat, butter and cheese. Yet the rations were generous, for Hitler well remembered how rationing had sapped morale in the First World War.

For some families, rationing led to an unexpected improvement in their diet. The Rodi boys were surprised to find that they got meat twice a week. On Saturdays their mother used the meat as a basis for making soup; on Sunday they ate the meat itself. The only drawback to rationing was the fact that prices remained high. Martha Luise could not afford the generous quantities of meat that they were allowed and used to give the family's ration cards to wealthier relatives.

People quickly mastered fending for themselves in wartime. The Rodis kept their own chickens and rabbits, as well as growing their own vegetables. The Aïcheles, too, grew potatoes and cabbages in the garden below the house, where there were also lots of fruit trees. For those living in apartments, it was more difficult to supplement their rations with home-grown produce, but most had friends or relatives in the countryside who supplied them with extra milk, cheese and eggs. The worst of the hardships were still many years away; indeed, it was not until the war's end that many families faced prolonged and severe shortages.

Windows now had to be blacked out at night, on the off chance of a bombing raid. Wardens patrolled the streets of Pforzheim throughout the hours of darkness to ensure that not a glimmer of light could be seen from the air.

Hannelore Schottgen's father found it too expensive to buy curtains for the big bay window in their living room, so he brought mats home from his school and stuck them against the glass. They looked nice enough by lamplight, but proved difficult to roll up in the daytime.

In the end, the family stopped using their electric lamps in the evening, as light still filtered out into the street, and started going to bed by candlelight instead.

Such measures seemed futile to the inhabitants of Pforzheim, who felt a world away from the hostilities. Many of the youngsters were disappointed when no foreign aircraft flew over the town.

Yet there were little reminders that Germany was now at war. There was daily training for air raids, and teenage girls were shown how to apply bandages and help children into gas masks. In the Eutingen branch of the Hitler Youth, new marching songs were added to the repertoire. The children were taught songs about England and Churchill, which described him as a fat pig.

The Eutingen youngsters were also obliged to go from door to door, asking for donations to the war effort. There was no question of opting out since it was all organised by the Hitler Youth. Sigrid Weber and her sister were forever being sent out with collection tins, and would be rewarded with a badge once the tin was full.

In the early years of the war, these collections were half-hearted affairs, but would become far more serious after the 1941 invasion of Russia. People were expected to donate everything they had. If they did not, it would be confiscated anyway.

In Eutingen, this policy of enforced donation would eventually create a great deal of ill-will against the regime. People began whispering, 'This cannot make you win a war,' but they were afraid to say such things openly.

With no bombing raids, nor even any planes flying over-head, there was a sense of unreality to the situation. The daily lives of Pforzheimers remained untouched by a conflict that was far away.

It was a feeling shared by people elsewhere in Germany. Even in Berlin, the war seemed to belong to another world. 'No excitement, no hurrahs, no cheering, no throwing of flowers, no war fever, no war hysteria,' wrote the American journalist William Shirer. 'There is not even any hate for the French and British, despite Hitler's various proclamations to the people.'

Wolfram's parents followed the progress of the German army with both disbelief and surprise. Poland was defeated. Then Denmark. Norway followed soon after. Finally Hitler turned on his enemies in the West, launching his spectacu-lar invasion of Belgium, Holland and France in the spring of 1940.

Suddenly, the country woke up to the realisation that this was to be a war on a grand scale. Now, at last, military strategy was the topic of the day, as in the conversation that the ten-year-old Frithjof Rodi overheard between two of his uncles, one of whom was serving in the army.

A colonel based on the Rhine, he said that he had worked out exactly how to overrun the Maginot Line. His home-spun approach, which Frithjof listened to in boyish fascination, was simply to circumvent the line. The French had concentrated all their resources on its defence. By driving to the north of it in a giant arc, the German army would render it obsolete.

This was exactly what Hitler had planned to do and it would prove a triumphant success. Once again, the German army swept all before it, entering the French capital in June 1940. At that time, Frithjof remembers sitting with his mother, listening to news on the wireless of the German triumph in Paris. When he turned to look at her, tears were rolling down her face.

He could not work out the reason for them. Was she affected by the solemnity of the occasion – the marching and the pageantry – or saddened by the thought that the French capital had been captured by forces loyal to Hitler?

Wolfram's thirteen-year-old sister, Gunhild, overheard a strange and sinister conversation in those early months of war that would disturb her sleep for years to come.

She was sitting in a train, listening to three adolescent girls chatting excitedly about the trip they were making to Ottensburg. All were in good humour. One of them in whispered tones spoke of the reason for their journey, which was to 'give a child to the Führer'.

The young Gunhild was puzzled at first, but she soon

realised the meaning of their words. They began giggling and saying how much they were looking forward to meeting lots of gorgeous-looking men whose babies they would have. And it was clear that they could not wait to arrive at their destination.

The teenagers were volunteers for Hitler's *lebensborn* or racial breeding programme, established in 1936. It was designed to produce pure Aryan children who would be raised as blindly loyal servants of the Third Reich.

Although their story remains a broken jigsaw, some inkling of the bizarre sexual awakening they were to experience can be gleaned from another *lebensborn* volunteer – a feisty teenager named Hildegard Trutz. In the late 1940s, Frau Trutz was questioned about the long months she spent in one of these establishments and she revealed what was expected of girls like those on the train to Ottensburg.

'The whole place was in the charge of a professor,' she said. '[He was] a high-up SS doctor who examined each of us very thoroughly as soon as we had arrived. We had to make a statutory declaration that there had never been any cases of hereditary diseases, dipsomania or imbecility in our family.'

Those giggling girls, each of them no more than eighteen years of age, would have signed a declaration renouncing all claims to the children they might bear. Once these formalities were complete, they would be introduced to the SS men who had been picked for the task of impregnating them. 'We were told to see to it that his hair and eyes corresponded exactly to ours . . .' recalled Hildegard Trutz. 'When we had made our choice, we had to wait till the tenth day after the beginning of the last period, when we were again medically examined and given permission to receive the SS men in our rooms at night.'

The young Hildegard admitted to being delighted to be serving the Führer in this way. 'I believed completely in the importance of what we were doing,' she said, '. . . [and] had no shame or inhibitions of any kind.'

She even harboured some affection for her chosen SS partner. 'He was a sweet boy, although he hurt me a little, and I think he was actually a little stupid, but he had smashing looks.' He slept with her for three evenings in one week. 'The other nights he had to do his duty with another girl.'

Hildegard fell pregnant soon after and eventually gave birth to a baby boy. 'It was not an easy birth,' she said, 'for no good German woman would think of having any artificial aids such as injections to deaden the pain, as they had in the degenerate Western democracies.'

The baby was taken from her soon after the birth and she never saw him again. She was nevertheless tempted to return the following year and have a second child, but she met and married a young SS officer in the intervening time. When she told her new husband about her *lebensborn* child, he was not particularly happy, '[but] he couldn't very well say anything against it,' she said, 'seeing that I had been doing my duty to the Führer.'

The Nazi regime was soon actively recruiting intelligent young girls as potential ideological child-bearers. One day, Hannelore Schottgen was sitting in the classroom at her Pforzheim school when she and her fellow students were visited by a lady from the Woman's Union. She had come to speak about giving a child to the Führer.

The girls were told that they would be offered free board,

lodging and food in a wonderful hotel or chateau, and would also be given the best care and attention.

This visit prompted a vigorous debate among Hannelore and her teenage friends. Some said it was immoral to have a child that would be separated at birth from its parents. Others argued that war demanded huge sacrifices. All were very confused. For years, they had been brought up with the vision of good, clean-living girls belonging to the League of German Maidens: with the picture of virtuous German mothers (with blonde plaits) surrounded by happy children. Now they were being told to give birth to babies outside wedlock who would be brought up without a family.

Eventually one of Hannelore's friends, who was against the *lebensborn* programme, spoke for the majority. 'At the end of the day,' she said, 'we've got to keep our *menschen-würde* – our human dignity.' Hannelore agreed. It was the first time the words 'human dignity' had meant something to her, rather than being an empty expression.

Her sentiment was shared by all the other girls in that Pforzheim classroom – even those who supported Hitler. No girl from her class gave a child to the Führer.

The Nazi propaganda machine stopped at nothing when it came to manipulating news, but there were some stories, particularly local ones, that could not be hidden. One of these, which occurred in Pforzheim on 22 October 1940, concerned a local doctor, Rudolf Kuppenheim, and his wife.

Dr Kuppenheim had been the chief physician at Pforzheim maternity hospital for more than forty years, in which he had assisted in the births of some 19,000 babies.

He was a respected figure in the town – much loved and widely known.

Among his circle of acquaintances was Wolfram's father. Both had belonged to the same freemasonry lodge and had met at numerous discussion evenings. It was how Erwin had got to know so many of Pforzheim's cultivated people, many of them Jews like Dr Kuppenheim.

Although the Reuchlin Masonic lodge had been closed in 1933, its former members made an effort to keep in touch with each other over the years that followed.

Dr Kuppenheim's troubles had begun some months after the closure of the lodge. At the beginning of April 1933, his Jewish background had required him to take early retirement from his job at the maternity hospital. He was still allowed to practise privately, in recognition of his distinguished military record in the First World War. In 1938, even this right was withdrawn. Pforzheim's Nazi authorities informed him that he was no longer allowed to work on account of his Jewishness.

Yet Kuppenheim was not a practising Jew. Indeed, he had not practised the creed of his birth for many decades. An enthusiastic convert to Protestantism, he had become a parish councillor of his local church in Pforzheim.

Kuppenheim and his wife, Lily, had no intention of leaving their home town. Although they had been deprived of an income and both their sons had emigrated to America, they vowed to remain in Pforzheim and wait for the Nazi menace to burn itself out.

On the morning of 22 October 1940, they were woken by two SA men ringing their doorbell to tell them that they were to be transported out of Germany, along with the rest of Pforzheim's remaining 195 Jews. They had two hours to pack a few belongings: one suitcase, one blanket, a little food and 100 Deutschmarks.

When Dr Kuppenheim asked the reason for their transportation, he was given no answer, although he must surely have known that the future looked bleak. The SA officials were extremely menacing, promising to return in two hours, then moving on to the next Jewish house on the list.

It was at this point that Doctor Kuppenheim and his wife took a momentous decision. They had no intention of being transported. The doctor laid out all his medals from the First World War, including the Iron Cross, First Class, then he and his wife swallowed capsules of poison.

When the SA returned later that morning, both of them were already in a deep coma. They were taken to hospital but the damage done to their vital organs was so serious that nothing could be done to save them. They died on the following day.

The news came as a great shock to Wolfram's father, for he had been on friendly terms with Kuppenheim for years and held him in high esteem. As the tale of their joint suicide spread through the town, there was widespread dismay. Their deaths seemed to symbolise the terrible injustice of Nazi anti-Semitism. Kuppenheim had brought so many new lives into existence. Now, his own had been taken.

A grim fate awaited the rest of Pforzheim's Jews that October morning. 'It is essential that Jews are properly treated at the time of their arrest,' read the directive handed out to those in charge of rounding them up. This, however, was only to avoid any protests from the local population.

Twenty members of the Maier family were arrested; nine from the Dreifuss clan and eight of the Reutlingers. There was no respect for age or sex; among those taken was Gustav Aron, eighty-five years old, and Blondine Emsheimer, who was eighty-eight. Everyone was subjected to the same brusque treatment.

Seven or eight Gestapo came to the house of Kathe Schulz, one of the families on the list to be deported. 'Get ready!' said the guards. 'In two hours you'll be taken to France.'

Kathe Schulz herself was be to be spared transportation for she was a *mischling* or half-Jew, but her father, Hellmuth, was arrested and taken to Pforzheim's freight station, the point of embarkation. Kathe, desperate to see him one last time, made her way to the station. After much wrangling with the Gestapo, she was allowed to speak with her father for a few snatched minutes. Then he and the rest of Pforzheim's Jews began a three-day journey to Camp Gurs, a bleak internment camp in the Pyrenees.

Once again, Robert Wagner had shown himself to be a ruthless exponent of anti-Semitism. The deportation of Pforzheim's Jewish population, along with Baden's other 7,000 Jews, occurred fully fifteen months before the Wannsee Conference that determined the extermination of all Jews living under Nazi rule.

Most Pforzheimers were only dimly aware of this process for several years earlier the town's Jewish community had been confined to a ghetto, well concealed from sight. 'The deportation of the Jews was carried out smoothly and without incident,' wrote Reinhard Heydrich in his report on the day's events. 'The population was hardly aware of the action taking place.'

Wolfram heard nothing more of the deportees once they had been taken away. No one asked any questions about them. It was the last people heard of them until after the war.

Nevertheless, news, of sorts, reached the Rodi family. Max Rodi had somehow heard that the deportees were being kept in barracks without any glass in the windows and was outraged.

Glassless windows were the least of their troubles. The prefabricated shacks were flimsy and freezing in winter, and the roofs leaked every time it rained. The inmates slept on straw, for there were no beds, and the food rations meagre.

'The barracks were very primitive,' wrote Herr Schulz, one of the few to survive Camp Gurs. '[There were] no windows and just a few air vents. When it rained or was cold, these had to be closed so there was darkness all the time.'

The food rations went from bad to worse during the winter months: 200 grams of bread per day, a bowl of watery soup and peas once every four weeks. Some 1,200 Jews died from malnourishment and dysentery. Of the 195 Pforzheimers deported to Gurs, 45 died of starvation. A further 78 were later killed in Auschwitz and 17 in other extermination camps. Only 55 would survive to the end of the Third Reich.

An equally uncertain future awaited their half-Jewish relatives who had been allowed to remain in Pforzheim. Forty were immediately categorised as 'non Aryans'. Their property was confiscated and a raft of discriminatory legislation was introduced, in which they were forbidden to use trams or bikes and prohibited from owning typewriters, cameras and radios, among many other things.

By December 1941, they were required to display a yellow star outside their homes, as well as having a yellow star sewn on to their clothes. Most were too scared to go out at all, which perhaps explains why Wolfram never saw anyone in the street wearing a yellow star.

He had left Pforzheim by this time and returned only sporadically to visit his parents. Now seventeen, he was inching closer to his dream of becoming a sculptor. After years of hoping, he had finally been accepted on a specialist wood-carving course in the Bavarian village of Oberammergau.

CHAPTER SEVEN

TRAINING FOR VICTORY

'You won't be rejoicing for much longer'.

T he little village looked at its most alluring in the icy winter months. The gabled homesteads and taverns wore a thick quilt of snow, and icicles dangled like frozen scabbards from the eaves of the church.

The winter of 1941 was bitterly cold. In the empty forests that surrounded the village and on the lonely slopes of Mount Ettal, the snow glowed a dull steely-blue. Locals shivered when they ventured into the marketplace and hoicked up their collars against the boreal blast; no one had ever known it so cold.

Wolfram had arrived in Oberammergau three months earlier to learn the ancient craft of Bavarian woodcarving. The village had been famous for its sculptors ever since the eighteenth century when local craftsmen idled away the long winter months with chisel and adze in hand. In the winking candlelight of their country farmsteads, they performed alchemy on wood, transforming chunks of rough linden into puckish cherubs and wizened prophets.

Wolfram had until now been captivated by the sober

gothic sculptures of medieval Germany but he was dazzled by the sheer flamboyance of Oberammergau's parish church. Angels arched their gilded feathers into the upper nave and pug-cheeked cherubs blasted their cornets at the shimmering high altar. The interior of St Peter and St Paul was a riot of rococo frescoes and *trompe l'oeil* trickeries.

The village was no less picturesque than the church. Oberammergau's façades were adorned with painted murals of prophets and patriarchs whose rich paunches and billowing gowns represented a cultural nod towards the worldly prince-bishops of Salzburg rather than the first-century martyrs of the Holy Land.

Wolfram, spellbound by what he saw, had never been happier in all his life. It felt as if this was where he was meant to be all along. The wooden sculptures that he found here, and the quality of the craftsmanship, could not have been further away from the kitsch imitations of later years.

The local population in and around Oberammergau was conservative in outlook and had supported Hitler enthusiastically for some time. More than 40 per cent of Bavarians had voted for the Nazis in the election of March 1933. Yet the realities of Nazism seemed less visible here than elsewhere. None of the students in Wolfram's class showed any relish for the politics of National Socialism. And although Hitler's mountain retreat at Berchtesgaden lay less than seventy miles away, it might have belonged to another world. The only reminder that Germany was a country in conflict came from Schloss Linderhof – one of King Ludwig II's private fantasy palaces. As Wolfram and his friends passed it, they noticed that its windows were boarded up and its entrance padlocked. Wartime had forced the closure of one of Bavaria's most famous attractions.

Wolfram should have registered for the Hitler Youth as soon as he arrived, but as no one actually ordered him to join, he decided to chance his luck by evading it completely. It was some months before the director of the school called all his students together to inform them that membership of the Hitler Youth was compulsory. Although he must have known that Wolfram was the only one not to have registered, he refrained from saying so. Wolfram reluctantly signed up, only to find that it was nowhere near as bad as he had feared. The man in charge of his age group had no interest whatsoever in Nazi ideology and left them to their own devices.

On Sundays, when there were no woodworking classes and no Hitler Youth, Wolfram and his friends would put on their hobnailed boots and gaiters, and take themselves off on mountain hikes into the high Wetterstein, over whose ice-topped crowns trailed wispy skeins of high-altitude cloud. With rosy cheeks and dripping noses, they would await the moment when the late-afternoon sun burst through the clouds, to reveal a new marvel. Wolfram had spent many days poring over maps and had worked out that there was a gap in the mountains through which you should be able to see the Dolomites, even though they lay more than one hundred miles to the south. To his great delight he was correct. On clear days, these distant peaks would nudge their gaudy pink summits into the sky.

In other moments of free time, Wolfram would head for the great Benedictine kloster of Ettal. This twelve-cornered abbey – another glittering pile of whimsical baroque – was also a functioning monastery – Wolfram loved to hear the rich liturgical chanting, the verse and echoed refrain that was sung from the daily psaltery. As the late-afternoon twilight spilled across the valley, and the winter solstice announced an even deeper chill, the choral voices of a dozen or more monks could be heard pouring forth into the darkness.

Wolfram had no idea that one of the Nazi regime's most outspoken critics, the Jesuit priest Rupert Mayer, was then being held under house arrest in the vaulted cloisters. The authorities wanted to kill Father Mayer but, worried that his death would make him a martyr to the faithful, they chose instead to incarcerate him in Ettal, where no one would ever see him.

Wolfram was under no illusions that he would be called into the Reich Labour Service when he turned eighteen. Yet the summons to report for a medical examination in February 1942 – the first inevitable step into the military – still came as a shock. The wording of the letter was brusque and official, signalling a dramatic transformation to his life. For months he had spent his days learning to wield his chisel with skill. Now, his woodcarving course was to come to an abrupt end.

Two of his Oberammergau friends managed to dodge the call-up. One suffered from asthma attacks and was pronounced too sickly to be drafted. The other had contrived to give himself blood poisoning by inhaling fumes from toxic metal and was sent to the local infirmary. The rest of Wolfram's comrades had their medical and were given certificates declaring them fit and well.

They all went for a beer afterwards. Some of the crowd made the best of the situation and pretended to be proud to be a part of the military. However, a couple of men in the tavern, who had already experienced the horrors of the front, introduced a note of sober reality to their celebrations, bluntly telling the lads: 'You won't be rejoicing for much longer.'

There was good reason for pessimism: the war on the Russian front was going from bad to worse. Hitler's invasion of the Soviet Union – spectacularly successful in the opening months – had faltered and failed as the mercury dipped to twenty below zero. Soldiers, many of them reluctant conscripts, began to ask themselves whether they would ever see their loved ones again.

It had been so very different at the beginning of the campaign. The German army had crossed the Soviet frontier at dawn on 22 June 1941 – the greatest land invasion in the history of warfare. Three million men, 3,300 tanks and virtually all the artillery units in the Wehrmaht were involved. The goal of the campaign was as ambitious as the size of the army: the conquest of the immense European slab of the Soviet Union.

Three army groups had thrust their way into Soviet territory on that bright summer's morning. Army Group North was to head for the Baltic areas of northern Russia and capture the great city of Leningrad. Army Group Centre was to advance towards Smolensk and Moscow, seizing the heartland of western Russia. Army Group South was to target the agricultural land of the Ukraine, capturing Kiev before wheeling sharply south-east towards the rich oilfields of the Caucasus. 'When [Operation] Barbarossa commences,' said Hitler, 'the world will hold its breath and make no comment.'

His confident predictions of a swift victory seemed prophetic. In the opening days of the campaign almost 4,000 Soviet aircraft were destroyed. By the end of the first week, advance units of the Germany army were one third of the way to Moscow. Vilnius fell on 24 June; Minsk was taken a few days later. By September, the siege of Leningrad was already under way.

Nevertheless, senior army commanders on the ground soon realised that Hitler had completely misjudged the strength of the Russian defence. 'The whole situation makes it increasingly plain that we have underestimated the Russian colossus,' noted General Fritz Halder just a few weeks after the invasion was launched. He had been told to expect 200 Russian divisions in defence of the motherland. In reality, there were almost double that number and they clung to every inch of Russian territory with a tenacity that took the German army completely by surprise.

'If we smash a dozen of them,' wrote Halder, 'the Russians simply put up another dozen. The time factor favours them as they are near their own resources, whereas we are moving further and further away from ours. And so our troops, sprawled over an immense front line, without any depth, are subjected to the enemy's incessant attacks.'

In spite of these difficulties, the German offensive achieved some spectacular successes. Kiev was captured in September and the Crimea was cut off from southern Russia. The German army had also reached the northern suburbs of Moscow and looked set to snap up Stalin's capital before the New Year.

However, it was at this moment of near-triumph that winter arrived in earnest, with freezing blizzards and biting winds sweeping in from the eastern steppe. While Wolfram and his friends were enjoying wintry hikes in the country-side around Oberammergau, the poorly provisioned troops outside Moscow were suffering from the effects of severe frostbite.

German casualties had topped half a million in the open-ing months of the campaign. Now, that figure rose dramatically. In one twenty-four-hour period in December 1941, 14,000 German soldiers had frostbitten limbs ampu-tated. Many of them would be dead within a few days.

It became increasingly obvious that conscripts drawn from Germany's youth would be needed to make up the shortfall in manpower. By the time Wolfram was called into service in 1942, there was little doubt that he would be despatched to the eastern front.

'We've spent days without potatoes,' wrote Wolfram's mother in a letter to her son. 'We've got the ration coupons to buy them but there are none available.'

In her kitchen in Eutingen, Marie Charlotte was trying to prepare lunch. In times of war and ever-stricter rationing, it was hard to conjure an appetising meal. Bread, pickled vege-tables and bottled fruit formed the basis of their daily diet.

It had been some months since she had last seen her church friend, Martha Luise Rodi. The Christian Community, where they used to meet each weekend, had been forced by the city's Nazi authorities to shut its doors permanently the previous June. The order had come in the wake of Rudolf Hess's bizarre flight to Scotland in the spring of 1941 – a solo peace mission on the part of Hitler's deputy whose true aims and purpose have never been satisfactorily explained.

Hess was declared *persona non grata* by the Nazi regime and all of his personal interests – which included mysticism, astronomy and homeopathic medicine – became tainted by association. Although he had never adhered to Steiner's philosophy, he was deemed to be sufficiently close to his ideas to warrant the closure and destruction of Germany's remaining Steiner churches. 'The end,' wrote Goebbels at the time, 'of occultism.'

Marie Charlotte visited her Pforzheim parish to find that it had been ransacked by overzealous officers from the Gestapo and stripped of all its furniture.

'You already know where I went on Tuesday,' she wrote. 'It was so upsetting to go there and see it again. On the previous day, the last pieces of furniture had been roughly removed.' Her only consolation was that Herr Becher, their now-unemployed pastor, had been given some work by a member of the Community.

As the campaign in Russia lurched from crisis to crisis, both Marie Charlotte and Martha Luise prayed for a speedy end to the conflict. Both had sons who would soon be conscripted to the battlefront and both of them hoped against hope that the invasion of Russia would be completed – or defeated – before their sons had to take their turn on the front line.

Martha Luise had one reason to be thankful in these difficult times. Her husband, Max, had been relieved of military duties within a few months of being drafted into the army and posted to Alsace, some sixty miles away, to teach German to the local Alsatian schoolchildren.

Max soon forged a close relationship with the villagers, in part because he spoke good French. When they learned that he had five children, they took pity on him, giving him cheese and smoked sausages to take home to the family each weekend.

When Martha Luise, a perfectionist, was not busy with the housework, she and her daughters spent their time wrapping scores of parcels for cousins and nephews who had been drafted into the army and were now fighting for their lives on the eastern front.

Martha Luise had almost a dozen young soldiers to whom she sent parcels and wrote letters. The family also sent food and warm clothes to these men when they realised that Hitler had taken no precautions in equipping his forces for the Russian winter.

As the first blast of winter arrived in Pforzheim – and news from the front became increasingly hard to obtain – the Rodi family speculated on how their cousins were faring out on the Russian steppe. The whole nation was now being asked to knit woollen clothing for the troops. Even eleven-year-old Frithjof learned to knit. Meanwhile, everyone whispered to themselves that Hitler should have profited from Napoleon's failures in 1812.

No one dared to speak of such things in public, but there was a growing feeling among Pforzheimers that Hitler had committed a grave blunder in invading Russia. These fears were to sharpen still further in the second week of December, when Germany found itself at war with the United States.

Frithjof looked forward with boyish enthusiasm to the occasional visits from the officer-cousins fighting on the Russian front, whom he admired greatly. They came in their military uniforms, bringing back dramatic stories of tank battles and hand-to-hand fighting in blizzards and snowdrifts. Such things made a deep impression on a young boy. He and his older brother always wanted to know whether or not they had been awarded the Iron Cross and whether it was first or merely second class.

Wolfram was increasingly concerned about what the immediate future held in store for him. Just a few days after his medical, he received his call-up papers, which told him to make his way to a training camp at Niederbayern, a few miles to the north of Munich.

The girls on his wood-sculpting course decided to give the young lads a joyous send-off, decorating sleighs with spruce branches and hurtling across the snow-covered Ettal valley. This good-humoured farewell did little to allay the anxiety and anger felt by Wolfram and his friends. Wolfram was particularly furious at being called up. For years he had dreamed of being a sculptor. Now, the war had become an indefinite interruption to his studies.

Life in the Niederbayern camp was physically exhausting. Gun training and enforced marches left him close to collapse each evening. Worse still, he was perpetually hungry as all available foodstuffs were now being diverted to soldiers at the front. 'Food is far more important for me than money,' he wrote in a letter to his parents. 'Please send me something to spread on bread – jam, honey – or some other food or some ration cards.'

The daily routine was punishing. The men in charge of the military training programme were petty tyrants who delighted in treating the fresh recruits harshly. Wolfram

and his comrades were woken at six: there was no breakfast. Having wolfed down whatever scraps they had
managed to save from the night before, they spent the
morning being instructed on gun maintenance and target
practice, something at which Wolfram excelled.

The importance of physical fitness was stressed again and
again. They were told that they could hope to survive the
Russian front only if they were in peak physical condition.

'I won't easily forget last Thursday,' wrote Wolfram in a
letter to his parents. 'We had to do a walk of nearly thirty-
five kilometres.' Winter had been dispelled in an instant by
a burst of spring sunshine and suddenly it was insufferably
hot – 'a real burning heat'.

An already difficult hike was made agonising by the fact
that none of the men had been issued with any socks. After
thirty kilometres, Wolfram could go no further: he, along with
several other men, collapsed from pain and exhaustion.

'As of yesterday,' he wrote, 'I'm lying in bed in the infirmary. On both my feet they've cut open my blisters and
drained them. The sores are really bad – the size of my
entire foot.' For the next seven days he was unable to stand,
but as soon as the blisters were partially healed he was sent
back into training.

There was usually a brief break for lunch at midday – a
one-pot meal, which was never enough for these growing
teenagers. After this then they had four hours of marching
and drilling in the afternoon. In the evening they would get
half a loaf of bread, a bit of margarine, and some cheese and
sausage. That had to be enough for the evening and the
following morning.

After a few days in camp, Wolfram was feeling homesick

and miserable. His most abiding memory of those eight weeks at Niederbayern was the lack of comradeship. It was the loneliest time of his entire life. In normal circumstances, he would have been recruited with friends from his own town or village. Having signed up with local farm lads from Bavaria and elsewhere in Germany, he had absolutely nothing in common with them.

As the end of May approached, Wolfram's time at the camp was fast coming to an end. All that remained was to find out where he would be posted. He longed to be drafted into the Alpine service, for he had a passion for mountains and had loved his hikes into the Bavarian Alps. 'If only I could at least see the Alps from a distance,' he wrote to his parents. 'How happy I'd be if I got to see the mountains again.'

It was not to be. At the beginning of June 1942, he learned that he was being sent to the East. The military situation there was critical and manpower in short supply. In the previous December, the Soviet army had regained a foothold on the Kerch peninsula, landing a large number of troops at Feodosiya. Sevastopol, too, was holding out against the German besiegers. Hitler decreed that the Crimea needed to be reconquered with immediate effect. Youngsters from the Reich Labour Service were to be sent to provide technical support, working alongside the army, in what was likely to be a prolonged military campaign. To the eastern front Wolfram must go.

Marie Charlotte was distraught when she heard this news, although she tried to put a brave face on it. 'In this day and age,' she wrote in a letter to her son, 'you have to take things as they come and try to see the positive side.' She was trying to remain upbeat, even though knowledge of his imminent departure to the East had dealt her a terrible blow.

'For me,' she wrote, 'in all experiences, I've recognised some sort of guidance and sense as to why things happened, including the painful things. You must remember that I shall still be thinking of you, even when you're abroad. Of course, I would love you to be spared anything unpleasant and difficult, but we have to remember that these things may contribute to making a stronger person out of you.'

Her advice was personal, heartfelt and born out of her Christian beliefs. She said that Germany was caught in a tremendous battle between good and evil. Although she did not mention Hitler by name, she was clearly referring to him as the diabolical figure who was leading Germany to ruin. 'Everyone has to remain strong in this day and age – in this fight between good spirits and bad.'

The bad spirits had certainly got the upper hand in the state of Baden. In Pforzheim, Karlsruhe and elsewhere, there were no longer any Jews left, except for the *mischlinge* (the half-Jews and quarter-Jews), plus those living a hidden existence in attics and cellars. Yet their absence did not stop the relentless anti-Semitism that was still being taught in universities and schools.

Frithjof Rodi was at school one day, being taught about the creation of the world. The teacher said that God was very tired after making Adam and Eve but that He still had a little lump of clay left over. He tried to make a third figure but it was extremely ugly and so He threw it violently into the corner. This made its nose crooked and its legs all bandy.

The children listened to the story wide-eyed, never having heard this particular version of the creation. The teacher then told them how this crippled and misshapen creature slowly came alive and started creeping towards God. God was appalled and said to it: 'Go to hell, you Jew!'

Once the teacher had finished with his story, he made all the children write it out in their neatest handwriting.

It was not just religion that was permeated with ideology. Science, too, was a target for the Nazis. They could do little to alter the chemistry and physics curriculum, but biology became an easy vehicle for anti-Semitism. In Hannelore Schottgen's class, race was the principal subject, focusing on the hierarchy of races. At the very top was the Aryan race: Nordic, tall, blond with blue eyes, a noble character, faithful, hard-working and the brightest part of the German population. Next down the scale were the Slavs, along with Latin and Mediterranean types. All other peoples of the world – especially those who were black or Jewish – were considered completely degenerate.

At playtimes, Hannelore and her friends would talk excitedly about how close they were to the proper race, although they were sorely disappointed when they worked out that hardly anyone turned out to be pure Nordic. The tall ones were dark, the blonde ones were little and the sole fair-haired girl who was tall had a crooked nose.

Hannelore felt uncomfortable in these biology lessons, largely because the teacher herself was uncomfortable, teaching the new curriculum without any enthusiasm while doing her best to keep a distance from it. Hannelore and her friends, aware that she did not agree with what she was having to teach, decided not to ask any difficult questions because they liked her.

History was also overlaid with racial theory. At school,

129

Frithjof learned that the Germanic race, with its blond hair and blue eyes, had destroyed the Roman Empire. Back at home, he and his brother used to joke about the fact that Hitler did not look at all Aryan.

This was true enough, but he was nevertheless portrayed as the embodiment, indeed the fulfilment, of Germanic destiny. In history lessons, teachers reproached the medieval kings of Germany for travelling to Rome for their coronations instead of using their energies to colonise the East. Only Otto the Great was singled out as an exception because he had expanded eastwards and fought the Slavs.

While Frithjof and his classmates were being instructed in anti-Semitism, his older brother, Peter, discovered that his full-time education was about to be abruptly interrupted. In April 1942, to his mother's great distress, he returned home with news that he had been drafted into the *heimatflak* or home defence. He was just sixteen years of age but, in these times of total war, even schoolboys were required to offer their lives to the service of the Fatherland.

Peter's job – and that of the other boys in his class – was to shoot down any enemy planes that happened to pass over Pforzheim. He was given a uniform and some basic training in how the guns were to be fired. Russian ones that had been captured at the front, they required three or four people to fire them. His task was to get the gun to the correct elevation.

The boys were woefully under-trained and their weapons were far from accurate. They had to be able to see the plane in order to shoot at it. Peter never had the opportunity to put his training into action. Indeed, he rarely saw any planes passing overhead.

His other friends were less fortunate. One was sent to Peenemunde on the Baltic coast, where Hitler's secret rocket programme was being developed. This was a regular target for the Royal Air Force, whose bombing raids were often heavy and sustained. His friend's group shot down many planes. One day he was given leave to go home because the family house had burned down in a raid. While he was away, his group received a direct hit and they were all killed.

Peter hated his time in the *heimatflak*. He still had to go to school each morning; then, after lunch, he changed into his military uniform and reported for duty. Worst of all, he was no longer allowed to live at home. He and his comrades shared cramped accommodation in barracks on the edge of town.

The food was not bad because it was being brought to Germany from the occupied countries. They had plentiful supplies of cheese and butter, which had been stolen from Denmark.

Personal hygiene, however, was non-existent. They were allowed home once a week and Peter was always desperate for a bath, but the family tub was kept permanently full of cold water, in case of fire.

CHAPTER EIGHT

DIRTY WAR

'We are not to publicise our objectives to the world.'

Wolfram and his fellow conscripts were to travel to the Crimea by train, a circuitous journey that would take them through the heart of German-occupied Ukraine. In different times and different circumstances, such a voyage would have been a fabulous adventure into the unknown for a group of wide-eyed young lads. As their destination was a war zone, the outcome was one of deep uncertainty.

They were to pass through many towns that had been brutally subjugated by the army and the SS, among them Brest-Litovsk, Kiev and Mariupol, before arriving at Dzhankoy on the Crimean peninsula. The 1,700-mile journey would take four weeks. For Wolfram, it seemed like four years.

Although the men were not aware of it at the time, they were unwitting pioneers in one of Hitler's more disquieting projects: to empty the Crimean peninsula of Slavs and transform it into a summer playground for the Germanic race.

'For us Germans,' he said in one speech, 'it will be our Riviera.' He planned to build a spectacular autobahn that

132

would stretch from Berlin to Sevastopol, entertaining visions of smiling German families climbing into their Volkswagen cars and driving southwards to the sun. He intended to call this new colony Gothenland. 'In the Eastern territories,' he said proudly, 'I shall replace Slav geographical titles by German names.'

For Wolfram and his comrades, their own voyage southwards fell dismally short of Hitler's rose-tinted vision. They were loaded on to overcrowded transport trains, forty men to a wagon. Each carriage was divided into narrow, boxed-off compartments, with boards, above and below, that created just enough space for ten men to sleep. It was like going to bed in a coffin.

The atmosphere in the enclosed carriage was fuggy and claustrophobic and it stank of stale sweat and unwashed clothes. There were no windows – just a narrow slit through which the inquisitive or bored could peer out on to the fleckled smudge of passing fields and forest.

The worst aspect of the journey was going to the toilet. The men had to suspend themselves over the gap between rattling carriages and, with the aid of a friend to anchor them, do their business on to the tracks below. As there was no toilet paper, they used the straw that covered the floor or, once they reached the Ukraine, the local banknotes, which were completely worthless.

Each of the conscripts had his own manner of dealing with the pangs of homesickness. Some told stories of happy childhoods. Others spoke with feigned bravado about the dangers that lay ahead. Wolfram spent his daytime hours in a trance, peering out through the letter-box slit that was his only link with the outside world.

'Brown cows in the fields, lots of houses, green meadows, a few hills, some windmills and derelict villages which from a distance looked quite nice to paint.' Such were his impressions in a letter he wrote to his parents.

There was a darker side to this idyllic picture – one that Wolfram was not able to include in the letter for fear of censorship. Alongside his memories of tumbledown villages and tidy potagers came the first hazy awareness of the more sinister reality that was overtaking these conquered lands.

He got his first shock as the train drew to a halt at the bleak frontier town of Brest-Litovsk, just a few miles inside Belorussia. A large number of Jewish women, all wearing yellow stars, were cleaning dirt from between the tracks. They were in a pitiful condition – their sallow faces and famished frames a visible testimony to long months of hunger and harsh treatment.

Wolfram, upset by what he saw, tried to speak with a group of girls, but no sooner had they begun to answer his questions than the bark of a German sentry echoed across the tracks. *Verboten! Verboten!* They were forbidden from communicating further.

Wolfram's eye was drawn to another group of Jews engaged in a desperate brawl over empty food tins that had been thrown out of the train windows by the German soldiers. They were wiping the insides of the tins with their fingers in the hope of finding some nourishment.

Wolfram and his comrades made their way from the station into town, where they became witness to a picture of human misery. Brest-Litovsk had been all but destroyed when the German army had attacked the Soviet garrison in the previous summer, subjecting defenders and civilians

Dirty War

alike to a lethal combination of mortars and flame-throwers. The liquid fire was particularly devastating. The few survivors from the citadel emerged with stories of a heat so intense that it melted bricks and liquefied steel girders.

The siege was only the opening chapter in a long saga of suffering and abuse. The newly installed German overlords were treating the enforced labourers, many of them Jews, with ruthless severity.

The most brutal guards were the ethnic Germans who had lived in Brest-Litovsk for generations. To Wolfram, it was as if they were unleashing centuries of repressed hatred on those whose lives they now held in their hands.

He was no less horrified to see how they behaved towards their Soviet prisoners of war. A group of captives was in the process of digging a trench through the centre of town, overseen by their vengeful guards. Wolfram was rooted to the spot, watching an old man throw shovelfuls of earth up from the trench. Each time he paused to catch his breath, the guard smashed him across the head with a spade.

Although Wolfram did not know it at the time, these prisoners of war were actually among the most fortunate of the hundreds of thousands captured by the German army. When Minsk had been taken, some 300,000 Soviet troops were taken prisoner. When Bryansk and Vyazma were seized, the Germans netted a further 650,000 men. Most were starved to death, murdered in cold blood or imprisoned without shelter in the cruel months of midwinter.

The inhumanity that Wolfram witnessed in Brest-Litovsk was but a pale reflection of the atrocities being carried out in the surrounding towns and villages. In the immediate aftermath of the invasion of Soviet Russia, four *einsatzgruppen* or paramilitary task forces had moved in with orders to execute small groups of Jews and partisans working behind their front line. By the autumn of 1941, these paramilitary groups were organising mass executions of the local Jewish population. The death toll had already topped 750,000 by the time Wolfram arrived in Brest-Litovsk.

The slaughter had been ordered by Hitler and Himmler, who made it clear that it was to be undertaken with a ruthlessness exceeding that of all previous killings. 'Even the child in the cradle must be trampled down like a poisonous toad,' said Himmler. 'We are living in an epoch of iron, during which it is necessary to sweep with iron-made brooms.'

Secrecy was imperative. Hitler issued numerous directives on the importance of ensuring that the butchery remained covert and hidden. 'We are not to publicise our objectives to the world,' he told his SS chiefs.

Wolfram witnessed scenes of barbaric treatment meted out to Jews in Brest-Litovsk. Although he knew all too well that vile things happened in war, neither he nor any of his comrades had any notion of the scale of the executions being carried out behind the scenes.

Even if they had known, they could do little, given their own unhappy predicament. There was an overriding feeling that everyone was trapped in the same terrible boat. Wolfram and the others lived in constant terror of what the future held for them.

They knew nothing of the *einsatzgruppen* death squads and were equally ignorant of the ethnic cleansing that was sweeping through the area around Brest-Litovsk. Not until after the war did Wolfram first learn of the mass murder of Jews, partisans and Soviet prisoners of war.

The ignorance of these young conscripts is not entirely surprising, given that deception was a key ingredient in the Nazi extermination programme. The gas vans used to kill some 350,000 Jews in the Soviet lands looked innocuous enough as they drove through the countryside.

The SS officer in charge of one such fleet of death vehicles, August Becker, ordered them to be made to look like mobile homes so as not to arouse suspicion: '[they were] disguised as house trailers, by having a single window shutter fixed to each side of the small vans and, on the large ones, two shutters, such as one often sees on farmhouses in the country.'

This folksy exterior belied the gruesome fate that awaited those within. The exhaust pipe was vented up through the floor of the rear cabin, enabling sixty people to be killed by poisoning and asphyxiation in each short ride to the mass grave.

The full horror of the outrages being visited upon the occupied territories was to remain unknown until 1946, when a small number of those who committed them were put on trial at Nuremberg. It was during the cross-examination of Otto Ohlendorf, head of Einsatzgruppe D, that the extraordinary level of planning and secrecy surrounding the policy of extermination was finally revealed. Ohlendorf spoke with precision, detachment and astuteness, proudly admitting that the 500 soldiers under his command had liquidated 90,000 men, women and children. He showed no remorse or regret, except when he spoke of his own men. His fear, throughout the killing process, was that they might become emotionally exhausted by conducting mass murder in secret and on a daily basis.

The train shunted slowly out of the sidings of Brest-Litovsk and began to push deep into Belorussia. There was a detectable change in the landscape as they headed southwards: at first, the fields were studded with coppices, which gradually merged into woods. Suddenly, one morning Wolfram awoke to find that the woods had thickened into forests whose giant spruce trees were wilder and darker than anything he had seen in the Schwarzwald.

'Vast forests and wild meadows,' he wrote in a letter to his parents. 'Houses made of wood with straw on the roof, or wooden slates.' This was a land that had yet to be touched by Stalin's plans for a modern agro-industry.

In one forest clearing Wolfram glimpsed his first Orthodox church. Its characteristic onion dome had a certain similarity to the Bavarian baroque, but its glittering cusp, topped by the double-barred crucifix of Eastern Christendom, signalled that they were now far from home.

Most of the churches in Belorussia and the Ukraine had been forcibly closed by Stalin some years earlier. One of the first actions of the invading German army had been to reopen them, earning them much gratitude from the pious faithful. Now, on Sundays and on feast days, the bells clanged in the crisp morning air and the faithful trooped to their re-established parishes.

Every railway junction and every siding was crowded with truckloads of soldiers being transported eastwards towards Stalingrad: Romanians, Italians, Spaniards and

Hungarians, as well as large numbers of Germans. The Italians yelled anti-Stalin slogans, while the Spanish volunteers sang and shouted, but the Hungarians and Romanians, more wary of their German allies, went past in silence.

At one point the train skirted the outer suburbs of Kursk, which had become a key tactical position of the German front line. The men were left in no doubt that they were close to the front when mortars started exploding all around them.

The train looped back into the Ukraine and Wolfram took comfort in a renewed familiarity with the landscape. In places, it looked like rural Swabia. 'Ukraine is beautiful,' he wrote in a letter. 'Really thick black earth, cornfields and sunflower fields everywhere. Sometimes we saw villages which I liked very much – lovely clean-looking whitewashed houses with big thatched roofs.'

The weather changed dramatically as they headed southwards towards Dnepropetrovsk and Mariupol. The cool spring breezes faded in an instant: now, summer arrived in a pulsating furnace of heat. It was stiflingly hot in the airless train compartment.

As Wolfram and his comrades neared Dzhankoi, on the Crimean peninsula, they caught their first glimpse of the distant Caucasus mountains, their silver-white backbone picked out like a bright line of chalk by the blinding August sunshine.

The men were by now so hungry and exhausted that the heat and brightness started to play tricks with their eyes. When they saw the most beautiful silhouette of a city, they all got excited, trying to work out which one it could be, but then, in a flash, it disappeared and they realised that the entire city had been a mirage.

Just a few hours after this enticing vision, the train pulled into a siding on a bleak area of steppe some distance to the north of Feodosia. After a journey lasting more than four weeks, they had at long last arrived at their destination.

Feodosia had until recently been a handsome Black Sea resort – a place of *fin-de-siècle* villas and luxurious sanatoria frequented by fat-bellied apparatchiks of the Soviet Communist Party. In the course of three successive battles, the town had been besieged, lost and then finally recaptured by the German army, suffering such severe damage each time that its once-elegant waterfront, all stucco and pillars, now lay in ruins.

Wolfram assumed he and his comrades would be billeted inside the town. Instead, they were transferred northwards to a remote spot within striking distance of the Sea of Azov.

His first impression was of dryness and heat; he had never been anywhere so hot. 'Sand and more sand,' he wrote in a letter to his parents. 'And no trees anywhere. It's really, really scorching; and the sea is nowhere near as beautiful as the North Sea. It's mostly calm – there are no shadows anywhere.'

He dreamed of the mountains above Oberammergau. 'I'd give anything to be on a big cold glacier,' he wrote. 'A waterfall or green meadows with fruit trees. I'd prefer that to the whole of the sea.'

The men's tented encampment was close to the military airfield – a desolate spot with no sign of the customary German efficiency. The camp itself was a blighted wasteland, its ditches and open sewers awash with fluvial waste. Swarms of flies spread disease and infection. Wolfram and his comrades had almost constant diarrhoea.

'There are a few people living here,' he wrote, 'but I don't know how. Nothing grows. We're close to a Ukrainian village. The houses are built of mud and the people are very poor. They spend the whole day lying on mattresses outside their house.' Wolfram had little contact with the locals, with the exception of the Tartars, who were friendly towards the Germans because of their hatred of Stalin.

The men were set to work on hard physical labour for twelve hours a day, digging trenches and constructing defensive earth banks. The only respite came in the morning and the evening when they were allowed to swim in the sea.

The front line was just across the Kerch Straits, less than fifty miles from Feodosia. As night fell, the men's sleep was disturbed by the menacing drone of Russian planes in the skies overhead, skirting low over the landscape as they looked for positions to bomb. 'It can be very loud when the Russians come,' wrote Wolfram. 'But so far, nothing has happened to anyone in our group.'

The hard work left the men continually hungry and thirsty. 'I'd love to have something sweet and fresh,' wrote Wolfram to his parents. 'There's no fruit here. If you want to send me something, please send me *brause* powder – the one where you add water and it tastes like lemon juice.'

He was feeling seriously anxious about the trials that lay ahead. Although he was relatively safe while still working for the Reich Labour Service, that safety would come to an end with the inevitable summons into the Wehrmacht.

'Here you can see what war is,' he wrote, 'even if the only danger at present is from bombs and sickness. But we are experiencing quite a lot and I can't say it's particularly nice. I wouldn't wish it on anyone.'

* * *

Wolfram remained in the countryside to the north of Feodosia for four weeks. He was then transferred to a village near Kerch, closer to the front, which had been recaptured from the Soviet army in the spring. 'All I can say,' he wrote in a letter home, 'is that this is the arsehole of the world. It's not a very elegant expression, but the only place more depressing can be the desert . . . everything is dead.'

Kerch, like Feodosia, bore the scars of the recent fighting. Soldiers and civilians jostled through the ruined streets, each carrying their personal burden of misery. 'Large numbers of German and Romanian soldiers,' wrote Wolfram, 'as well as men from the Reich Labour Service. And there are also lots of Russians sitting on the pavements . . . young girls with make-up and very dirty children.' The civilian population was trapped in a war zone with no money, no shelter and precious little food.

Food was a constant problem. With supply lines cut and transport bogged down in mud, there was never enough to eat. 'With the sugar you sent me, I cooked myself a very nice apple compote', wrote Wolfram. 'And I also made sauté potatoes with butter.' However, the rare additional rations that survived the journey to the Crimea were soon consumed and he was once again hungry.

He had been in Kerch for only three days when he started to feel ill. He took himself off to a military doctor who dismissed his sore throat and temperature, accusing him of exaggerating his sickness. When his temperature rapidly developed into a fever, he became so weak that he could hardly pull himself out of bed. Even now, despite all the tell-tale signs, the medical staff still did not realise that he had contracted diphtheria.

There was no transport to take him to the infirmary, which was situated in a nearby village. The doctors told him that he would have to make his own way there. He found himself standing in the street, trembling with weakness, burningly hot and with a high fever.

He was most fortunate that a passing driver, a German military officer, took compassion on him, picking him up and driving him to the infirmary, which he reached just in time. His sickness had by now developed into a life-threatening condition that could be alleviated only by a huge dose of serum.

The doctors injected him on his arrival but it made little difference. He was still in a poor state the next morning, so they gave him a second injection. Wolfram overheard the doctors talking about him as he lay there with a dangerously high temperature. 'Look! A typical Labour Service lad. He has no idea that you come here to die.'

One of the side effects caused by the serum injections was a temporary paralysis of the nerves. In other patients, this had triggered heart failure, but it also brought moments of temporary respite. It was during one of these that Wolfram was transferred by hospital train to Cherson in the southern Ukraine, crossing the Dneiper by boat. The first thing he saw on his arrival was a funeral procession, the first of many. In Cherson, death was ever present.

The journey provoked an even higher fever. 'I'm still in hospital but I'm okay,' he wrote to his parents in October 1942. 'That's the way with diphtheria. Some days you've got high fever and feel really, really bad. And then you get a serum injection and you feel fine, although you still have to lie down for a week.'

The Ukrainian nurses working in Cherson hospital cared little for the German soldiers under their charge. Wolfram shared a room with another conscript who was seriously ill. Whole days would pass with no one coming near them. They were brought no food – nothing. When they complained, the nurses shrugged their shoulders and said they had forgotten they were there.

Wolfram heard nothing from the battlefront during his time in hospital and had no inkling of the clash of arms that had begun in the outskirts of Stalingrad, where troops were engaged in relentless fighting in temperatures that had already dipped well below zero. Soviet forces were still clinging to the west bank of the River Volga, despite near-constant bombing raids. 'The whole sky was full of aircraft,' wrote one German infantry man serving on the front line. 'Every flak gun firing, bombs roaring down, aircraft crashing, an enormous piece of theatre.'

'I haven't got news,' wrote Wolfram to his parents at the very moment when the battle was entering its critical phase. 'I don't hear or read anything of what's going on in the world.' Nor did he know that all of the comrades from his year group had been conscripted into the army and were on their way to the River Donetz, where they were to fight in the rearguard battle for Stalingrad.

The military hospital in which Wolfram was confined lay directly opposite an Orthodox church. Each day, from dawn until a late dusk, he could hear the doleful chant of funerals. *'The choir of the saints have found the fountain of life and the door of paradise . . .'* The voices of the basses were mirrored in reverse by the upper-octave tenors – a polyphonic chorus that transported him. 'Such wonderful singing,' he wrote to his parents. 'So much more solemn than you find in the Catholic churches.'

In his illness and depression, he had at last found something to raise his spirits. As he gazed down from his bedroom window upon the Orthodox funeral processions, he was so struck by their solemn beauty that he had a sudden urge to attend one, even though the doctors had forbidden him to leave his bed.

'I've got a healthy heart,' he wrote to his parents, 'so it should be okay.' He crept downstairs in his pyjamas and, with the help of a friend, managed to clamber over the fence into the churchyard. 'There were a few men and women – really few – but they sang with such beauty. The priest was a very old man with a big white beard and sometimes he sang on his own. He was wearing a beautiful robe of embroidered gold and had a big high black hat.'

As the white coffin passed, Wolfram noticed that it was decorated with delicately intertwined flower motifs with clusters of colourful blooms on the top. However, it was the low, mournful chanting that made the most lasting impression on him. 'Such sad and nostalgic songs,' he wrote. 'They seem to go so well with the dark black earth. How I would have loved to come here before the war.'

His visit to the church had lifted his soul but seriously weakened his fever-ridden body. A few days after attending the funeral, his muscles locked into rigidity and he collapsed to the floor. When he tried to move, he found that all his limbs were immobilised. 'Now it's happening,' said the doctor to the nurse. 'It'll last a long time.'

Wolfram was paralysed from head to foot. He could not eat, so the doctors tried to feed him through tubes pushed up his nose. When this failed to work because he was unable to swallow, they injected food directly into his gut. They now realised that the only chance of him recovering was to transport him to Germany by plane, even though this meant a hazardous train journey to the military airport in Nikolaev, some fifty miles to the north-west.

Wolfram was by now in such a dangerous condition that he had to be accompanied to Nikolaev by a nurse, whose cheery demeanour immediately attracted the attentions of the soldiers in the next carriage. When she went off to chat with them, Wolfram overheard the men making coarse jibes about him. 'He'll soon have a cold arse,' said one. What this meant was that he did not have long to live.

While Wolfram was left on his own, he was preyed on by other men in the carriage. Someone stole his watch. He watched the man take it but was unable to move or cry out. He heard him saying to his mates: 'Why not? He'll be dead soon.'

He was not surprised by their behaviour. When someone needed new trousers and came across a person who was dying, they simply clawed them off and stole them.

Wolfram was still alive when they pulled into Nikolaev, but the journey had weakened him still further. By now he was only partly conscious and could no longer speak. 'Herr Professor Aïchele,' wrote the doctor in a letter to his father. 'I am writing on behalf of your son ... he himself cannot write because he is too weak. He is meant to be moved by plane but at the moment the weather is too bad. Therefore he has had to stay here, but we will look after him.'

Just days after Wolfram's parents received this letter, they were sitting at home when the telephone rang. It was

Frau Hoch, the post lady in Eutingen, who informed Marie Charlotte that another letter had just arrived from Nikolaev. Marie Charlotte tore down to the centre of the village – she would later recall that she had never run as fast in all her life – and ripped open the envelope.

She had hoped against hope that it would be from Wolfram, but saw immediately that it was not his handwriting. She was even more devastated when she read it. The letter had been written by a nurse, Sister Dorothea, who was caring for her son.

It told her and her husband to brace themselves for the worst. Wolfram was going to die.

CHAPTER NINE

A MATTER OF LIFE OR DEATH

'The enemy is listening!'

Wolfram's mother left no account of how she coped with the anxieties of knowing that her nineteen-year-old son lay hundreds of miles away in the last throes of life. When, many years later, she sat down to write a memoir of her experiences, she lingered on the good things that had happened. This was part of her philosophy of life. She believed that there was a reason behind everything – that the dark wheel of fortune was not quite as fickle as the gloomy chroniclers of medieval Germany would have her believe.

Marie Charlotte certainly had plenty to worry about in the autumn of 1942. While her youngest son was dying of diphtheria, her eldest, Reiner, had been posted to Tikhvin, a grim military base some one hundred miles to the east of Leningrad. As sleet sluiced down relentlessly on the exposed Russian marshlands, and the canvas tents dripped and leaked, Reiner wrote home of a war that could never be won.

Wolfram's mother also had troubles of her own. Just weeks before receiving news of Wolfram's impending death, she had received a summons to the local Gestapo head-quarters in Pforzheim. Although she had no idea what she had done wrong, and no clue as to why she was to be inter-rogated, she was alarmed by the mere prospect of being called in for questioning and was half sick with fear by the time she entered the building.

The conversation that took place was to remain a mystery for some years as she was under strict orders not to reveal anything that had been discussed. It later transpired that the Gestapo had been keeping a watchful eye on the family and had assembled a substantial dossier about their dangerous eccentricities, particularly those of Marie Charlotte. They knew all the details of her attendance at meetings organised by the Steiner movement as well as of her involvement in Pforzheim's anthroposophical society. They also had copies, faithfully transcribed by hand, of all Marie Charlotte's pre-war correspondence with the Soucrains, a French family whose son had previously been a lodger in Eutingen.

After lengthy questioning, Marie Charlotte was warned to tread with extreme care. She was forbidden from travel-ling more than five miles from the Pforzheim area without prior permission from the Gestapo and told that her move-ments would be monitored at all times by the state police.

Marie Charlotte feared that this was the prelude to some-thing far worse: that the regime was preparing to punish her and her freemason husband, at a time and in a manner yet unknown, for persistently refusing to join the Nazi Party.

The catalyst for her interrogation was almost certainly the assassination of Reinhard Heydrich, director of Reich Security, in the late spring of 1942. Ever since, the state police had been ruthlessly clamping down on 'enemies of the state'. Marie Charlotte's membership of the Christian Community and her connections with France automatically placed her in a high-risk category.

Other members of the parish also came under increasing harassment from the Gestapo. At the same time that Marie Charlotte was called in for interrogation, Martha Luise Rodi received an unannounced visit from two uniformed officers at their house on Spichernstrasse.

Her eldest son, Peter, was at home when they knocked on the door. The men did not wait to be invited inside but barged their way in and brusquely informed Martha Luise that they were under orders to confiscate all her anthroposophical books – anything, indeed, that might be connected with the Rudolf Steiner movement.

Martha Luise had never been shy to speak her mind and she saw no reason to act differently when confronted with the Gestapo. She expressed her indignation about this invasion of the family home, making very clear to them her unhappiness at their manner and behaviour. In Hitler's Germany there was no room for manoeuvre. The officers helped themselves to the offending volumes, as well as to other books that had nothing to do with Steiner.

Martha Luise said firmly, 'No, those ones aren't to be taken.' Ignoring her, the men took two of the family's laundry baskets, filled them with books and set off with them down the garden path. As they did so, Peter's sister called after them: 'No, you're not to take those. We'll expect them back!' She was referring to the laundry baskets, but the men thought she was talking about the books and replied sarcastically: 'Oh, no, I don't think you'll be getting these back.'

Such events, set against a backdrop of perpetual war,

were a source of constant anxiety for seven-year-old Barbara, the youngest in the Rodi clan. The regime's first intrusion into her childhood had been the call-up of her father on the day that war broke out. Then, her brother Peter had been drafted into the *heimatflak*. Now, with every month that passed, life seemed to become darker and ever more disturbing.

She started to seek refuge in books, where life was peaceful, happy and often romantic – as well as divorced from reality. She began to live more and more in a dream world, even though the war was continually intruding on those dreams, and often cried herself to sleep for no obvious reason. Her mother would pray with her each evening, asking God to protect her father and brother and all who were dear to the family.

In distant Nikolaev, Wolfram was hovering between life and death. Paralysed and extremely weak, he kept slipping in and out of consciousness.

The German army deemed it bad for morale for soldiers to see their comrades die, so those who had no hope of recovering were segregated from their friends shortly before the end. By mid-November 1942, the doctors, seeing Wolfram at death's door, moved him into a room of his own. His fellow patients awaited the inevitable news.

Two days passed and still Wolfram clung to life. His medication was continued, even though it seemed to have no effect. However, after a few more days, his broken body suddenly showed signs of responding. The doctors were surprised and expressed cautious optimism. They also took the decision to move him back on to the ward.

By the third week of November 1942, it was clear that Wolfram had passed the most critical point of his illness. He regained full consciousness and, though extremely weak, was soon able to sit up in bed. The hospital's chief physician was confident enough to write a letter to Wolfram's father, voicing his belief that Wolfram was on the mend.

'Herr Professor Aïchele, I am writing this on behalf of your son who sadly is not well enough to write. But he's improving very fast and soon he'll be in a position to write himself.'

Wolfram had eaten nothing for weeks; now, he developed a voracious appetite and was soon attacking giant-sized portions of roast chicken and mashed potato, washed down with glasses of excellent red wine from Bordeaux. Recuperating soldiers were given all the resources that the German army could buy or steal from the occupied lands. He was also plied with lots of coffee – a rare luxury in times of war – as it was believed to stimulate the nerves.

At the beginning of December, Wolfram was strong enough to haul himself out of bed. A few days later, he took his first tentative steps with the aid of a nurse. He managed a circuit around the bed, which seemed like a long and exhausting mountain hike.

The doctors knew then that he would make a full recovery. 'He's developed quite a healthy appetite,' wrote one of them in a letter to his parents. 'Each day he has to take a few steps with the nurse . . . he's still young and in two or three months he'll have forgotten that he was ever ill.'

The medical staff in Nikolaev hospital prescribed electric bath therapy that would reinvigorate his shattered nerve endings, but no such treatment was available in Nikolaev.

Wolfram needed to be transferred to one of the German spa centres.

Moving him back to Germany in wartime and in midwinter was a tall order. Hitler had ordered all available planes to be diverted to Stalingrad, where the Luftwaffe was engaged in a final, desperate mission to save General Paulus's doomed Sixth Army.

The countdown to catastrophe in Stalingrad had begun at the very time when Wolfram's illness was at its most critical. A vast Soviet offensive, Operation Uranus, had crushed the Romanian Third Army, which had been protecting the northern flank of General von Paulus's troops.

A second offensive, from the south, had enabled the Soviets to form a ring of steel around the Sixth Army. Some 300,000 German soldiers found themselves trapped inside a pocket that they called the *kessel* or cauldron. Among them were thirteen infantry battalions and three motorised divisions, along with the headquarters and entire command structure of the Sixth Army.

Their only hope of survival was to break out while they still had fuel, ammunition and food. However, when Goering assured Hitler that the troops could be supplied from the air, the Führer responded by ordering General von Paulus to defend his positions to the death.

Goering's air-supply mission proved a chimera to the men on the ground. Driving blizzards, coupled with technical failure and anti-aircraft fire, caused the loss of some 500 German aircraft. The desperately needed food never arrived.

As the Soviet army pushed home its attack, the German army's rations were slashed to starvation levels. Jaundice, diphtheria, dysentery and typhus picked off the weakest while frostbite killed many more as they sought in vain to flee their attackers. 'And so they streamed by,' wrote one German soldier who was eyewitness to the catastrophe. 'The remains of the shattered and decimated formations . . . with vehicles that were being slowly dragged and pushed by wounded, sick and frostbitten men. There were emaciated figures among them, muffled in coats, rags; pitiful wrecks painfully dragging themselves forwards, leaning on sticks and hobbling on frozen feet, wrapped in wisps of straw and strips of blankets.'

When Soviet forces captured the last two airfields inside the *kessel*, at Pitomnik and Gumrak, the fate of the German soldiers was sealed. Even General von Paulus realised the situation was hopeless. As Soviet troops closed in on his bomb-shattered headquarters in the basement of the GUM department store, he knew the end was nigh.

At 7.45 a.m. on the last day of January 1943, he and his staff signalled that they were surrendering. The battle for Stalingrad was over.

The military airfield at Nikolaev had been deserted during the attempted relief of Stalingrad; it was to remain silent for many weeks. In the aftermath of the disaster, all available planes were diverted eastwards to transport wounded men away from the battle front.

At the end of January 1943, to everyone's surprise, a lone aircraft broke through the foggy skies above Nikolaev and touched down on the runway. On board was a senior-ranking German officer who needed an urgent operation on his tonsils. He had sufficient status to be able to order the plane's diversion to Nikolaev where he knew he could have it done quickly and under anaesthetic.

Wolfram's doctor was prepared to perform the operation on one condition: that afterwards the officer take fifteen of the most seriously ill patients back to Germany. When this was agreed, Wolfram was selected as one of the fifteen. He was promptly handed a uniform, told to get dressed and helped to the plane on the following morning. Four hours later, they landed in Lemberg (Lvov), in the western Ukraine.

Wolfram's experience of Lvov was a blur of images snatched from the window of a military ambulance. Grey slush, grey streets, grey buildings – along with large numbers of seriously wounded soldiers. He spent the night in Lvov hospital, sharing a room with a soldier dying of his wounds. The man's parents had somehow managed to travel all the way from Germany to see him in his final hours. They sat in the darkened room, talking in whispers to their son as he slipped away. To Wolfram, it seemed painfully sad.

The man was still clinging to life on the following morning when Wolfram was taken to the station and put on a train to Dresden – a three-day journey in a carriage filled with more sick and dying soldiers.

The winter canvas was monochrome and bleak. Ukraine and Poland were shivering under thick snow, yet the frozen landscape held none of the romance that Wolfram had sensed in Oberammergau. Here, the terrain was hostile and cold, and the scouring easterly wind had smoothed the snowscape into an icy carapace. The occasional tree, skeletal and blasted with frost, made an eerie silhouette against the gun-metal sky. Everyone, everywhere, had tales of suffering and defeat.

On their arrival at Dresden, they were told to make their way to a makeshift infirmary. On the following morning, there was a change of plan and they were all ordered back to the station, to be put on another train.

The men had no clue as to their final destination. They kept asking where they were going but no one seemed to have any idea. To these sick and wounded soldiers, it seemed as if the entire German army was in terminal decline.

The train rattled on through the next day and night. Then, at dawn, as the weak winter sun rose above the horizon, they pulled into the spa town of Marienbad in the Sudetenland. After a confusing, zig-zag journey across Eastern Europe, Wolfram had at long last made it to a sanatorium. 'This morning, at 4 a.m., I arrived,' he wrote to his parents. 'I met lots of people in the train who were coming back from Stalingrad.'

These hardy survivors recounted harrowing stories of frostbite and starvation, as well as lingering deaths from jaundice and gangrene. 'I think I'd rather not mention in this letter the things they said to me,' he wrote. 'They were completely exhausted, especially their nerves.'

The defeat at Stalingrad was a disaster for the Nazi regime. Not only had the Sixth Army been wiped out but, in an added humiliation, its commander, General von Paulus, had been captured alive by the Soviet army.

The solemn news of the defeat was broadcast as a special communiqué on 3 February 1943. 'True to its oath of allegiance,' began the announcement issued by Goebbels' propaganda ministry, 'the Sixth Army, under the exemplary leadership of Field Marshal Paulus, has been annihilated by the overwhelming superiority of enemy numbers.' The communiqué added: 'They died so that Germany might live.'

Two weeks after this grim intelligent, the Aïchele and Rodi families switched on their radios in order to listen to a second broadcast that was to be made by Goebbels himself. Delivered live, before a huge audience in Berlin's Sports Palace, the much heralded speech was intended to be a triumphant call to arms for the German nation. Goebbels told his wildly enthusiastic audience that the time had come for total war.

'Do you believe with the Führer and with us in the final total victory of German arms? . . . Are you determined to follow the Führer through thick and thin in the struggle for victory and put up with the heaviest personal burdens?' His rhetorical questions were met with frenzied cries of 'Yes! Yes!' and loud chants of 'Sieg Heil'.

A large part of Goebbels' speech was devoted to his favourite theme – the treachery of and danger posed by the Jews. It was they, he claimed, who had been responsible for the defeat at Stalingrad and they were also working hard to ensure the ultimate defeat of Nazi Germany. 'Jewry represents an infectious phenomenon which is contagious,' he said. 'Germany . . . has no intention of bowing to this threat, but means to counter it and, if necessary, with the most complete and radical *exterm—*' At this point, Goebbels paused momentarily and corrected himself: '*elimination* of Jewry'.

Goebbels' barbaric sentiments were heard with weary resignation by the Aïcheles and the Rodis. There was nothing new in his vicious anti-Semitism: he had been expressing such views for years. Nor did the two families take any notice of his slip of the tongue. Indeed, no one in Pforzheim who listened to his speech on that February evening had any notion of the fact that Goebbels had meant to say 'extermination', not 'elimination'. Even his Sports Palace audience had failed to heed the slip; tellingly, they responded to his words with cries of '*Out* with the Jews', not '*Death* to the Jews'.

Nor did anyone in Pforzheim know that Goebbels' 'radical' policy was already under way – that Jews were already being exterminated in vast numbers. No one, that is, until Max and Martha Luise Rodi received an unexpected visit from a distant cousin. Albrecht Scholl pitched up at their front door at some point in the early months of 1943, having just returned from a tour of duty in occupied Poland. In the privacy of Max's study, he poured out a chilling tale of brutality and death.

Albrecht had been posted to Poland at some point in 1942. He was an officer in charge of bookkeeping, a purser who had been sent to serve in the East. It is impossible to know how he found out what was going on. It is most unlikely that a purser in the regular army would ever have been admitted to a death camp; he must surely have taken his account from an eyewitness – someone who had seen it happen.

The camp that he was told about may well have been Treblinka, sixty miles to the north-east of Warsaw, which had opened its gates on 24 July 1942. In the first six months of operation, some 700,000 Jews had been murdered here – a number that was to rise still higher in the early months of 1943.

The killings had become a dreary routine for the SS guards in charge of this and the other five camps in occupied Poland. Victims were pulled from the arriving freight trains, segregated according to gender and then ordered to strip naked.

The fittest were taken to one side to serve as workers; the rest were led straight to the gas chambers. 'On their way to their doom, they were pushed and beaten with rifle butts . . . dogs were set upon them, barking, biting and tearing at them.' So wrote Yankel Wiernik, one of the Jews forced to work as a labourer in Treblinka. 'The chamber was filled, the motor turned on and connected with the inflow pipes and within 25 minutes at the most, all lay dead, or – to be more accurate – were standing up dead.'

The information that Albrecht Scholl passed on to Max Rodi was sketchy and incomplete. Whilst he certainly did not know the name of the extermination camp, he was shocked to the core by the fact that the Nazi regime had consecrated itself to mass murder.

Max and Martha Luise were also profoundly shaken by what they had heard. They had long known of the political camps like Dachau, where Communists, Socialists and Jews were imprisoned and sometimes killed. They were also aware of the transportation of Jews from all over Europe. Indeed, people were told quite openly that these deported Jews were being held in labour camps and would soon be able to build new lives in the occupied lands. It therefore came as a thunderbolt for the Rodis to discover that they were actually being massacred.

They still had no idea of the scale of the extermination programme and undoubtedly did not know about the existence of the gas chambers. It was not until the end of the war that the family learned about other camps, such as Auschwitz and Bergen-Belsen.

Shortly after Albrecht's visit to the Rodi house, Peter and his sister were called into their father's study and saw immediately that something was wrong. With a grave expression, Max said that he had a matter of great importance to tell them.

Although he spared his children whatever grim details he might have gleaned from Albrecht, he wanted his two eldest to be aware that the Nazi regime was committing murder on a grand scale in the lands of the conquered; that Jews were secretly being killed in their thousands.

It was too dangerous for Max to inform his neighbours, friends or even other close members of the family. Such subjects were strictly taboo – and for good reason. Whoever they told would want to know from whom they heard it. If the implicated person was denounced, he or she would end up in Dachau.

The consequence of this culture of secrecy was that everyone kept their mouths shut. Even the Nazis had a slogan: 'The enemy is listening.'

For reasons that remain unclear, Albrecht Scholl was demoted in rank after his tour of duty in Poland. Soon afterwards he was sent to the battlefront, where he was killed.

He had been told terrible things that had left him deeply, profoundly shaken. The assumption in the Rodi family was that he had chosen his own death.

Wolfram spent five months at the Marienbad sanatorium. The doctors prescribed rest, food and exercise. There was to be no early return to the battlefront.

At the beginning of February, his father paid him a surprise visit; a whole year had passed since he had last seen his son. 'I stood in Wolfram's room where two other comrades were lying,' he wrote in a letter to his wife. 'Wolfram was lying in his bed with a cold pack over his chest and he had a wonderful massive smile on his face when he saw me . . . he doesn't look bad, but you can see that he's just come out of a really serious illness.'

Wolfram proved a popular patient and kept the nurses amused by doing impersonations of Hitler. The laundry lady, who was fanatically pro-Hitler, was moved to tears by these performances, closing her eyes and imagining that the Führer was talking to her personally. However, the soldiers, whose battlefield sufferings had turned them vehemently against the Nazi regime, just laughed, all thinking it a huge joke.

As the time for convalescence rapidly ran out, Wolfram knew he would be discharged before the summer. 'The doctor cannot stand it when men are healthy but remain in hospital,' he wrote.

The day for his release came soon enough. In mid-May, he was sent back to Pforzheim. Eight weeks later, after an unexpectedly long leave of absence, he received his call-up papers. He was sent away for training, first to Strasbourg and then to Münsingen. Nine months had passed since he had first contracted diptheria.

The new recruits were divided into groups when they arrived. The better-educated were to be trained as *funkers* or wireless operators. All the rest were to be taught how to use guns.

As there were not enough *funkers*, the officer in charge asked for one more volunteer. Wolfram put up his hand and was accepted immediately.

The *funker*'s role was to transmit and decipher messages between the officers and their troops. Having been sorted into teams of two, the trainees began the slow process of learning Morse code. Wolfram was paired with Erwin Miggel, a mild-mannered Viennese organist with no interest whatsoever in the war. Their opposite team consisted of Lang and Ritzy, who shared similar sentiments.

For Wolfram, it was like being back among family. Werner Lang came from Oberammergau and his uncle had been Wolfram's tutor.

The two lads found they had friends in common and they enjoyed spending their evenings remembering happier times. Together with Miggel and Ritzy, they would sneak off to alehouses whenever possible, or race up the meadows behind the camp in order to catch a glimpse of the distant Alpine panorama. They could just make out the Zugspitze and Hörnle, the very mountains that Wolfram had climbed when he was in Oberammergau.

The greatest annoyance was their training commander, known to everyone as Lieutenant W. A petty tyrant, he did his utmost to humiliate the men under his charge, making them crawl through muddy puddles at the beginning of each day. Then, when their uniforms were sodden and they were soaked to the skin, he would send them to their Morse lessons.

Lieutenant W was a diehard Nazi. He used to insist that the trainees should report their parents to the Gestapo if they did anything that was ideologically unsound. He also punished his recruits for minor misdemeanours, like not saluting him correctly, and would frequently withhold food as a penalty.

He would eventually get his come-uppance. Accused of mistreating the men under his command and found guilty, he was severely disciplined. 'He's been given two years in prison and demoted to a simple soldier,' wrote Wolfram in a gleeful letter to his parents.

It was during his training that Wolfram received news from Franz Bader, one of the men with whom he had travelled to the Crimea. Bader's letter was a litany of suffering. Soon after Wolfram had collapsed with diphtheria, all of his comrades had been drafted into the army and sent across the River Donetz to join the rearguard battle for Stalingrad.

'So many killed,' wrote Wolfram to his parents. 'And lots of my comrades died.' In fact, he later discovered that the only one known to have survived, apart from himself, was Franz Bader. He had managed to get out alive because his feet froze and he was semi-paralysed. In terrible pain, he had crawled to an army infirmary where he was treated for severe frostbite before being sent to fight on the Italian front.

As Christmas approached, Wolfram felt increasingly depressed. Food was scarce and morale lower than ever.

'The shit starts again,' he wrote to his parents. 'In all the pubs and inns, all the food is eaten up by six . . . the Italians soldiers here eat raw potatoes and think it tastes nice!' These new recruits, with their impish, tramontane features, fascinated Wolfram. 'They've got such interesting faces,' he wrote, 'and some of them have these huge beards, like the old Tyroleans with their felt hats and capes . . . they look like shepherds in the baroque cribs.'

Christmas left him in a deep gloom. 'It's degenerated into

one big drinking session,' he wrote. 'Then, when the soldiers are completely drunk, they all sing stupid songs. There is absolutely nothing here to do with the Christian feast. They don't care at all.'

His spirits were temporarily lifted by a hike into the hills high above the training camp. In the sharp winter air, he once again glimpsed the Bavarian Alps, their soaring crags now powdered with snow.

One day, the youths were woken by sudden activity, followed by the announcement that a new regiment was being formed – in fact, an entire infantry division. The 77th was to be assembled from several undermanned infantry regiments, along with an artillery battalion, a signal battalion and a divisional supply unit.

Wolfram and his friends were to be a part of this new division, serving in the 1021st Grenadier Regiment under the command of Colonel Rudolf Bacherer, a tight-lipped Nazi with a balding head and piercing eyes.

He came from Pforzheim and Wolfram had been at school with his son, but the connection stopped there. Bacherer was a loyal servant of the Führer, an ideological Nazi who looked forward with relish to the battles ahead.

Just a few weeks after Bacherer's appointment, Wolfram was told that they were on the move. 'On Saturday, we're leaving this place,' he wrote in a note to his parents. 'But I've no idea where we're going.'

CHAPTER TEN

SURVIVING THE HOME FRONT

'He'd prepared his young wife and his brother, who managed
to contain their grief.'

Wolfram's sister, Gunhild, could not stop shivering. In the autumn of 1943, the family's
dwindling supplies of coal finally ran out.
Erwin was unable to buy any more and, as the first blast of
a Schwarzwald winter slammed into their exposed hilltop,
the villa turned almost arctic.

Gunhild's bedroom, in the eaves of the house, was so cold
that she would cry herself to sleep. As the mercury dipped
far below freezing, all the windows iced up on the inside.

An additional source of misery to Gunhild was the family's meagre diet, which grew less appetising with every
month that passed. Feeding a family in wartime required a
considerable degree of household planning and organisation, skills that did not come easily to Marie Charlotte. She
did her best to prepare dishes that provided some nourishment but Gunhild quickly tired of the same monotonous
meals in which potatoes were the principal ingredient.

She started mixing yeast with stale breadcrumbs and

water – a staple in times of hardship. This would then be blended into a paste so that it could be spread on toast. It was supposed to taste like meat; in fact, it tasted of yeast and stale bread.

Household management became more problematic still when the family found themselves playing host to an endless stream of strangers left homeless by the RAF's relentless bombing raids of German towns and cities.

'Uncle Walter wrote from Lubeck,' recorded Marie Charlotte in one of her many letters to Wolfram. 'He tells us that in the last raid there were 3,000 dead, 3,000 wounded and 30,000 left without homes.'

Many of these homeless were despatched into the country-side to be lodged with families whose houses were still intact. The Eutingen villa played host to a constant ebb and flow of temporary lodgers – single women, families, children and old men. Sometimes they stayed for just a few weeks; at other times, they would remain for a month or more. Gunhild knew better than to complain, yet it was nevertheless disconcerting to share the family home with complete strangers.

One morning, a whole new busload of homeless people were brought to Eutingen and assembled in the school playground. Everyone in the village was told to go and pick a family that could be lodged in their homes.

Marie Charlotte, busy with household chores, sent her sixteen-year-old daughter down to the lower village in order to make the choice. When Gunhild arrived at the school gates she found a crowd of refugees, all in need of shelter. Clueless as to which ones to pick, she eventually selected a mother with three children because she was impressed with the way the little ones said *mutti*.

The arrival of these temporary lodgers coincided with that of a new home help. Sigrid Weber lived in the lower village of Eutingen and her parents were close friends of the Aïcheles. When she turned sixteen and had to do her compulsory *Pflicht-jahr* or Duty Year Service, the two families conspired to arrange for her to spend that time being a maid in the Eutingen villa.

It was an arrangement that suited both sets of parents. Marie Charlotte would have someone she already knew to help with the numerous domestic chores, while the Weber family would be able to keep their daughter close to home. The only person who was not particularly happy was Sigrid herself. For much of her childhood she had been best friends with Gunhild; now, suddenly, she found herself a domestic servant in her old friend's household.

It was still bitterly cold and the house's size made it difficult to keep clean. Sigrid was constantly being told to sweep the floor and clean up but it remained a hopeless mess. The new lodgers and their young children contributed to the chaos. The kitchen was filthy from overuse and there was always a pile of greasy crockery in the sink.

Sigrid soon found herself entangled in a fraught relationship with Marie Charlotte. The tensions were due, in part, to the hunger and extreme cold, but they were also fuelled by Marie Charlotte, who had been living under immense stress for many months.

She was suffering, perhaps, from acute depression – and with good reason. Her two sons were both at war; she herself was being monitored by the Gestapo; and the greatest joys in her life – reading, art and music – were now firmly controlled by the Nazi regime.

Sigrid was constantly intrigued and often exasperated by Wolfram's parents. She had always known them to be eccentric but now that she was living under their roof, she realised they were completely different to all the other Germans she had ever met.

It was as if they were living in a fairy-tale world – in their own private castle, in a land that was completely divorced from reality. Sigrid was left with the impression that refined conversation and music were all that mattered – that intellectual exchange and culture were far more important than food and drink. Indeed, it was as if they did not care about what was taking place in the wider world. They certainly never spoke of politics or war, although these were taboo subjects for everyone.

Yet war constantly intruded on them, especially as a growing number of their circle lost their loved ones in battle. The most recent to die was Rolf Elsässer, whose parents were close friends of both the Aïchele and Rodi families.

His religious memorial service had to be conducted in secret because of the ban on the Christian Community. 'Even though it wasn't in a church,' wrote Marie Charlotte, 'it was very beautiful and solemn. The Rodi children and the Elsässers played music very beautifully and [then] they read the gospel of the Resurrection.'

Young Rolf had always told his family that he did not expect to come back from the front. 'He'd prepared his young wife and his brothers,' wrote Marie Charlotte, 'who all managed to contain their grief. It was much more moving than if they'd been in hysterics.'

In Eutingen, as in Pforzheim, public morale had by now

dipped to its lowest ebb since the conflict began. By the winter of 1943 most people had realised that Germany was going to lose.

Hitler knew from his experiences of the First World War how important it was to keep up public spirits. Cinemas, theatres and concert halls remained open and virtuoso musicians were spared war service so that they could entertain those with loved ones at the front.

Marie Charlotte's spirits were temporarily lifted by an evening of opera at the Pforzheim concert hall. The renowned tenor, Wolfgang Windgassen, was making his debut as Don Alvero in Verdi's *La forza del destino*. His bravura performance electrified the Pforzheim audience; Windgassen was the heart-throb of thousands of young local girls. When he emerged to greet his swooning fans at the end of the concert, Gunhild was among them. She was presented to him and even got close enough to touch him, a rare and exciting privilege.

Wolfram's parents continued to visit close friends in these troubled times, but no amount of entertainment could disguise the fact that the war was going from bad to worse. The humiliating annihilation of the Sixth Army at Stalingrad had been the first cruel blow. The only consolation was the saving of General von Kleist's forces in the Caucasus, which had been able to cross the Don and reach safety before they too became trapped.

There had been more grim news throughout the course of 1943. In July, the Germans had launched their much vaunted offensive against the Kursk salient. It proved a catastrophe; the largest tank battle in history ended with the German army losing a staggering 2,900 tanks. By early autumn, Soviet forces had advanced into the Ukraine and driven the German army back to the River Dnieper.

The Allies, meanwhile, were taking advantage of their victories in North Africa, launching a seaborne invasion of Sicily in July 1943. The island was in their hands by mid-August, by which time Mussolini had been dismissed from power and promptly arrested. Within weeks of the victory in Sicily, the Allied Fifth Army was landing 170,000 men at Salerno, just to the south of Naples. With rumours of an impending Allied landing in northern France, where coastal defences were still not completed, Hitler looked increasingly vulnerable on every front except the home one.

As they boarded the train at Münsingen station, Wolfram and his comrades still had no idea where they might be sent. Some thought they were heading for the Ukraine. Others said they were off to Italy. All the speculation proved in vain; their destination remained so secret that even their commanders did not know.

The journey seemed to last a lifetime. The lads would sleep, then be jostled awake, then fall asleep again, and still they were on the move. At one point, one of Wolfram's friends peered out through the window and thought he recognised the Paris skyline. However, the train rattled on through the night and it was only when it finally came to a halt in Bayeux that they realised they had been posted to Normandy.

The men were told to walk to Caen, some twenty miles to the south-west. On their arrival, weary and footsore, Wolfram and his comrades were told to continue on towards Audrieu, a little village that lay a few miles from Caen.

They blinked in disbelief when they finally arrived there. Chateau Audrieu, their billet, was an elegant manor built in the formal classicism of pre-revolutionary France. The Livry-Levels, hereditary chatelaines since the early eighteenth century, had made few changes to its unstudied grace.

In the dim light of its oak-panelled salons, there were enough antiques to have kept Wolfram occupied for days, but the house was so dark that he could snatch only brief glimpses of the ancient trunks and settles, and portraits of the family's Louis Quatorze armigers – chevaliers of impeccable pedigree – remained as incorporeal as ghosts.

The German officers got to stay in the chateau while Wolfram and his fellow *funkers* were lodged in the outhouses, surrounded by acres of formal gardens, parterres, fountains, topiary, orchards, meadows and woodland.

As winter gave way to an early spring, they were sent on training exercises into the nearby woods and coppices, with constant reminders of the need to be absolute masters of their machines. Men's lives would depend on the speed with which they could transmit messages on the battlefield.

They were woken at three in the morning in order to prepare their horses. The animals had to be harnessed to a cart that carried their Morse machine – a clunking great piece of equipment that was far too heavy to be transported by hand. The men themselves packed everything else they needed into rucksacks: weaponry, cooking equipment and a *zeltbahn* – cleverly designed triangular structures that could be put together and made into a tent.

The Morse excursions took them through many picturesque farming communities. As the dawn sun broke through the woodland, and they sent and received messages, they were hotly trailed by infantry. These foot soldiers would fire blanks at them so that they could experience what it was like to be operating the machine in the heat of battle.

Once the exercise was finally over, the men made their way back to the chateau in their own time, often stopping at the farmhouses to try to buy eggs, milk and butter. A few of the farmers expressed their displeasure at the sight of German soldiers training on their land, but most were friendly, especially towards Germans who spoke a smattering of French. Wolfram's team-mate, Miggel, asked one farmlady: '*Avez-vous du lait?*' She emitted a peal of gay laughter, placed her hands on her withered bosom and told him that her cows had milk but that hers had dried up years ago.

On one occasion, Wolfram went with one team member into a village store in St Come-de-Fresne. The shopkeeper shook her head sadly, saying, 'So young,' to the lad that was accompanying Wolfram. She asked his age and, taking pity on him, gave him a little bag of sweets.

One morning, the men peered out of the window of their billet to see a band of exotic new arrivals shuffling up the chateau's long driveway: volunteers from Uzbekistan and Turkmenistan who had been drafted in to help Wolfram and his comrades transport their unwieldy Morse machines.

Wolfram stared in amazement. Here was a band worthy of the Golden Horde – Tartar and Mongol warriors with tapering eyes and wispy beards. Seven centuries earlier, they would have arrived on horseback, wielding arced bows and damascene scimitars. Now, they were armed with more familiar weaponry, automatic Lugers, yet their Far Eastern appearance lent a touch of foreignness to a quintessentially French backdrop.

'Turkmen!' wrote Wolfram to his parents. 'There's *nothing* European about them.'

These Asiatic soldiers, who had yoked themselves to the German war machine out of their hatred for Stalin, brought a renewed sense of adventure to the training exercises. Wolfram was bemused by their lack of knowledge about the war. 'They're taking part in this conflict even though they have absolutely no idea what it's about. Nor do they have any clue as to which country they're in and they certainly couldn't point to it on a map.'

The arrival of warm weather injected a note of optimism into the men's lives. 'Now we have such lovely spring mornings,' wrote Wolfram, 'and the bird chorus in the morning is just like at home. On the lawn beyond the chateau, the daffodils are beginning to bloom. At long last, spring is really coming.'

At the beginning of April, Wolfram's spirits were raised still further by a visit to Caen. It was market day and the town was packed with farmers peddling their local produce, prompting memories of the distant days of peace. 'There's still lots to buy here. And there's such a lovely, joyful life in the streets and loads of civilians everywhere. It reminds one of the times that haven't existed in Germany for so many years.'

He was staggered by the variety of items on sale in the shops, quite unlike the empty shelves of Pforzheim, and decided to send things back to his parents. 'I've bought you 250g of cocoa powder . . . I also bought myself two woollen socks, which I'll send you to keep for me. When I next go into town, I want to buy some angora wool which you can get here. And when I've saved up enough, I'll get myself a big rucksack. I saw a fantastic one in a shop window for 1,350 French francs.'

On Holy Friday, at the end of April, the men were given a day off. Miggel managed to tune their wireless to a certain radio frequency and suddenly there was a wonderful burst of music. It was Bach's *St Matthew Passion*, broadcast live from Leipzig. They could not hear it very well for the line was crackly, but they sat glued to their headphones. The music transported them back to civilian life and reminded them of happier times.

The next day was Wolfram's twentieth birthday; it was also his last at Chateau Audrieu. The threat of an Allied invasion from England was increasing with every day; now, the men were to be transferred to Brittany to protect a stretch of coastline that was dangerously exposed.

They headed to Dinan by train, a journey of extreme discomfort. There were no compartments or even carriages, just a platform on wheels, open to the elements.

However, the apple and pear trees were still in bloom, and the landscape was at its bucolic best. 'Sometimes from the train we get the wonderful scent of the blossom,' Wolfram wrote to his mother. 'It reminds me of Franconia, except that instead of timber houses they're built of Normandy stone.' He was delighted to catch a glimpse of Mont St Michel, its black silhouette outlined dramatically against a luminous, copper-red sky. 'Just as we passed, the round disc of the setting sun was hovering above the church spire. I couldn't take my eyes off it.'

The train came to a sudden halt in the middle of the countryside and everyone was told to get out. They were ordered to unload everything, but no one explained why. Guns, crates of ammunition, and straw and oats for the horses – all had to be taken off the train. Just as they lifted off the last few boxes, the order was countermanded and they were ordered to reload them.

Everything had to be done in a great hurry for the train needed to continue to its destination, giving no time to reload all the fodder for the horses. The officer in charge took the decision to leave three men to guard these supplies. Wolfram and two others were chosen to remain behind, lodged in an empty house.

They had no idea how long they would be there, were given hardly any food and had no papers justifying their presence. Having assumed someone would return for them on the following morning, they were surprised when no one showed up.

A second day passed and still no one came. By now, they had eaten the last of their rations and were getting hungry. It was while they were considering what to do that a young lad from the nearby farm paid them a visit.

Looking longingly at the supply of oats, he told Wolfram that his horse had not eaten properly for more than two years. The Germans, he said, had confiscated all the best fodder. Now, he had a proposition to make: if they gave him some oats, he would supply them with food in return.

Such an exchange was strictly forbidden, but Wolfram thought it sounded like a sensible idea. He checked with the others and they agreed, but they warned the lad to burn the sacks as soon as they were empty, because they knew he would be shot if such incriminating evidence was discovered on his farm.

The boy took a sack and promptly returned with eggs. He also asked the Germans whether they would like to dine with his parents in the farmhouse that evening.

Wolfram and his two comrades were delighted to accept, if a little embarrassed. As they sat at the table next to a roaring fire, the farmer's wife made them dozens of pancakes, all washed down with cider. At the end of the meal, conducted in the soldiers' broken French, they were invited for lunch on the following day.

The farmer was quite open about his views on the German occupation, telling them that whilst it had brought many changes to their daily lives, it was the small things that irritated him the most. The ban on firearms was a source of particular annoyance. The farmer had long been accustomed to hunt and shoot for the pot, but his rifle had been confiscated by the Germans on the day they had occupied the area.

When Wolfram and his comrades heard this, they offered to help him out. One of the three, a keen shot, promised to shoot wood pigeons. During the following morning he managed to bag dozens. From then on, Wolfram and his comrades were invited to share the roasted wood pigeons with the family each evening.

Word of their excursions soon spread through the local villages. The owner of a little bistro near by asked them to shoot pigeons for him as well, so they started to provide him with a regular supply.

The three Germans were by now on such good terms with the farmer that they were invited to attend the first communion of one of the youngsters in the family. 'We can't possibly come,' Wolfram told the farmer. 'We're the Bosch.' However, the farmer pressed them, telling them it would be fine.

They went to the celebration in their uniforms but left all their weapons behind – an offence that was punishable by death by firing squad, although they did not think of the danger.

The locals stared at the three soldiers dressed in their khaki fatigues, until the farmer assured the congregation that they were good Germans. Afterwards he invited them back to eat sausages and cake made with real butter and real eggs.

One evening, when they had got to know the farmer well, they asked him why he was being so kind to them. He told them that he had served as a conscripted soldier in the First World War and had hated it. 'It's not your fault,' he said. 'You didn't choose to fight.'

As they all drank more and more cider, and grew ever more merry, they drew caricatures of Hitler, Stalin and Churchill, pinned them to the wall and threw rubbish at them. There was general agreement that the people at the top were all the same: criminals, every last one of them.

For more than a fortnight, no one came to look for Wolfram and his friends until eventually one morning, a German military car pulled up. A professional officer by the name of Glasser stepped out and announced that he had come to fetch them.

When he noticed the nearby farm and poked his head into the pantry, he was sorely tempted by the sight of their eggs, butter and cream. With some hesitation, he drew

Wolfram to one side and asked him whether he thought the farmer would be willing to sell him a little food. Wolfram feigned ignorance and said he had no idea.

Glasser went and asked the farmer, who reacted with great discretion, making no mention of his close relationship with Wolfram and his friends. Instead, he expressed surprise at the suggestion but readily agreed. 'That's amazing!' said Glasser to Wolfram when he returned with a sack filled with eggs and cheese. 'Look what they've given me.'

Once Glasser had loaded the food into his car, he drove Wolfram and the others to their new billet at St Brieux, on the north coast of Brittany. Wolfram was happy to be reunited with Miggel, Lang and Ritzy although less pleased that the relaxed routine of life, which he had become used to, now came to an abrupt end. He was billeted in an underground bunker with a metal ladder as the only exit. As it was airless and claustrophobic, the men spent much of their time outside.

They passed the last two weeks of May doing yet more Morse code exercises, transmitting messages about the forthcoming weather conditions. Finally, on the morning of 6 June, they were brought news that was to change their lives for ever. In the early hours of dawn, a massive armada of ships had been sighted approaching the northern French coastline. *Invasionstag*, or D-Day, had begun.

CHAPTER ELEVEN

SLAUGHTER FROM THE AIR

'You lie there helpless . . . like a man facing a firing squad.'

Wolfram knew nothing about the Normandy landings when he was jolted from his sleep by the army reveille on Tuesday, 6 June 1944. He swung his legs wearily out of bed and glanced outside. The leaden sky was smudged with clouds and a fine drizzle was washing in from the sea. Another miserable summer's day in northern France.

It is a mark of the German army's lassitude that even as Allied forces were storming on to the beaches of Normandy, the majority of Wehrmacht soldiers were unaware that the largest seaborne landing in the history of warfare was occurring on their doorstep.

Wolfram was still in the dark when he ate breakfast that morning; indeed, he first learned news of the landings at around midday. Even then, there was no sense of urgency or panic. None of the men was instructed to pack his equipment and there was no talk of their being sent to the beachhead. It was business as normal.

The sluggish German response to the landings is all the

more surprising, given that Field Marshal Erwin Rommel, responsible for defending the Normandy coastline, had long argued that Allied soldiers must be attacked while they were still on the beaches. 'The enemy is at his weakest just after landing,' he said. 'The troops are unsure and possibly even seasick. They are unfamiliar with the terrain. Heavy weapons are not yet available in sufficient quantity. That is the moment to strike at them and defeat them.'

The dismal weather, so depressing to Wolfram that summer's morning, was one of the principal reasons for the German army's lack of preparedness. An Allied invasion was certainly expected at some time in the near future, but the previous evening's weather report had been so bad that the German high command in Normandy scoffed at any notion of an imminent landing. 'Rough sea, poor visibility, Force 5–6 wind, rain likely to get heavier. Most probably we shan't even get our usual raids.'

It was not just the weather reports that led to inaction on the ground. Most of the senior German commanders in Normandy were not at their posts at the time of the landings, leading to confusion and paralysis. Rommel had left on the previous morning in order to pay a surprise birthday visit on his wife in Germany. Many other commanders were attending a war games exercise in Rennes, among them General Friedrich Dollmann and General von Schlieben. The latter was charged with defending the stretch of coastline that included the landing area of Utah Beach.

Another key person missing was General Wilhelm Falley of the 9th Infantry Division. 'Nothing's going to happen in this lousy weather,' he said as he set off to Rennes.

The German high command took comfort from the fact

that if the landings did not take place on 6 June, then they were most unlikely to happen for several weeks. 'The various conditions of tide, moon and general weather situation necessary for a landing here in northern France won't coincide again until the second half of June.' Such was the opinion of Admiral Hennecke, the Normandy naval commander.

While the German commanders enjoyed themselves, and Wolfram slept through the night at his Brittany barracks, *invasionstag* became a dramatic reality for a small number of German troops. On a bleak stretch of beach close to the village of Sainte-Marie-du-Mont, Lieutenant Jahnke and his men were seated inside Strongpoint W8, a concrete bunker, listening to the drone of enemy bombers. For many weeks, Allied aircraft had been bombing depots, military installations and gun emplacements. On this particular evening they were bombing with greater force than usual.

Jahnke saw no undue reason for alarm, informing his men that the Allies would never attempt a landing without an aerial bombardment of the coastal landing areas.

It was as he uttered these words – he would later recall – that a wave of 360 Marauder medium bombers screamed in from the sea. Their bomb-bays opened as they passed above Strongpoint W8. There was a blinding flash as a series of rapid explosions thumped into the beach, causing Strongpoint W8 to shudder and groan before cracking open like a nut. Jahnke was flung against the wall of the bunker before being buried in deep sand. He dragged himself outside just in time to see the ammunition bunkers receive a direct hit.

Strongpoint W8 had been the principal fortification on Utah Beach. Now, it lay in smouldering ruins. The

75-millimetre anti-tank gun was twisted beyond repair and all the machine-guns were entombed in sand.

However, the attack was not yet over. A new wave of aircraft roared in from the sea, firing 50-millimetre rockets at the two bunkers that still remained intact.

'Everything's wrecked! Everything's wrecked!' screamed one of the German mess orderlies.

Jahnke remained cool under pressure. He rallied his shaken men, offered some encouraging words and then peered through his telescope towards the gunmetal sea. At this point, he got his second unwelcome surprise of the morning. A floating argosy could be seen steering directly towards the beach – a truly massive fleet of destroyers, gunboats, battleships, minesweepers: ships both big and small. Each one was flying an ungainly barrage balloon from its stern, as protection against attack from the air.

Most alarming was the fact that they were coming at low tide. Rommel's entire coastal defences had been planned with the expectation that the invading army would land at high tide. It meant that all the underwater obstacles – wired ramming blocks, stakes and mines – were exposed and clearly visible.

Jahnke's men vowed to put up a spirited defence. Lance Corporal Friedrich was crouched behind a machine-gun in the turret of a buried Renault tank. Others were tinkering with the last remaining 88-millimetre gun, desperately trying to coax it into life.

'Fire!' The gun suddenly sprang into action, volleying a shell at the first American tank to roll on to the beach, instantly crippling it. That, however, was the first and the last shell to be fired: the gun was too badly damaged for further use.

'It looks as if God and the world has forsaken us,' muttered

Jahnke to one of the German army runners. He was not wrong. Vast quantities of men and *matériel* were being disgorged on to the beach and German resistance was almost at an end. An explosion flung Jahnke into the sand for a second time that morning. When he awoke from his fleeting unconsciousness, an American infantryman was standing over him, rifle in hand.

More than six hours before Wolfram knew anything about D-Day, Lieutenant Jahnke was already a prisoner of war.

Wolfram's regiment, the 1021st Grenadier Regiment, was ill-equipped for battle. So was the 77th Infantry Division to which it belonged. Many of its men were conscripts like Wolfram and few had seen any battlefield action. The division lacked officers, equipment, vehicles and supplies. Furthermore, a very high proportion of the men were *volksdeutsche* – ethnic Germans from the occupied territories. There were also large numbers of Poles, Tartars from the Volga region, Georgians, Azerbaijanis and Turkmen. The loyalty of these men to the Third Reich was, at best, questionable. Most were fighting on the German side out of loathing for Stalin, not loyalty to Hitler. Thousands of miles from home and uncertain of the cause for which they had taken up arms, they were an unreliable force to throw against the Allied forces now pouring on to their beachheads.

Notwithstanding their lack of experience, it was imperative for as many German divisions as possible to move northwards to counter the invading Allies. As news from the coast deteriorated from bad to worse, the 77th Infantry Division's commander, Major-General Rudolf Stegmann, prepared to send his troops into battle.

It was around midday on 7 June, a day after the landings, when Wolfram and his friends were told to pack their belongings. They were on the move.

There was by now a real sense of urgency among German commanders on the ground. The Allied landings may not have gone according to plan but they had succeeded in their principal goal of establishing a strong beachhead. On Utah Beach more than 23,000 men had been brought ashore on the first day, along with 1,700 vehicles. The cost had been fewer than 200 American lives.

On Omaha Beach, the other American landing place, a stiff German defence had led to extremely high casualties: American V Corps alone lost 3,000 men – killed, wounded or missing – and large numbers of tanks and artillery lay crippled on the beach. Yet the Americans fought valiantly and managed to secure a small beachhead by the evening of that day.

The other three landing points – the British army's Gold and Sword Beach and the Canadian Juno Beach – had also been captured after initially heavy fighting. By midnight on D-Day, 155,000 Allied troops were ashore.

Rommel was quick to recognise the strategic danger posed by the landings on Utah Beach, the most westerly of the five landings. If the Americans succeeded in pushing inland, they could cut the Cotentin peninsula in two and isolate all of the German forces stationed in 'Fortress Cherbourg' on the northern tip of the peninsula. To prevent such a disaster, the 77th Infantry Division was ordered northwards with the aim of blocking any American advance into the Cotentin.

Wolfram and his comrades set out on foot, with their horses carrying the heaviest of the communication equipment. It was a long and exhausting march to their goal, the River Meredet, more than 150 miles to the north, and they needed to get there at high speed. The men covered up to fifty miles a day with almost no break. After forty-eight hours on the march they were exhausted. At one point, Wolfram was so tired that he rested his head on the belly of the horse and fell asleep as he walked mechanically along the road. On the rare occasions when they stopped, everyone slumped to the ground and was asleep within seconds.

For the first two days the men marched in daylight, but as they neared the Utah beachhead, the skies overhead became increasingly dangerous. There were fighter bombers constantly above them that would fly in extraordinarily low and shoot at anything on the ground that moved. The men's nerves were tested to the limit. They would be forced to scatter and hide, diving into copses, hedgerows or abandoned farmhouses.

'Even the movements of smaller formations . . . are immediately bombarded from the air with annihilating effect,' read one of the weekly situation reports submitted to the German high command. 'Neither our flak nor the Luftwaffe seems to be in a position to check this crippling and destructive operation.'

The difficulty of marching under fire quickly became apparent to Wolfram and his comrades. The regiment found itself advancing northwards not as a single body but as dozens of little bands, many of them leaderless. They had very little idea of where they were heading, nor did they know what they were supposed to do when they reached their destination. These groups of men were increasingly vulnerable to attack from the sky and were forever flinging themselves into ditches to escape being strafed by machine-gun fire from the Allied fighter-bombers. The hail of bullets so intense that each new raid brought fatalities.

Wolfram and his men were walking along a narrow country lane when they stumbled across the bodies of two dead soldiers lying by the roadside. The putrid stench and their blackened faces betrayed the fact that they had been killed some days earlier, probably in one of the raids that preceded the landings. Yet no one had bothered to give them a decent burial. The men decided to cover the corpses with earth. Wolfram went to pick one of them up but as he grasped the body, his hand went straight through the flesh. Already in an advanced state of decomposition, it could no longer be moved without falling apart completely.

The difficulties of advancing en masse, and with tanks and artillery in tow, was compounded by the terrain. The Normandy bocage – a landscape of meadows and copses criss-crossed by hedgerows – brought severe logistical problems for the movement of defensive forces, slowing the men to a snail's pace. Tanks and vehicles got bogged down in the lanes while the heavy artillery, constantly strafed by fighter-bombers, was forced to scatter far and wide.

The Panzer divisions could only just squeeze along the narrow country roads and were forever getting stuck between the hedgerows. Whenever this happened, long columns of vehicles would have to turn around and seek a different route. At such moments of disorder, they were extremely vulnerable to attack.

As the men got nearer to the front, they saw huge numbers of abandoned tanks and vehicles that had been hit from the air. On one occasion, curiosity got the better of Wolfram and he opened the hatch of one of these stricken vehicles to peer inside. It was a picture of horror: charred and carbonised bodies lay on the floor of the tank. They had been shrunken by the intense heat and reduced to the size of babies.

After five days on the move, Wolfram and his comrades were completely lost. They knew only that they were nearing the coast because of the sound of cannon coming from the warships at anchor in the English Channel: a regular dull noise – thump, thump, thump – as they bombarded the land.

On their sixth day, the men started to encounter wounded soldiers fleeing from the battlefront: a sure sign that they were nearing their goal. They had just bivouacked for the night when a little group of German soldiers came staggering towards them, covered in blood. A few were able to walk but others were so badly injured that they were being carried. It was a chilling omen.

Wolfram's parents knew nothing of the clash of arms in Normandy. Marie Charlotte turned on the radio that Tuesday morning to listen to the news, but there was no mention of any Allied landings. Nor were there any reports in the local Pforzheim newspaper: the late edition had gone to press many hours before Allied troops had begun pouring on to the beaches.

It was not until the following day that the local newspaper carried a short report about the invasion, although there was very little detail about what was actually happening and no sense that the German army had made a catastrophic blunder in not reacting more quickly to the invasion. Under the headline, 'Historic Plan Stopped by German Defence', the report stated that the Allies had suffered appalling casualties as a result of a masterful German counter-attack. 'Horrible losses under German fire.'

The following day's newspaper took purposeful misinformation one step further, reporting that the German army had pushed the British and Americans back into the sea. It conceded that a second wave of troops had managed to get ashore and were now clinging precariously to a small strip of coastline: 'But not at all deep . . . and at the cost of shameful quantities of men and material.'

By day three, the regional Baden newspaper was gleefully reporting tens of thousands of Allied deaths. Like so many in Pforzheim, Marie Charlotte assumed that the British and American landings – the only real hope of a swift end to the war – had been a catastrophic failure.

As Wolfram and his fellow *funkers* neared the front, they came under increasingly heavy fire. They had spent many months training for just such an eventuality and had learned how to keep cool heads. However, now that they were on the field of battle, they discovered that real bullets were very different to simulated fire. They also realised that the enemy were going out of their way to destroy their radio machines. The *funkers* would find a safe place, install their antennae and dig themselves into a deep hole, but no sooner had they started transmitting and decoding signals than they came under sustained fire.

The Americans were indeed targeting battlefield communications in order to maximise the confusion for the German forces. It took them an average of two hours to locate the position of *funkers* like Wolfram. Once they had done so, they would begin shelling these positions with great intensity.

The scene at the battlefront was one of total chaos. No one had a clear idea how to halt the American advance and no one was even sure whether the Normandy landings were indeed the long-awaited invasion, or merely the first of several. Hitler had long predicted that the Allies would land in the area around the Pas de Calais. A week after the initial invasion, he was still expecting a second set of landings.

Much of the initial confusion among the German forces in Normandy had been caused by the American airdrops in the hours that preceded the landings. Soldiers from two airborne divisions, the 82nd and the 101st, had been landed in the countryside behind Utah Beach. The drops had not gone according to plan, for the troops had been widely scattered and found it difficult to reconnoitre in the little fields and hedgerows of the bocage.

And yet, ironically, in failure lay their greatest success. The airborne assault caused absolute confusion among the German defenders. Some officers thought that the Americans were deploying an entirely new military strategy, disrupting their defences by engaging in sporadic action behind enemy lines.

The German defence, if disorganised, was spirited and the Americans had to fight their way into every village. St Mère Eglise, the bridge at La Fière, Azeville and Crisbecq: one by one they fell into American hands and small numbers of Germans were killed or taken prisoner.

The Americans had originally intended to swing swiftly northwards from Utah Beach to capture the port of Cherbourg, but they now saw the advantage of pushing westwards across the peninsula, thereby cutting the Cotentin peninsula in two and trapping large numbers of German troops.

The drawback to this strategy was that there were many natural obstacles to overcome. The Meredet and Douve rivers, as well as strong German positions on the ridges of high ground, made the American advance a daunting one for the newly landed troops. Yet it was conducted with gritty determination on two flanks.

The front line kept moving with every hour that passed and Wolfram and his men were obliged to move with it. Even though they were the ones relaying all the battlefield signals, they could get no clear idea of what was happening.

As the Americans drove westwards, the plight of the German forces in the Cotentin grew desperate. The loss of Carentan, a strategically important town in the south of the Cotentin, came as a heavy blow. This was quickly followed by the American capture of the Quinville ridge in the north.

The Allied control of the skies was also presenting a growing threat. Not only were they continually strafing and killing troops on the ground, but they had also managed to cut all the supply routes into the Cotentin peninsula. The German army stationed in the Cotentin required 5,250 tons of food each week to keep its soldiers fed. By mid-June, it was receiving just 200 tons.

Ten days had now passed since the Allied landings and the German forces in the peninsula were facing disaster. It was at this moment of crisis that Hitler decided to take personal control of the situation. On 16 June he made a trip to Soissons, east of Paris, in order to discuss strategy with the senior commanders of Germany's western forces, including Rommel and Rundstedt.

'He [Hitler] looked sick and tired out,' wrote Hans Speidel, Rommel's chief of staff. 'Nervously he played with his spectacles and with coloured pencils which he held between his fingers.' Speidel thought he resembled a broken man. 'His old personal magnetism seemed to have gone. After brief and cool greetings, Hitler, raising his voice, first expressed sharp dissatisfaction with the successful Allied landings, found fault with the local commanders and then ordered that Fortress Cherbourg be held at any cost.'

Rommel and Rundstedt begged Hitler to rethink this approach. It made no strategic sense to keep troops holed up in positions that were not under attack. What was needed was for troops to confront the American invasion head-on, hitting hard at every spearhead into new territory.

Rommel eventually decided, without Hitler's explicit approval, to use elements of Wolfram's 77th Infantry Division to construct a defensive wall on the western bank of the River Meredet. In that way, he hoped to forestall the American plan to cut the Cotentin peninsula in two.

Wolfram and his men began their deployment on 16 June, the same day as Hitler's visit to Soissons, by which time the American advance had proved so successful that the defensive wall had to be moved even further west, to La Haye-du-Puits, a little village just a few miles from the coast.

They were dug in along the road that linked Montebourg and Valognes. It was Sunday morning, 18 June, and there was a lot of gunfire, for the Americans had taken the land just to the south. Wolfram and the other men were told to pack up and get on the move as quickly as possible. *Schnell!*

Hurry! Hurry! They were in great danger of being completely isolated by American troops.

The withdrawal took place amid scenes of absolute chaos. Wolfram's unit had no news of what was happening, nor did they have any maps. Even the road signs had been removed, so they had no idea where they were going. It was only by memorising the names of some of the villages that Wolfram was later able to work out where he had been.

The 77th Infantry Division took everything with them as they tried to escape the clutches of the Americans, including artillery, armoured vehicles and tanks. What they did not know was that their retreat southwards would lead them through territory that had already been captured by advance units of the American army.

Among the little market towns that Wolfram and his comrades passed through was Briquebec, which lay some eight miles from the coast. As they made their way down the main street in the early-morning sunshine, they were wholly unaware that the Americans had already dug in and were watching the German retreat from their foxholes.

The men passed through the town without seeing a single American soldier. There was no one around, not even civilians. The place was deathly silent and eerily deserted. The only sign of conflict was the dozens of abandoned parachutes that had blown into the trees and were billowing from the branches.

Wolfram and his comrades were by now in serious trouble. American forces had reached the western coast of the Cotentin peninsula and captured the resort of Barneville-sur-Mer. It was an extraordinary achievement. Twelve days after landing on Utah Beach, they had succeeded in entrapping tens of thousands of German soldiers stationed on the northern coastline.

The Americans had no intention of engaging the enemy as they moved south. Instead, they were planning to lure them towards the hamlet of Le Vretot, which was the perfect place for an ambush.

Wolfram was blissfully ignorant of the danger as he and the other men marched through the rich farmland. The country lane that led to Le Vretot seemed little different to the thousands of other byways that criss-crossed the peninsula: it lay below the level of the fields and was lined with flowering hedgerows. The foxgloves and cow-parsley proved a source of constant temptation for the horses, which kept trying to munch on these vergeside snacks. The men were thankful that the weather was crisp and bright, unaware that the clear sky was about to rain death upon them.

Panzers, artillery, horses and men – all were making their way along the road to Le Vretot. Their path was frequently blocked by crippled and burned-out vehicles, which halted their progress. Each one had to be dragged away before the men could continue. It was during one of these enforced halts that Wolfram happened to notice a subtle change in the landscape. The road no longer passed through the bocage. On one side there was a steep bank and on the other a sharp drop. They were suddenly very exposed.

Then, quite without warning, there was a screeching roar in the sky to the north. Scores of American fighter-bombers hurtled towards them at extremely low altitude.

Wolfram flung himself into a low ditch and buried his head. As he did so, all hell broke loose. Exploding shells, grenades and machine-gun fire rattled down on the men, cracking through the air with a hail of fire and shrapnel. The artillery column came to an abrupt standstill as soldiers leaped from their vehicles in blind panic and urgently sought cover. Only now did they realise why the Americans had chosen this spot to launch their attack. With its steep drop and sharp bank, it was a death trap, making it almost impossible to avoid the fragments of flying metal.

As Wolfram lay cowering in the ditch, tanks, guns and mortars exploded around him. At one point he raised his head slightly and saw that the little lane had been turned into a scene of bloody carnage. The horses were neighing and whinnying in terror and pain, desperately trying to escape their harnesses. Unable to break free, they were being ripped to pieces.

The attack was relentless. Wave after wave of fighter-bombers screamed overhead, peppering everyone on the ground with machine-gun fire. Survival depended on potluck. Some of the best-concealed men were killed instantly. Others, more exposed, managed to escape with their lives.

Wolfram lay in the ditch for what seemed like an eternity as the *jabos* – the dreaded fighter-bombers – strafed everyone. His Morse equipment lay scattered across the road, smashed into hundreds of pieces, and he had no idea whether his fellow *funkers* were dead or alive.

'You lie there, helpless...' wrote one German soldier after surviving a similar attack just a few days earlier, 'pressed into the ground, your face in the dirt – and there it comes towards you, roaring. There it is. Diving at you. Now you hear the whine of the bullets... Not till they think they've wiped out everything do they leave. Until then you are helpless. Like a man facing a firing squad.'

At one point there was a slight let-up in the shooting. During the raid, Wolfram had been lying next to another lad and exchanging a few words with him. When the bombing relented for a moment, he shouted to him: 'Quick! Let's get out!' When there was no answer, he realised that the lad was dead.

Wolfram knew the planes would soon be back so he got up quickly, clambered out of the ditch and ran ahead to slip down a side road. As he crouched in a ditch that was deeper and less exposed, there was another roar of planes and the strafing started all over again. The soldier next to him had a piece of his earlobe neatly shot off. If he had been hit just a few millimetres to the left, he would have been killed instantly.

The fighter-bombers seemed determined to destory everything on the ground below. A sergeant who had previously fought on the Russian front lay next to Wolfram and told him that his experiences in Normandy were far worse that anything he had experienced in the East. In Russia, the shooting was slow and measured because of a need to conserve weaponry. Here, the Americans loosed off everything they had – a massive quantity all at the same time.

In less than one hour, the 77th Infantry Division was decimated. It suffered such heavy casualties, along with the loss of almost all its vehicles and artillery, that it was no longer a viable fighting force.

Only one group of men attempted to fight back, attacking the advancing American infantry in the fields around St Jacques-de-Néhou. They were firing at close range and, for a short time, caused severe damage. However, the Americans soon counter-attacked, pounding them with 81-millimetre mortars. Some 250 Germans were killed and a further sixty taken prisoner. Among the dead was the 77th Infantry Division's commander, General Rudolf Stegmann. He was driving along the road when a fighter-bomber swooped down from the sky and opened fire with such force that Stegmann's car was torn open like a tin can. The general was killed instantly – the fourth senior commander to lose his life since the landings of 6 June.

Then, after about two hours, the bombardment suddenly stopped. The planes retreated towards the horizon and silence returned to the countryside. The only sound came from the terrible moans of the wounded and dying.

The survivors were in a daze for there was a sense of unreality to what had just happened. One minute they had been walking along a country lane in the sparkling sunshine; the next, they were being torn apart by bullets and exploding shells. Stunned by the intensity of the battle, as well as completely lost, they were unsure where to go. All they knew was that they were trapped inside American-controlled territory and would have to fight their way out if they were to avoid death or capture.

The next thing Wolfram heard was German motorbikes roaring towards him, the riders shouting out orders as they drove through the wreckage. 'Get to the next woods! Regroup up there! You'll be protected there.'

Wolfram and the other survivors made their way to the woods, pausing momentarily to take stock of the carnage. There were bodies everywhere. Corpses that already stank, and scores of horses with their bellies ripped open and their guts spilling on to the road. And everything was still burning. It made for a terrible sight.

Dusk had fallen by the time the survivors had made it to the relative safety of the woods. They sought comfort in the penumbral shadows, aware that no American soldiers would risk their lives in coming to attack them here. It was eerily quiet, for no one dared to speak. The only sound was the whispering of the leaves and the occasional muffled rumble of a distant explosion.

Command of these shell-shocked survivors had fallen to the most senior regimental commander, the Pforzheimer, Colonel Rudolf Bacherer. He was determined to save the remaining men under his command and presided over an impromptu meeting of the few unit commanders who could be found. Several of them proposed retreating northwards towards Cherbourg in order to assist in the defence of the port. Bacherer refused to countenance this idea and wanted to continue to resist the American advance, still hoping for final victory. 'Every house must become a fortress,' he had said just a few days earlier, 'every stone a hiding place, and for every stone we must fight.' He ordered a breakout through the American lines that was to take place that very night.

Wolfram and the others were ordered to bind together all their possessions. It was crucial that there was no sound of banging or clattering. They were also told that no one was to say a word while they were on the move. The men were also forbidden from eating – a precaution in case they were wounded and needed emergency medical treatment.

They walked and walked in total silence, passing through villages that had already fallen into American hands and now sported a few banners declaring *Victoire*. At one point, they stumbled across thousands of American propaganda leaflets calling upon all German soldiers to surrender.

Filled with pictures of beautiful women, the pamphlets claimed that life was better in America, adding that even prisoners travelled in Pullman carriages.

Although the majority of villages were deserted, in one the men sighted a few American troops who were relaxing and caught off their guard. A brief shoot-out instigated by the German vanguard left all of the Americans dead. Then the telephone cables that they had laid were cut. Wolfram and his comrades passed on unopposed through the village.

They were by now utterly exhausted and could go no further. The order for rest was given and everyone slumped on to the banks of the sunken lane. A few men were posted as sentries, keeping a watchful eye on the American positions ahead.

Colonel Bacherer knew that he could not risk leading his weary men into nearby Barneville-sur-Mer. Instead, he decided to punch his way southwards, hoping to break through the American forward lines on the banks of the River Ollande. In a radio signal sent to the German 243rd Division, less than three miles away, he requested armoured support.

They responded within minutes, bombarding the American positions and enabling Bacherer to lead his men down to the river. However, as they reached the muddy estuary and peered through their binoculars, they realised that there was a new problem to be overcome. The only bridge, which they had to cross, was already being patrolled by heavily armed American sentries.

All of a sudden, Wolfram heard shooting up ahead. Bacherer's forward units – men from the 1st Battalion, 1050th Infantry Unit – had started to engage the Americans at close range. It was a bloody, hand-to-hand struggle fought with fixed bayonets under the cover of light machine-gun fire.

The battle did not last long, perhaps twenty minutes, at the end of which news came that the bridge had been captured. The American soldiers, quickly grasping they were massively outnumbered, had beaten a hasty retreat, leaving their fallen comrades on the bridge. Bacherer ordered his men to cross as quickly as possible, before the Americans could bring up reinforcements.

More than 1,400 German troops managed to escape from their trap that morning, taking with them 100 American prisoners. Once they had crossed the bridge, they were told to head southwards, away from danger.

They reached a village with a big manor house that had been commandeered by the German army. When Wolfram walked into the great hall, which was now serving as a field hospital, he saw battled-wounded Americans and Germans lying side by side – some with fractured bones, others suffering from shrapnel injuries or burns. The doctors were hastily examining each one in turn, trying to work out who was most in need of treatment.

Wolfram had remained with Miggel, his fellow *funker*, during their flight from the American zone. When they first arrived at the manor house, Miggel had darted down into the cellar. A few seconds later he was back upstairs with a broad grin on his face. 'Look what I found,' he said to Wolfram, holding up two pots of jam. Wolfram was struck by the incongruity of the scene. On the one hand there were the wounded and dying; on the other there was the triumphant Miggel with his jars of preserve.

The men were told to regroup outside and to start heading southwards, away from the front. They passed through rich pastureland and meadows, whose bucolic beauty was marred by a constant and ghastly noise. The cows in the fields were emitting low and anguished wails of pain, not having been milked for many days. Among the conscripts marching with Wolfram were several farmers who could not bear these terrible cries. As they walked, they would run into the fields and milk the cows, in order to relieve them from their misery. With no time to collect the milk, they just let it run into the earth.

Many of the animals were also suffering from festering bullet wounds sustained during the constant raids by Allied fighter-bombers. These animals were shot to put them out of their misery.

There was no sense of order or discipline as the men trudged along the country lanes. Indeed, they made their way southwards in complete disarray. Men would drift away and disappear, never to be seen again. On other occasions, Wolfram and his group would find themselves joined by troops who had become separated from their commanders or lost their way. At one point, the bridle path they were following divided into two. Miggel said to Wolfram: 'Carry on. I'll catch up with you.' He never did so. It was the last Wolfram ever saw of him.

Later in the afternoon of 19 June, Wolfram learned that the postal service between Normandy and Germany was still working. He hastily scribbled a letter to his parents in order to let them know he had survived the breakout and was back in German-held territory. He also revealed that he was deeply shaken by the horrific scenes he had witnessed. 'The many fallen comrades,' he wrote. 'I can still see them in my mind. I now know the meaning of "fallen in battle".'

Like so many who survived intense firefights, he was left with a feeling of both guilt and gratitude. 'They have fought and fallen for us, just for us – to give us something more beautiful; a better life.'

However, he also knew that his current situation was far from secure and we was particularly upset to have been separated from Miggel and two other close friends. 'I've got nothing left except what I'm wearing. And I'm missing my comrades – especially the three who I'm always thinking about – the sergeant Matusiac, the artist, Miggel, and Lang . . . I keep thinking of these three and I'll never forget them. I miss them so much. Hopefully – maybe – I will see them again soon. Hopefully this horrible materialistic battle will soon come to an end. All I see is planes and devastation.'

Wolfram's experiences over the previous few days had convinced him that the war was lost. The meagre resources of the Third Reich were no match for the equipment and manpower of the Allied forces. He had been astonished by the quantity of weaponry. The Americans seemed to have endless supplies of everything, whether planes, guns or ammunition.

The Germans, by contrast, did not even have enough food to eat. The men would sneak into abandoned farms and carry off whatever they could find. They often took the crates of butter and cream that were awaiting transportation to Paris, cutting off great slabs of butter and wrapping it in cabbage leaves to keep it fresh.

Wolfram had been told by his commanding officers that

he and his comrades were free to help themselves to supplies from uninhabited French houses, but they were under strict orders to take only the least valuable items in such houses. Although they could take a spoon if they needed one, if there was a choice between a cheap spoon and a silver one, they were to take the former. An unusual gesture in times of war, it was most certainly not the norm in the German army.

Wolfram was to spend five long weeks in the southern part of the Cotentin peninsula, continuously in retreat and never sure as to his exact location. The men had no maps and no equipment. They could only ever work out their whereabouts by entering abandoned farmhouses and looking for the PTT (post, telegraph, telephone) calendars distributed free to every house in France. These calendars had maps of the local area printed on them and gave the men some clue as to their position.

On 24 July, Wolfram and his comrades were stopped on the road by a senior German officer who ordered them to gather around him as he had an important announcement to make. With an impassive face, he informed them that an attempt had been made on Hitler's life. Four days earlier, Count Claus von Stauffenberg had tried to kill the Führer during a meeting at his Wolf's Lair headquarters in Rastenburg.

The bomb had detonated at 12.40, exactly as planned, and had ripped through the room, killing and wounding many of those present. Hitler, however, was not among the dead.

The officer told the men this news in brief and then went on his way without another word. No one who was with

Wolfram dared to say anything. Indeed, no one spoke at all for several hours, although one of the men later muttered to Wolfram and a few trusted confidants: 'See, it's the beginning of the end.'

Colonel Bacherer was working hard to re-form the 77th Infantry Division in order to strike back at the Americans. It was proving a forlorn task. The men were now scattered over a wide area of countryside and were constantly being forced southwards, first to La Haye-du-Puits, then to Périers and Coutances. Just a few months earlier, Wolfram had been entranced by this picturesque market town. Now, its medieval centre was a heap of debris. 'Only the gothic cathedral stands,' he wrote. 'Everywhere there's a picture of sadness and destruction.'

The bombing raids grew in intensity with every day that passed. On one occasion, Wolfram looked up to see the sky black with Allied planes. They were probably heading for St Lô, which was completely annihilated at exactly this time. Wolfram was suddenly struck by the thought that in the weeks since *invasionstag* he had seen only four German aircraft.

Most families in the region had fled their homes to escape the fighting, but there were the occasional incongruous discoveries. Wolfram and his men broke into one house that was very close to the front line. In the dining room, they found the table already laid in expectation of the owners' imminent liberation.

The family sheepishly emerged from the kitchen. Although unpleasantly startled to find themselves confronted by German soldiers, rather than American ones, they were courteous and friendly to these unwanted guests. Wolfram chatted with them and they gave him some cider to drink. In the near distance, he could hear the clanging of church bells – a clear signal that the Americans had already liberated the villages just to the north.

By the end of July the Germans had been pushed back to Avranches and Wolfram once again glimpsed Mont St Michel in the distance. 'Don't be surprised by this writing paper,' he wrote to his parents. 'It lives in the same earthen hole as me. And don't be surprised if you don't get any more news – it would be hardly unusual given the circumstances. I'll write as often as I can but I'm at the front where anything can happen.'

He ended his letter in cryptic fashion: 'How often have I already been led. I've had someone taking me by the hand and showing me the way, just as Tobias was led by the angel in the Botticelli painting.' It was, perhaps, his idiosyncratic way of informing his parents that he was preparing to let himself be led northwards. He had decided it was time to surrender to the Americans. There was no point in continuing. Without his Morse equipment, he was useless and could do nothing. Now, he just wanted to get away from it all.

There had been an unpleasant incident two days earlier that had helped him make up his mind. One of his conscripted comrades was being admonished by the staff sergeant as they stood close to the American front line. The sergeant was bawling at the lad, telling him he was useless and a good-for-nothing wimp.

It was as he said these words that the conscript received a direct hit in the chest. He stood rooted to the spot for a second before slumping to the ground. It was difficult for the men to absorb what had happened. One minute he was standing there being shouted at; seconds later, he was dead

– hit by a stray bullet. Even the sergeant felt terrible. The man had died at the very moment that he was being told he was useless.

Surrendering to the Americans was a perilous business. Wolfram knew that he would be executed if he was caught by one of his own officers. There was also the danger that he would be killed by those to whom he was trying to surrender. There were numerous stories of trigger-happy GIs shooting men who had offered themselves up as prisoners.

The next morning was Sunday, 30 July. Wolfram heard church bells again, which could only mean that the Americans were very close. Then he heard the rumble of American tanks: they were driving along the main road just a few hundred metres from his position.

He and his comrades were exhausted after weeks on the move. They were also dispirited. No one wanted to carry on, especially the Austrian soldiers. They were all saying: 'What's the point? It's going to be over soon.'

When the men came to a farmhouse later that day, they knocked on the door and asked the owner if they could sleep there for the night. The Frenchwoman told them that they could use her barn on condition that they got rid of their guns. The men dismantled them and buried them. It was a dangerous thing to do; discarding weaponry was tantamount to desertion.

The next morning was clear and dazzlingly beautiful. Wolfram and his comrades were ravenously hungry and wondered how they could get their hands on food. They spoke with the farm lady, who told them there were several well-provisioned Americans in the next village who were guarding a small group of prisoners.

The men begged her to go and tell them that they wanted
to surrender, but she refused to get involved. They spent
the rest of the day pondering what to do. By the time
evening fell, they were all so famished that they decided to
give themselves up just so that they could eat.

They made their way over to the village, catching the
American soldiers completely off guard. The Germans
could have easily overwhelmed them but no one could see
the point. Instead, Wolfram and his colleagues simply
walked up to them and asked whether they could surrender. The Americans were friendly and kind. After frisking
the men and reassuring themselves that they had no weapons, they gave them cartons of cigarettes and a little food.

As Wolfram and his friends joined the other prisoners
sitting on the ground, there was a moment of comedy that
broke the tension. All heads turned towards the main street
of the village where a lone Turkmen serving with the
German army could be seen emerging from a house. With
his Mongol eyes and wispy moustache, he looked as if he
had just arrived from the Central Asian steppe. Yet he was
dressed from head to foot in traditional Normandy costume
and was trying to pass himself off as a French civilian.

The Americans all burst out laughing, as did Wolfram
and his comrades. 'You,' said the Americans, 'are not
French!' And they took the Turkmen prisoner.

CHAPTER TWELVE

PRISONER AT LAST

'How dare you . . . how dare you complain!'

Marie Charlotte had no idea that Wolfram had been captured. Each morning, long before dawn, she would creep up to the attic and secretly tune in to the BBC to listen to the long lists of German soldiers that had been taken prisoner by Allied forces. The names were read out in random order, starting at 4 a.m. She would sit there for several hours in the hope of hearing that of her son, although she never did, even after Wolfram was in safe American hands.

In the summer of 1944, a new family of homeless people – from the north of Germany – were installed in the attic of the Eutingen villa. At the same time, Marie Charlotte agreed to house the furniture of their friends, the public attorney, Kurt Weber, and his wife.

The Webers, who lived close to the centre of Pforzheim, feared that the town would at some point come under attack, which would place, their house and all their belongings at risk. As a precaution, they carried all their antique tables, chairs, wardrobes and escritoires up the High Path and stored them in the largest salon of the Aïchele villa.

Marie Charlotte spent much of her time in the garden, tending her vegetable plot and listening to the monotonous drone of British planes high above. Although they passed overhead almost every day, they nevertheless attracted the attention of Eutingen villagers. People would cast nervous glances at the sky and hope that they were heading elsewhere.

One bright August morning in 1944, a small group of villagers was chatting in Hauptstrasse, the main street in the village, when a fleet of RAF bombers was sighted in the cloudless heavens, returning to their home bases after a daylight raid on the nearby city of Stuttgart. As they crossed directly over the Eutingen hillside, one of the planes got into serious trouble.

Among those who had gathered in the street was fifteen-year-old Werner Rothfuss. He saw a brilliant flash as one of the planes dramatically exploded in the air.

He and the others scuttled into a nearby cellar as the plane fell to earth in a shower of burning metal. Then, when the skies were once again quiet, they emerged blinking in the sunshine to see where the wreckage had landed.

Young Werner was the first on the scene and found the twisted metal at the northern end of the village. It was a British four-engine bomber, whose debris was scattered across a number of gardens. He dashed back to alert all those who had seen the plane come down.

Doris Weber, sister to Sigrid, had been playing down by the river at the time of the crash and saw nothing. It was not until she walked back up the street towards the centre of the village, that she realised something was wrong. She caught sight of a large gathering of people on

Hauptstrasse, in front of the village offices next to her family's house.

There was great excitement among the crowd and it did not take long for her to discover why. One of the British pilots had miraculously survived and had been brought as a prisoner to the Eutingen offices. He was badly injured and in considerable pain, suffering from a broken leg and severe concussion.

Doris did not get to see the pilot, but young Werner was whisked inside the building. His father was head of the local Red Cross and he needed his son's help in translating from German into English.

Werner was led into a ground-floor room, level with the street, where the pilot was being held. He was lying in a corner, his leg resting on a wooden splint.

Werner translated all the questions in the ensuing interrogation. He asked how many engines the plane had and how many crew were on board. The airman told him that it had four engines and seven crew, at which point someone said: 'Good, then we have them all.'

Werner's father was in the process of bandaging the man's crippled leg when there was sudden commotion in the hallway outside. Several men entered the room, one of whom rushed at the Englishman and demanded roughly: 'Does your leg hurt?'

The pilot answered: 'Yes, it's broken.'

The man in question was Julius Zorn, a senior functionary in the local Nazi Party and an infamous troublemaker. Angered by the mere fact of the pilot's survival, Zorn clutched him by the throat while uttering threats and abuse.

Werner's father was extremely disquieted by Zorn's

behaviour. Unable to stop him and sensing that something terrible was about to happen, he told his son that they should go, even though it meant abandoning the pilot. 'Come, let's get out of here,' he said. 'Such things have nothing to do with us.' The two of them left as hurriedly as they had arrived.

The crowd outside had by now dispersed, having been ordered by the local authorities to return to their houses. The sunlit street was completely deserted. An uneasy calm had descended on the village. The only sound came from the rustle of the trees and the distant barking of a dog.

Doris Weber was sitting in the kitchen, whose a window overlooked the village offices, when the silence was suddenly broken by a piercing, high-pitched scream, coming from the adjacent courtyard. She was shocked and terrified by it. It stopped as abruptly as it began and the village once again lapsed into silence. Doris could not forget the scream that kept ringing in her ears.

It was some hours before she learned what had happened to the rescued airman. She was peering out of the kitchen window when she noticed a long wooden box in the yard behind the wall. She asked a lot of questions until finally one of the neighbours saw no point in concealing the truth any longer: 'The pilot is dead. That's his body in the box.' The scream had been his death cry, the very moment of his murder.

The story was hushed up by the local authorities and the villagers knew better than to talk about it in public. Yet there were whispered conversations in many Eutingen homes that night as people came to terms with the fact that a cold-blooded murder had taken place on their very doorstep. It provoked widespread revulsion, even though the pilot was British.

Four years were to pass before news of the murder spectacularly resurfaced. British military officials got to hear of the incident and alerted the Hamburg tribunal that was in the process of investigating war crimes.

Werner Rothfuss and his father were suddenly summoned to Hamburg as witnesses. Among the interrogated was Julius Zorn, the former Nazi official whose fiefdom had included Eutingen. Werner immediately recognised him as the man who had bent over the pilot.

The trial was due to begin on the following morning but when the witnesses assembled in the courtroom one person was missing. The judge called for silence: he had an important announcement to make.

He told the assembled crowd that Julius Zorn had killed himself. He had committed suicide by slashing his wrists.

While unsavoury events were unfolding in the village of Eutingen, Wolfram was experiencing his first hours as a prisoner of war. These were to prove even more dangerous than when he was serving as a *funker*. As he and his comrades were marched northwards by their American guards, they found themselves walking along a country lane just a few metres from the German front line. The next thing they knew, dozens of fighter-bombers were flying overheard and blitzing the German positions with heavy machine-gun fire.

The gunfire and explosions brought back disturbing memories of the carnage that Wolfram had experienced six weeks earlier on the road to Le Vretot. One of the Turkmen travelling with him was so petrified by the noise of the shooting that he panicked and rushed into the field in order to pray. Those prayers were to be his last. He was immediately gunned down from the sky and killed.

The prisoners pressed on northwards and soon reached the market town of Ducy, captured by the Americans just a few days earlier. Four years of German occupation, followed by sudden liberation, had sparked a spontaneous outpouring of joy. The local inhabitants were all completely drunk. They were singing patriotic songs and dancing in the street but as soon as they saw the procession of German prisoners they started shouting insults and hurling stones. The prisoners might have been lynched on the spot, had it not been for the presence of the American soldiers who protected them from the mob.

The ranks of prisoners swelled as they shuffled their way northwards until there were several hundred of them. Some miles to the north of Ducy they were picked up by a fleet of army vehicles and driven towards Utah Beach, where a makeshift prison camp had been established in the scrubland behind the dunes.

It was a bleak and windswept spot: there were no tents, nor even any blankets. The detritus of war lay all around – crippled tanks, mangled artillery, discarded guns and reams of barbed wire. The men were herded into a large, fenced-off area guarded by American soldiers that would serve as their home for the next six days.

They were divided up according to nationality. The Germans were told to assemble on one side and the Georgians, Turkmen and Azerbaijanis on the other.

As dusk fell, the Americans began to distribute food

boxes to the prisoners. The German soldiers immediately formed themselves into an orderly queue and awaited their turn. The Asiatics, however, began arguing and jostling, and it was not long before a scrap broke out.

As punches were thrown and insults hurled, the fight developed into a near riot. Some of the stronger prisoners walked away in triumph with several boxes of food tucked under their arms. Those who were left empty-handed could expect a long and hungry night.

As the German soldiers watched in incredulity, Wolfram heard one of the Turkmen calling his name. It was Babei, who had been in charge of their horses while their unit was on the road. He was standing by the fence, clutching a blanket that he had somehow managed to get hold of.

He asked after Lang, one of Wolfram's fellow *funkers*, who had been in charge of the Turkmen and always treated them well. '*Lang gut,*' he said. 'Lang's a good one.' Wolfram replied that unfortunately he had no news of Lang. Babei then threw the blanket over the fence and said in his broken German: 'It's for you.' Wolfram was extremely touched by his generosity, aware that the Turkmen could have done with the blanket himself.

The prisoners arranged themselves on the rough ground as comfortably as they could, but there was little shelter from the wind and driving sand. Even though it was midsummer, the air grew damp and chilly as the last light faded. The men resigned themselves to a sleepless night.

It was about two in the morning when the Georgians in the adjacent camp lit a bonfire that they had made from bits of old crates. Once they had a settled blaze, they all started to sing.

The singing was quiet at first, but the sound steadily grew in crescendo as more and more of the men joined in. It was piercingly beautiful – an intricate polyphonic chant that drifted across the night, like a mournful and plaintive outpouring of all their sorrow. Wolfram could not help asking himself how the same people who had been so wild just a few hours earlier could now give voice to such haunting and complex melodies.

He remained in the camp on Utah Beach for the next six days. Each morning, the Americans asked for work volunteers, promising double rations as an incentive.

When the volunteers returned to the camp each evening, they invariably said that they had been burying decaying corpses all day, but Wolfram noticed that the last group of workers never came back. He had also observed that cargo ships arrived from England each morning with men and military hardware to be unloaded and assumed that the volunteers who did not return to camp had been taken away on the returning cargo ships. Desperate to escape from the war zone, he made it his goal to get aboard one of these vessels.

To his surprise, he found that a number of his comrades did not share his desire to get away from the battlefront. Many believed that the war was almost over and were hoping to return to their families in Germany as quickly as possible. They had no wish to end up as prisoners in England or, worse still, find themselves transported to America.

A few confessed to believing that Hitler's much vaunted wonder weapons would soon be unleashed on the Allies. If so, they wanted to be in a position to break out from their prison camp and continue the fight.

On 7 July 1944, the American guards once again called

for volunteers. When the necessary number had been assembled, the rest of the men, including Wolfram, were told to make their way down to the beach. They were going to be shipped to England on the next available vessel.

Later that afternoon, they were taken to an enormous cargo boat that was being used to transport tanks and artillery from Britain to France. There were no decks inside – just a cavernous, hollow shell, like a gigantic warehouse. The guards told the men to find a space on the floor and sit down. A row of buckets at the far end of the hall would be their latrines.

The German soldiers retained a strict hierarchy of rank even in captivity, with the officers sitting in a little group by themselves. Each time the men needed to use the latrines, they had to pass these officers.

On one occasion, those answering the call of nature included a private named Goesser who had been at Wolfram's training camp in Strasbourg. Wolfram, seeing him now wearing the badge of a sergeant, assumed he must have been promoted on the battlefield.

The officers also noticed the badge as he passed and began jeering at him. 'Congratulations!' they shouted amid peals of laughter. 'So you're a sergeant now!'

It transpired that Goesser, hearing a rumour that the American army required work only of the lower ranks, had promoted himself by removing the badge of rank from a fallen sergeant and sewing it on to his own uniform.

The genuine officers teased him mercilessly but with good humour. One of them said: 'Come, come over here. Have you got your papers? I've still got my stamp and I can validate your promotion.'

Goesser was embarrassed but nevertheless had his papers stamped, upon which the officers extended a general invitation to the others. 'Hey, does anyone else want to be a sergeant? Come over here and we can sort it out!'

The ship sailed through the night, docking in Southampton at the break of dawn on the following day. Wolfram and the other prisoners were escorted off the ferry in the early-morning sunlight and led down on to the quayside at exactly the moment when the English harbour staff were heading to work. All reacted similarly to the newly arrived Germans, turning their heads to stare, but no one said a word. It was so different from what the men had experienced in France, where villagers had shouted abuse and thrown stones.

Their guards on land were a different matter, however. On board the ship they had been civil and courteous, but here in Southampton they were overtly hostile, screaming at the men, calling them pigs and insulting them in German.

They were almost certainly Jewish immigrants who had fled their homes in the wake of Nazi persecution. Having been given refuge in Britain, they now vented their rage on the German captives in their charge.

The prisoners were ordered to strip naked and their clothes were taken to a special oven to be heated to a temperature that would kill all the lice and fleas, while the men were led to a shower block where they could at last wash away weeks of sweat and grime.

First, they were told to put all their personal belongings into a little bag with their name and number on it. An officer told them to report anything that went missing while they were in the showers.

A few of the men, discovering that items had indeed been rifled, duly reported it but soon realised their mistake. The guards were furious, yelling at them: 'How dare you – how dare you complain?'

The prisoners were completely bewildered by this. Why had they been told to report missing items if they were just going to be abused?

After two nights camped out on the Southampton quayside, the men were told to gather their belongings and prepare themselves for a long train ride. They were to travel at night so they would have no idea where they were going.

The journey seemed to take a lifetime, for the train kept shuddering to a halt in the darkness. Wolfram slept fitfully, even though he was exhausted. When dawn broke and the train started moving again, the men were told to close the curtains and not to look out.

After few more uncomfortable hours they finally arrived at their destination: a prisoner-of-war camp at Driffield, near Hull, on the north-east coast of England. It was a makeshift establishment, a tented encampment laid out in a field. With eight men to each circular tent, it was so crowded that they had to sleep with their feet pointing into the middle. When it rained, the tent leaked.

Wolfram was constantly hungry for the canteen staff never produced enough food, but one unexpected treat came in the form of real coffee. None of the men had drunk it for years; Wolfram had last tasted it in Nikolaiev, in November 1942. Now, there was an unlimited quantity and they drank so much that they all got stomach ache.

The worst element of life at Driffield was the constant boredom. There was absolutely nothing to do. One of the men brought out a deck of playing cards but that amusement soon wore off. Wolfram had a little pocket knife and started to carve chess figures out of lumps of chalk. He had only enough time to make three pawns before it was announced that they were once again on the move.

This time, their destination was infinitely more exciting. They were being taken to New York.

Pforzheim had undergone many changes in the three months since the Allied landings in Normandy. The summer vacation had been become permanent as schools and universities across Germany were closed.

The teachers were sent to work in factories producing weapons, where children were also given jobs. In the Rodi family, fourteen-year-old Frithjof and his two older sisters were required to go to work each morning, Frithjof to make clockwork pins for anti-aircraft grenades. When the clock started ticking, it was fired skywards into a convoy of planes and would then explode, sending fragments of metal everywhere.

Anyone who was too old to be conscripted into the army had to serve in the munitions factories. At the same time that Wolfram was being transported to Driffield prisoner-of-war camp, his father, Erwin, was told to report for duty in a weapons factory in Pforzheim. He was not there for long. As summer gave way to autumn, he was drafted into the Volksturm or Home Guard and posted to Alsace, where he was placed with a small group of men his age whose job was to construct defences on the frontiers of the Reich.

Each morning, Erwin and his comrades were woken at dawn and handed pickaxes and spades. For the next ten hours, they were required to dig deep trenches and construct earthen embankments high enough to stop a tank. It was tough physical labour for old men and quickly took its toll. Erwin had never been physically strong, even when young. Now, aged fifty-seven, he was in poor shape. After a few weeks of back-breaking work and very little food, he was close to collapse.

It was extremely fortunate that the head of the Eutingen Volksturm group happened to be Max Weber, a friend and close neighbour. Aware of the debilitating effect that such hard exertion was having on Erwin, Herr Weber wrote a special letter, permitting him leave of absence.

Erwin arrived back in Eutingen to find Marie Charlotte struggling to find enough food to feed herself and her daughter, let alone the various house guests. As time went on, meat, dairy products and vegetables had become more and more scarce; now, total war was constantly disrupting supplies from farms to markets.

The shortages affected families in Eutingen, Pforzheim and every other town in the area. In the Rodi household, one of the daughters, Gisela, was put in charge of food. The family nicknamed her their Minister for Foreign Affairs. She would regularly head into town and try to stock up on essentials like flour and cereals, which would be placed in a huge wooden cupboard that the family called the *mehltruhe* or flour trunk. Even so, the Rodis, like the Aïcheles, could not have survived without the fruit and vegetables they grew in their garden.

The family's eldest son, Peter Rodi, was two years younger than Wolfram and had so far escaped being drafted into the army. Now, however, after a brief stint in Poland, he was conscripted into the infantry and sent to Montbéliard, in eastern France, where resistance fighters were proving a new and menacing threat to national security. Many of these fighters had joined the French Forces of the Interior, formed in the aftermath to the Normandy landings. They would turn out to be an effective fighting force, despite their poor discipline, and the German army in France would come under increasing attack in the autumn of 1944.

In the weeks that followed Peter's departure, the family received no news as to his whereabouts. His mother used to tune in to the BBC every day to get the latest information on the fighting. The news was always announced by a loud and distinctive *bumb-bumb-bumb-bumb* sound. Whenever people heard that noise, they instantly knew that someone was listening illegally to the BBC.

One morning, a few weeks after Peter had left home, two men from the local Nazi Party turned up unannounced at the Rodis' house. The family had by now become so accustomed to listening to the BBC that they had forgotten that it was punishable by several weeks of harsh treatment in Dachau.

Martha Luise had left the radio on by mistake and, as the Nazi officials stood in the hallway, there suddenly came a loud *bumb-bumb-bumb-bumb*. It was the BBC news.

Fortunately the men passed no comment and, equally, Martha Luise managed to keep her cool. Calmly turning to her daughter, she asked her to switch off the radio.

She found it rather more difficult to keep her composure on discovering the reason for their visit. Peter, the officials told her, had been involved in a shoot-out and was missing in action. It was unclear whether he was dead or had been taken prisoner.

Many months were to pass before the family heard that Peter had been captured and was being held by the French. It was even longer before they learned the details. The moment of his surrender, heavily outnumbered and outgunned, had been extremely tense. His captors had lined him up against a wall with two others and pulled out their guns. Peter was convinced that they were about to be executed.

The three Germans stood in abject fear as the French soldiers joked among themselves and played with their pistols. Then, unexpectedly, the Frenchmen started to laugh. The mock execution had been nothing more than a little joke. Satisfied that they had made their three captives sweat, they put away their guns and led them off to a barn where many other men were being held prisoner.

They were eventually transported to the citadel in Besançon. For fully eight days they had nothing to eat. With just one tap for water, there was always a massive queue of men made desperate by thirst. On the ninth day of their captivity, they were given bread and a cauldron of watery soup.

Peter and his fellow men were first transferred to Camp de Thol, a prisoner-of-war camp close to the town of Pont d'Ain, then, shortly afterwards, moved once again, this time to Genissiat, just a few miles from the Swiss border. Here, they were to work as labourers on the construction of a new hydroelectric dam across the Rhône.

Although the barracks were marginally better than in Camp de Thol, with at least beds to sleep on, there was never enough food for young lads doing hard physical labour and they were famished from dawn until dusk.

Meals consisted of *pois de champs* – hard, brown peas. If the men had chewed them, they might have got a little nourishment, but being ravenously hungry they wolfed them down in a matter of seconds. An hour later, the peas came out exactly in the same state as they had gone in.

The French had suffered four long years of occupation and saw no reason to treat their German prisoners anything other than harshly. The lads worked for at least eight hours a day, shovelling sand and mixing cement. It was back-breaking work, especially on such a meagre diet. There were few rest breaks and the guards overseeing them would beat anyone they felt to be slacking. On one occasion, Peter was so exhausted that he could no longer summon the energy to lift his shovel. He pretended to faint in order to give himself a few minutes' respite. When the guard realised that he was faking, he hit him.

The chill mountain air, hard labour and wretched gruel quickly took their toll. One morning, Peter noticed that ulcers had started developing on his feet and arms. Soon after, his legs began swelling from hunger oedema, a swelling that then spread to his face. It was not long before he was in terrible shape; he was beginning to waste away from a lack of protein.

The non-existent hygiene also contributed to the miserable state of these weary and hungry men. Because they were unable to wash, their skin erupted into livid rashes and sores. Each morning, when they had to walk up a hill to their workplace, all the French girls would hold their noses against the stench of their unwashed bodies.

After a further week of hard labour, Peter was declared unfit to work. His oedema had worsened to such an extent that he was no longer able to pick up a shovel. He was taken back to the camp in Pont d'Ain and sent to the camp infirmary. It was where people went to die: the entire place stank of death.

There were thirty prisoners in the infirmary; each night one or two of them would expire. Peter knew when someone in the neighbouring bunk had died because the lice would leave the corpse as soon as the warmth had gone from it and make their new home on his body.

The inmates were left unattended for most of the time. A prison guard usually appeared twice a day – once to deliver a saucepan of inedible slops and once to take out the toilet pail. It was not long before Peter was little more than a skeleton. He weighed less than fifty kilograms, despite being well over six feet, and much of that weight was from water retention. As he lay there in the darkness, surrounded by groaning and dying men, he told himself that he had less than two weeks to live.

CHAPTER THIRTEEN

WORKING WITH COWBOYS

'We can't all be cheats!'

Wolfram and his comrades were transferred by train to Liverpool in the second week of August 1944, then escorted to the city docks, where a large troopship lay at anchor. This was to be their floating prisoner-of-war camp for the next fortnight as they were transported across the Atlantic.

For the first few days of the voyage the men were allowed out on deck for only half an hour at a time, but this rule was relaxed once they were at sea. The American officers assembled the men outside each morning and asked for volunteers to work on the ship. The outer hull was covered in rust, which needed scraping off. As an incentive, volunteers were promised extra rations of food.

Wolfram offered his services immediately, infinitely preferring to be out of doors, in the fresh sea air, to being confined below decks. He was roped to the side of the vessel with scraper and brush in hand, and spent hours in the late-summer sunshine, watching the frothing breakers beneath his feet.

After almost two weeks at sea, the men were once again confined to their cabins; they realised they must be nearing their destination. All were excited about the prospect of landing in America. It was as if a whole new adventure was about to begin.

One evening, an excited cry went up. Some of the men had managed to prise off the cover of one of the ship's portholes and could see that they were at long last approaching land.

In Wolfram's corridor there was a flurry of activity as everyone dashed to the porthole. Naturally, they all formed an orderly queue so that everyone could have his turn.

The sight that greeted Wolfram's eyes was breathtaking. The entire skyline of Manhattan was lit up – a sparkling, twinkling panorama of skyscrapers and lights. It was incredible to behold. The blackout had been a fact of life for so many years in Europe that everyone had forgotten what it was like to see lights at night.

As the vessel boomed its way into the harbour and prepared to dock, the men were assembled on deck and given standard landing forms that were normally intended for civilians. Wolfram found the questions on the form extremely strange, with things like: 'What would you like to do in America?' The other men were no less perplexed, having all assumed they would be enforced labourers.

The prisoners were told that an officer would shortly be arriving to debrief them and they awaited his arrival with growing impatience, excited at the prospect of meeting their first genuine New Yorker. There was by now a real sense of anticipation; everyone felt as if he had arrived in an exotic new land. It suddenly seemed as if anything was possible.

Five minutes passed, and then ten – and then, at long last, a whisper began spreading through the ranks. The officer had arrived, wearing an immaculate military uniform that had been carefully starched and pressed. The prisoners had not seen anyone looking so spick and span for many months. You could hear a pin drop in the silence as he walked across the deck. Everyone was waiting to hear him speak.

The officer tapped his cane and prepared to address the men. The prisoners craned forward to catch his opening words. All were expecting a cool New Yorker speaking with an American drawl.

No drawl was forthcoming; he did not even address them in German. *'Jetzt heered emal alle här,'* he said in a Swabish dialect so thick that most of the men could not understand a word. *'An schreibed uuf alles en grosbuchschdaben.'* (Now all pay attention, you need to write everything in capitals.)

As he spoke, the assembled prisoners burst out laughing, some to the point where they had tears streaming down their faces. 'Speak English,' they shouted. 'At least we'll be able to understand you!'

For the few Swabian prisoners, it felt like a homecoming. Wolfram was trying to work out from his dialect exactly which town the officer was from. Eventually, someone said: 'Günsburg, it's definitely Günsburg.' Then everyone started whispering this information to his neighbour: *Günsburg, Günsburg, Günsberg*.

When the laughter finally died down, the officer was able to explain what was about to happen. The men were going to be transported to Texas but first they would have to walk across New York to get to the station. He said that on no

226

account were they to accept the sweets and cigarettes that people were sure to offer them.

The men were completely baffled. Why would anyone want to give them gifts? Only later did they learn that New York had a large German population who would turn out in force to greet prisoners whenever they disembarked. They felt sorry for their fellow countrymen, aware that many of them were conscripts with no enthusiasm for Hitler's war.

The number of German prisoners being shipped to America had been small in the first few weeks that followed the Normandy landings, but it increased dramatically in the months that followed. By the end of August, when Wolfram arrived in New York, more than 30,000 were disembarking each month. This huge influx led to a rapid expansion of camps right across the country – in Ohio, Texas and California, as well as many other states. The number of Axis prisoners on American soil would eventually top 420,000, the vast majority of them being German.

The friendly reception given these prisoners was Wolfram's first surprise. His second was the train in which they were to travel. Seven weeks earlier, in Normandy, he had picked up a propaganda leaflet with the unlikely claim that soldiers would travel in Pullman carriages if ever they were prisoners in America.

Now, he discovered that this was indeed true. He and his fellow prisoners could not believe their eyes when they saw the train. There were four plush seats in each compartment but only three prisoners. When they asked why the fourth place was kept empty, they were told it was so that they would not be too crowded.

The food, the endless resources of America and the sense

of abundance left a profound impression on men who had suffered from years of rationing and hardship. When they were served their first meal on board the train, the American guards distributed brand-new paper plates and cups. As soon as the prisoners finished eating, they tried to wipe the plates clean to use them again for the next meal.

The Americans stared at them in bewilderment and asked them why on earth they wanted to reuse the plates. 'They belong in the trash,' they said. 'You need to throw them away.'

Wolfram and his friends expressed their surprise at such waste, only to be given a lecture on the American economy. 'Plate manufacturers also have to make a living,' said the officers in charge of them. 'If you reuse the plates, they won't need to make new ones and then they won't have a job.' The prisoners were amazed. It was their first contact with an entirely different way of thinking.

The three-day train journey took them on a meandering, 1,800-mile trek through seven states. Wolfram's previous long train journey, two years earlier, had traversed the monochrome snowscape of the Ukraine and Belarus. Here in America, the wooded glades of Pennsylvania and West Virginia glowed with the luminous reds and golden yellows of late summer.

After a fortnight spent at a holding camp – Camp Maxey in Texas – they were on the move again, this time to Oklahoma, in the heart of the Great Plains. As Wolfram stared out of the window for hour after hour, he was struck by the vastness of the canvas, as well as its emptiness. The train rattled along through terrain without any sign of human habitation, save for the occasional ranch that was lost in the middle of nowhere.

At last, one afternoon, a large settlement appeared in the distance, with buildings, shacks and prefabricated barracks. The men had finally arrived at Camp Gruber, a vast military training compound with a prisoner-of-war camp attached – one of thirty in the state of Oklahoma.

The camp sprawled over 60,000 acres and provided training for infantry, field artillery and tank units. When Wolfram arrived, the 42nd Infantry Division, known as the 'Rainbow', was in the middle of training for combat. Within months it would be fighting inside the frontiers of the Third Reich, liberating Dachau and setting free its 30,000 inmates.

Camp Gruber was far more comfortable than anything that the men had previously experienced. Although there were forty-five men in each dormitory, everyone had solid beds and there was a gas heating range, which they could light if they felt cold.

The surrounding landscape suggested the frontier territory of the Wild West. The nearest settlement of any size was Muskogee, a one-horse trading settlement that was home to large numbers of Creek American Indians. The majority of the population lived in isolated farms deep in the countryside, in conditions that were basic and primitive, and years of hard physical labour had left them exceptionally tough.

These blunt-tongued settlers were the pioneering descendants of peasants from Ireland: O'Caseys and O'Shaughnessys from Cork, Kerry and County Clare. Although the families themselves were poor, Wolfram and his fellow prisoners were constantly struck by the boundless resources of America. When they had arrived in Normandy, they had been supplied with badly made uniforms that quickly fell apart. Now, they were reclothed in American uniforms that were well sewn and made out of soft material. Indeed, the only thing that distinguished them from their American guards was the fact that their uniforms had PW stencilled on them in big white letters.

The camp food was nourishing and served in plentiful portions. More pleasurable still to Wolfram, the camp's library contained books that had been banned for many years in Germany, including Thomas Mann, Lion Feuchtwanger and Stefan Zweig.

The men were told that they had been brought to Oklahoma in order to help with the harvesting of cotton, peanuts and strawberries. Wolfram was allotted to the cotton fields. Each morning he and his comrades would assemble into groups of thirty and wait at the gates of the camp for the pick-up that would drive them for an hour or more along dusty tracks to the plantations.

Each prisoner was expected to pick 150 pounds of cotton a day – a quota that most of them had reached by early afternoon. The work was made easier by the fact that they swiftly learned to cheat their superiors. They would distract the guard as each sack was weighed, adding heavy stones to increase the weight. Then, once the sack had been lifted off the scales, they would surreptitiously remove the stones and slip them into the next sack.

What they had failed to realise was that the entire van was also weighed before and after it was loaded. Nor did they know that the driver was putting his own stones into each sack in order to get paid more. He quickly twigged that the men were engaged in the same trickery as he was and expressed his annoyance.

'We can't all be cheats,' he said and suggested that they come to an agreement, whereby everyone added a pre-agreed amount of stones.

Wolfram worked in the cotton fields until the harvest came to an end, at which point everyone started to ask themselves what they would have to do next. They were surprised that there was so little work to be done.

The prisoners were once again divided into groups. Some worked inside the camp, cooking, cleaning or making popcorn for the camp's cinema. Others, like Wolfram, joined a small team of civilians working in the tyre repair workshop.

The workshop's owner, Mr Hebel, in cowboy boots, stetson and checked shirt, might have dropped straight out of a western. Furthermore, he stank. Wolfram felt sure that he had never washed.

The civilians working for Mr Hebel were friendly towards the prisoners and frankly expressed their delight that the war was going on for so long, as it had created a lot of work in and around Camp Gruber – work for which they were paid good money.

To Wolfram, it was as if everyone based in the vicinity of the camp was on the make. One soldier, a sergeant from Texas, returned from his home leave with old tyres from his family's farm machinery, swapping them for new army tyres, which he sent back to his parents.

Other soldiers started to do the same – with the tacit approval of Mr Hebel – and it was not long before the prisoners were also involved in the scam. One of Wolfram's comrades spent all his days sitting in the tyre workshop, removing the words US ARMY from the stolen tyres.

*   *   *

Wolfram and his companions received little information about the war in those first months as prisoners. Newly arrived German soldiers brought them the occasional scrap of news but it was always many weeks out of date by the time it reached Camp Gruber.

The men themselves rarely talked of the war and their experiences at the battlefront. Nor did they speak about politics, which was considered a taboo subject and strictly off-limits. Wolfram got along particularly well with one prisoner and had many lengthy conversations with him. Yet it was not until long after the war, when he met up with the man in Munich, that he discovered that he had been a fervent Nazi. The Third Reich had created such a culture of secrecy that men learned not to talk of their political convictions, even when imprisoned.

The little news that Wolfram did hear from the battle-front confirmed what he had known for a long time: that Germany had lost the war and Hitler's defeat was inevitable. Although Allied forces were having to battle for every inch of ground, they were steadily and relentlessly advancing towards his homeland. Brussels, Antwerp and Lyons had all been liberated in September, while the Allies were also driving northwards in Italy.

October and November brought further gains: Athens, Zeebrugge, Metz and Strasbourg were all captured after a fight. The German army attempted to retake Antwerp in December, in the infamous Battle of the Bulge. Although their offensive temporarily halted the Allies, as well as causing large numbers of casualties, the American and British forces would continue their relentless push towards the German border in February 1945.

Wolfram knew none of this at the time; indeed, the war could not have seemed more remote from Oklahoma. Although desperate to start woodcarving again, he was hindered by a lack of tools and equipment. This was remedied when, with the help of friends, he managed to prise off some of the metal slats from his bed, with which he was able to make himself a set of knives and chisels.

He was delighted. At last, after almost three years of interruption, he was doing precisely what he most wanted to do. As Christmas approached, he began sculpting a traditional crib, just like the ones he had been trained to make in Bavaria. It was an exquisite piece of craftsmanship, carved from a thick wooden crate that had previously contained mandarins. Wolfram became known to everyone as 'the carpenter' and news of his talent soon came to the notice of the camp's senior officer, a man they had nicknamed Captain Melchior.

Wolfram risked punishment for having made his set of knives, but when Melchior saw the crib, he was taken aback by the quality of the carving. Keen to encourage the other prisoners in their skills and hobbies, he decided to stage an exhibition inside the camp. Wolfram's crib was to win first prize in the resulting competition.

When Mr Hebel learned of Wolfram's talent, he asked him to make furniture for his daughter instead of repairing tyres. Wolfram had to be careful not to get caught. He always had a tyre lying next to him so that he could pick it up and pretend to be mending it if an army officer came to inspect them.

At the beginning of December 1944, the men learned that the genial Captain Melchior was to be replaced by a different guard, a Russian Jew, whose behaviour was decidedly eccentric. In the days before Christmas, he confiscated all the cigarettes and sweets that the men had bought at the camp tuck shop. On Christmas Day, he came in, wished the prisoners a Happy Christmas and placed on the dining table everything he had confiscated, telling them it was a little present.

No one ever went short of provisions in Camp Gruber. With prisoners working in the kitchens and having access to the store cupboards, there were constant opportunities to filch tins of food and pots of jam. The civilian workers at Camp Gruber were forever asking the prisoners to steal things for them, knowing that they would lose their jobs if found out but that the Germans would escape punishment.

The prisoners were also paid a little money for their work, which they spent in the camp's tuck shop on books, cigarettes and ice cream. Wolfram had never eaten so much ice cream in all his life. The men were given it almost every day. In winter they used to melt it to create a vanilla-flavoured hot drink.

The prisoners were responsible for washing and ironing their own clothes, a chore that many of them found tiresome, until they worked out how to avoid it altogether. Several of their comrades had been given jobs working alongside civilians in the army's clothes store. Each week, these men would allow their fellow prisoners to come and help themselves to new uniforms. They would then throw away their dirty kit and stencil the letters PW on to the new one.

Wolfram had received no news from his parents in the six months that he had been a prisoner, nor had they heard from him. Indeed, they did not even know that he was still alive, although they had read in the Pforzheim paper that Colonel Bacherer had been captured, along with most of the men who had survived the breakout from the American beachhead.

As winter gave way to spring, the men began to ask themselves how much longer they would be prisoners. Their guards told them that Allied forces were rapidly advancing towards the Rhine, so the war was clearly entering its final stages. As the German army inched ever closer to defeat, Wolfram spent his evenings wondering how his home town of Pforzheim was faring.

CHAPTER FOURTEEN

FIRESTORM

'And then . . . all hell was let loose.'

T he night was as clear as glass. The moon hung low in the sky, a great silver bauble that shimmered in the icy air. Wolfram's mother, Marie Charlotte, was far too busy in the kitchen to take any notice.

The clock in the dining room had just chimed 7 p.m. and supper was about to be served. Family meals had lost all of their conviviality over the previous three years and daily life had become one long waiting game. Marie Charlotte had no idea when the family would be reunited and could not predict what the future held. The US Third Army had crossed the River Saar on the previous morning and was now just ninety miles from Pforzheim. On the Reich's eastern frontier, the Soviet army had captured Poznan. Nazi Germany was fast crumbling and although it was obvious that the end was near, it was less obvious how the victors would treat the vanquished.

Although there was much to worry about, Marie Charlotte did her best to put on a brave face. She still had her husband, Erwin, and her beloved daughter, Gunhild. And on this particular night, she also had a friend in the house. Frau Weber – wife of the Pforzheim attorney, Kurt Weber – was staying, together with her young children. The little ones had already eaten and were safely tucked up in bed. Now, the grown-ups were preparing to dine. In the wood-panelled dining room, the table was set and the potato pie was being kept warm in its dish.

Friday, 23 February 1945, had been more stressful than usual. Allied planes had been passing overhead for much of the afternoon and the air-raid sirens had sounded with monotonous regularity. These had been a feature of life for more than three years but they had grown increasingly menacing over the previous weeks. This particular day had been the worst in a long while. Everyone in Eutingen had spent hours at a time crouched in their cellars waiting for the sound of the all-clear. Marie Charlotte and her husband often chose to ignore the warnings. Aloof in their villa, they felt more or less secure.

Marie Charlotte had continued with the household chores, keeping a nervous eye on the skies above. The drone of planes grew in crescendo as the adults sat down to eat, although there was no sound of bombing and it came as a huge relief that the air-raid sirens did not sound again while they were at the table. They did their best to enjoy the pie but their conversation was periodically drowned out by the noise from the sky.

It was a few minutes after 7.30 p.m. when Erwin, who had finished eating before the others, stepped outside to get a key from his workshop in the garden. This was one of his favourite places on earth; in daytime there was a spectacular view across the wooded river valley towards Pforzheim.

Now, in the pale glow of the moonlight, Erwin cast his eye towards the south-west, expecting to see the town's distant roofs and gables bathed in silvery light. As he gazed across the valley, he was shocked by what he saw. He looked again – as if to double-check – and this time he had to pinch himself, scarcely able to take it in. Then, realising that his eyes were not deceiving him and that he and his family were in imminent danger, he ran breathlessly back towards the house.

'*Christbaums!*' he gasped as he burst into the dining room. 'There are *christbaums* all over Pforzheim!'

The cosy intimacy in the house was shattered in an instant. *Christbaums* – Christmas trees – were the magnesium flares used as target markers by Britain's Royal Air Force. Just ten days earlier, those same flares had lit the skies above Dresden – the prelude to a catastrophic bombardment and firestorm that had reduced the city to rubble and some 25,000 of its citizens to corpses. Erwin had a terrible premonition that the same fate was about to be unleashed on Pforzheim. If so, their own village was also likely to be in danger, for the British raids were notorious for their inaccuracy.

As if in confirmation of his fears, the whine of the local air-raid siren suddenly pierced the night air.

'Frau Weber quickly went to get the children out of bed,' explained Marie Charlotte in a letter that she later wrote to her eldest son. 'Everyone took what they needed – a coat or bag – and Gunhild got the dogs. We all went into the cellar. And then –' There is a slight pause in the letter, as if she had to collect her thoughts before continuing. 'And then – all hell was let loose.'

*   *   *

Some four hours earlier, a young sergeant named Doug Hicks had glanced anxiously at the skies above Lincolnshire before climbing into his Lancaster bomber. It was rare to be taking off in daylight but tonight's target was a distant one: it lay close to the Black Forest in the south-west corner of Germany. Hicks and his crew were heading for Pforzheim, a provincial market town in the northern part of Baden. It was a place of such insignificance that most of them had never heard of it.

Even the strategists in the Royal Air Force had hesitated when selecting it as a candidate for bombardment. Some months earlier they had drawn up a list of potential cities to be targeted. Pforzheim fell into the lowest of the five categories.

Now, on 23 February 1945, Operation Yellowfin had finally been given the green light. Pforzheim's watch-making industries were believed to be producing precision weapons and needed to be destroyed. They raid would be carried out by 379 aircraft carrying almost half a million high-explosive bombs.

Among those planes was a Lancaster bomber known by its crew as 'D for dog'. This was Sergeant Hicks' aircraft and it was his fifth mission with 505 Squadron. He was the rear gunner, charged with protecting the plane from attack from behind. It was a lonely role: for the next eight or nine hours he would be crouched in a tiny plexiglas turret, staring into the clouds for any signs of enemy aircraft. His only contact with the rest of the crew was through the wireless intercom system.

All the ground staff assembled outside the Nissen huts to wave the men goodbye. Hicks had just turned eighteen and had no interest in king and country. He and his fellow airmen saw these bombing raids as a big adventure.

The Lancaster roared down the runway before climbing steadily over the Lincolnshire countryside. It banked slightly as it did so, affording a bird's-eye view of the airfield at North Killingholme and the little villages of Brocklesby, Great Limber and Croxby Top. The runway steadily contracted until it was nothing more than a pencil-thin line; the surrounding fields shrank to smudged green miniatures.

As the squadron headed out across the North Sea, Hicks' thoughts flashed back to his previous mission, just ten days earlier. The same crew had taken part in the bombing of Dresden, unleashing their incendiary bombs with relentless intensity and turning the city into a fireball.

The Dresden raid had been one of the most devastating of the war. From his position at the rear of the aircraft, Hicks had been stunned by the conflagration ignited by their payload. He had also been struck by the scale of the raid and the number of planes involved, hardly believing that so many could fit into such a tiny area of sky. Now, as his Lancaster once again made its way across Belgium, he could only wonder about the new destruction that they were about to unleash.

The trip was uneventful and the planes reached Pforzheim exactly on schedule. There had been no anti-aircraft fire from the ground and no encounters with German fighter aircraft. They were flying at 20,000 feet and although it felt icy cold inside the aircraft, the men were wearing their electrically heated suits, which kept them warm enough.

As the plane circled the target and the tail swung through 180 degrees, Hicks caught sight of little fires on the ground below. These were coming from the magnesium parachute flares that had been dropped by pathfinders – the elite squadrons that located the exact target and sent down flares to mark the ground.

The Lancaster circled the town once again, descending to 8,000 feet – so low that the town's larger buildings appeared as looming shadows in the moonlight. Hicks, a Canadian recruit to the Royal Air Force, heard the voice of the master bomber crackle over the radio. The calm voice and pronounced English accent of the pilot were a reassuring. He could almost imagine the pilot describing a polo match as he issued the order to start bombing: 'Bomb on the red target indicators' – 'Good show, men' – 'We are right on target' – 'Jolly good show'.

Wolfram's parents were not the only people to panic when they saw the *christbaums* light up the sky over Pforzheim. Their close friends – who, like their house guests, were also called Weber – lived just a few hundred yards away in the heart of Eutingen village. They too were at dinner when there was a frantic knocking on their front door. It was the tenant who lived in the apartment above them, wearing nothing but his underwear and clutching his trousers. 'Go as fast as you can into the cellar,' he screamed. 'There are *christbaums* all over Pforzheim.'

The family rushed to their basement shelter, which had been lined with straw mattresses and stocked with provisions. Soon after, the earth began to tremble and shake with ominous regularity. Although they were three miles away from Pforzheim, the foundations of their apartment block shuddered from the force of the first explosions.

Sigrid Weber said goodbye to her life. She was numb with fear.

Other friends of Wolfram's parents would have to endure a more terrifying evening still. Their church friends, the Rodis, lived much closer to the centre of Pforzheim. Although their house lay just outside the phosphorus grid laid out by the British pilots, all of their extended family lived in the heart of town, which now exposed them to the greatest possible danger.

Martha Luise Rodi had turned on her wireless shortly after 7.30 p.m. and had heard the ominous sound of a ticking metronome – the usual prelude to the announcement of an imminent air raid. Then came the news that there were thirty planes to the west of Pforzheim, crossing the Rhine and flying very low.

Martha Luise immediately telephoned her mother and sister who lived in a little apartment in Nagoldstrasse, at the bottom of the hill, warning them to take shelter. Shortly after, at about five minutes to eight, the family heard another announcement, alerting them that the planes were marking the city. The last words that they heard were: 'Bombs are being dropped.' Then there was silence.

Martha Luise ushered her children into their shelter as soon as they heard that the city was being marked with flares. With her husband away, her eldest son missing in action and one of her daughters, Ev-Marie, on Reich Labour Service, she felt acutely protective towards her remaining three children.

However, many local people reacted to the air raid with weary indifference. The sirens sounded every day and yet the bombs always fell elsewhere. There was a feeling that

Adolf Hitler visits Pforzheim and Eutingen, en route to the fire-damaged village of Öschelbronn, in September 1933. The Aïchele family were criticised by neighbours for declining to join the cheering crowds.

The Nazi leader of Baden, Robert Wagner, inspects a rally in the market square of Pforzheim, November 1934. Wagner was one of the most fanatical regional leaders.

Election poster, 1932. Women were instructed to vote for Hitler. Wolfram saw posters like this all over Pforzheim.

Poster celebrating the League of German Girls – the female branch of the Hitler Youth. Girls went from door to door collecting money, in this case for 'youth hostels and homes.'

A 1933 street march of the League of German Girls in Hornburg, near Pforzheim.

Uniformed officers confiscate books in preparation for burning them. The scene on the right took place in Hamburg: similar scenes occurred in Pforzheim in June, 1933.

Nazi policy was to deport all Jews in Germany (left). Among the first communities to be deported was that of Pforzheim in October 1940.

State sponsored anti-Semitism was ubiquitous: here, one of Pforzheim's Jewish owned shops, Ehape, is guarded by uniformed Nazis. 'Scoundrel' reads the banner outside.

Deutsche Bauern-jiddisch gesehen---

Hitler held inflexible views about art. National Socialist art (right) was championed by the state, while 'degenerate' art (above) was displayed for public ridicule at the infamous Munich exhibition, 1937. The caption reads: 'German peasants viewed through Yiddish eyes.'

Hans Knab was the local Nazi leader in Pforzheim – the eyes and ears of the regime. Gestapo officers and informers helped him monitor all aspects of life in the town.

Sebastopol, above, was seriously damaged during its capture by German forces. In 1942, Wolfram saw similar scenes of destruction in Kerch, at the eastern end of the Crimean peninsula.

Wolfram recuperating in a military hospital in Marienbad, 1943. As soon as he was better he was sent to Normandy, arriving in time for the D-Day landings.

Wolfram served as a 'funker', or wireless operator, working in a small team similar to the one pictured. It was dangerous front-line work as wireless operators were specifically targeted by Allied forces.

'*Schnell*! Quick! Take cover!' On 17 June, 1944, Wolfram and his comrades were attacked from the air. Wolfram was one of the lucky few to survive.

Wolfram and his comrades gratefully surrendered to American forces. They were taken to a makeshift encampment, similar to above, adjacent to Utah Beach.

German prisoners of war were transported from New York to their prison camps in Pullman trains.

German prisoners painting the letters PW onto their uniforms. The American uniforms were of a far superior quality to the German ones.

Wolfram and his fellow prisoners were obliged to watch a film showing Allied forces liberating an extermination camp. They were deeply shaken by what they saw.

Pforzheim, 1945. The historic town centre was obliterated by RAF incendiary bombs on the evening of 23 February. Among the 17,000 dead were many acquaintances of the Aïcheles.

Wolfram returned to his studies in Oberammergau in 1946. His sculpture of Christ on a donkey was carved for the parish church of St Peter and St Paul. It remains there to this day.

Pforzheim would be spared. After all, it made no strategic sense to bomb a provincial town on the fringes of the Black Forest.

Among those who ignored the sirens was Hannelore Schottgen. She was returning to Pforzheim after a long stint in the Reich Labour Service and was cycling through the easternmost part of town when she suddenly heard the familiar sound. As she was just fifteen minutes from home, she decided to keep going but was stopped by an air-raid warden and ordered into the nearest public shelter.

Her arrival was met with much grumbling, for the cellar was already overcrowded. On the point of tears, she went back upstairs and begged the man to let her continue on her way.

The warden reluctantly agreed to let her get back on her bike but he did so on condition that she take cover as soon as she saw planes overhead.

As she turned into Kiehnlestrasse, in the centre of town, she was stopped for a second time. A warden ordered her off her bike and into a shelter. 'Come on, miss,' he said. 'You can't carry on any more. They've already sent down the Christmas trees.'

Hannelore told him she feared being greeted once again by outright hostility, but he reassured her that the girls in this particular shelter were very friendly. 'You'll be treated well. Go in quick.'

As she descended into the cellar, she heard the low rumble of the vanguard planes passing overhead, followed by the sound of flak from the local air defences.

She was indeed given a warm welcome by those already in the shelter – eight Reich Labour Service girls and a warden – who were huddled over a wireless listening to the news.

They heard the radio announcer describing the situation as desperate. Suddenly the voice became stronger: 'Big groups of enemy planes are coming nearer our area.'

The girls glanced at one another and prayed that the aircraft were heading elsewhere.

Eight thousand feet above Pforzheim and crouched into the rear turret of his Lancaster, Sergeant Doug Hicks was still listening to the crackling instructions being issued by the master bomber. 'We are right on target . . . jolly good show.'

It was as he heard the words 'jolly good show' that the aircraft lurched violently to the left and started a sickening downward spiral. Sparks and flames began streaming past his turret and his intercom went dead. He assumed they had been hit by flak, for he could see tracer fire arcing up from the ground. In fact, the Lancaster had been hit by an incendiary bomb released from a plane flying directly above them.

Peering out of his turret, Hicks realised that the rear of the plane had also been hit by fire from the ground. He counted six holes in the left side of the tail and another five on the right.

The pilot was fighting hard to keep the aircraft under control. As it flew over the town at an alarming angle, Hicks got a dramatic panorama of sky and land. The whole target area was a sheet of white light. When he looked upwards into the fire-lit sky, he could see dozens of Lancaster aircraft with their bomb-bays open.

*   *   *

In the Aïcheles' hilltop villa, Wolfram's parents were still sheltering in the cellar. There was a continuous thumping that shook the entire hillside. To Marie Charlotte, it felt as if a giant was punching the floor of the valley with his fist. 'Bomb after bomb,' she wrote. 'The whole house was shaking.'

At one point during the bombardment, she and her husband crept upstairs and poked their heads outside, only to find that they were scarcely able to breathe. The firestorm in the valley below was so intense that all the oxygen was being forcibly sucked from the air.

Marie Charlotte was suddenly very frightened. 'The air pressure was so strong that the door was flung out of our hands.' In Dresden, the same suction had wrenched windows and doors from their frames, allowing the fire to spread with unchecked rapacity.

As Wolfram's parents stared down into the valley, it seemed to be one luminous sheet of flame. It was mesmerising, even hypnotic. They would have watched for longer, had they not been sent dashing back to the cellar by a stray incendiary bomb that smacked into the damp earth of a neighbouring field, setting it alight.

At their house on Spichernstrasse, the Rodi children were also crouched in their cellar, hands jammed in their ears in an attempt to block out the deafening thumps. They could not see anything, but they could hear the planes roaring overhead.

Barbara, just nine years old, was shaking with terror. To make matters worse, the electricity was suddenly cut. Now, all they had for light was a pocket torch.

Then, incongruously, there was a frantic knocking on

their front door. It was Uncle Karl, a cousin of the family, who had run all the way from his house in order to see whether they were still alive.

He brought a tale of such destruction that it seemed inconceivable anyone in the town centre would survive.

Sergeant Doug Hicks was thinking much the same thing as his crippled Lancaster bomber circled Pforzheim. With every passing second, another sector of the city exploded into flames. Soon, the scores of individual fires conjoined into one massive conflagration that turned the ground into a spiralling, whitish-gold pool of flame. The bombs being dropped contained a mixture of high explosive and phosphorous incendiary that gave a curiously cold colour to the heat of the fire.

Hicks, isolated in the tail, was desperately trying to make contact with the pilot but the intercom system remained dead. Convinced that the plane was going to crash-land, he prepared himself for the terrible ordeal of parachuting to the ground, unplugging his electric suit and getting ready to open the turret doors. As he peered into the void, he was brought to his senses by the horrendous sight below him. The entire town was a raging, pulsating fireball. He decided that he would rather ride the aircraft until it hit the earth than jump into the burning hell that was Pforzheim.

As if to confirm that he had made the right decision, the plane suddenly righted itself and levelled off. Severely damaged, but brought under control by the skill of the pilot, it swung in a westerly direction and headed for home.

The firestorm that it left behind was awesome, with great tongues of flame leaping and writhing into the winter sky.

So bright was the glow, indeed, that it was still visible to Sergeant Hicks when his plane was more than one hundred miles from Pforzheim.

On the ground, the flames devoured utterly everything in their path. More than 90 per cent of the buildings in the centre of town were now ablaze. As the fire ate through supporting timbers, so the exterior stone façades collapsed in on themselves. In the eye of the firestorm, the temperature approached a staggering 1,600 degrees centigrade – so hot that even metal beams and girders were turned to liquid.

The firestorm could be heard sucking in oxygen with greedy relish. Then, like a spiteful bellows, it belched out a noxious concoction of sulphur-yellow gases.

Many of the 17,000 Pforzheimers who would not survive that night were already dead. Pulverised by bombs, crushed by collapsing buildings or starved of oxygen, their end was terrible but mercifully swift. However, in one small cellar in the centre of town, caught in the heart of the firestorm, Hannelore Schottgen was still alive.

'We were sitting there, huddled together. All we could hear was bomb after bomb; screaming and screeching and noises of things breaking down. The whole house seemed to be moving. A bit of ceiling fell down . . . there was disgusting dust everywhere. More things fell in. Was the house going to collapse on top of us? Was it going to bury us alive?'

She later recalled her fears as she sat crouched in the cellar. At one point there was a momentary pause in the bombing and a ghostlike voice could be heard on the wireless, announcing that the raid was coming to an end. The

girls experienced a moment of elation, but the announcement was swiftly followed by a second one that warned that
a far larger formation of planes was now heading their way.

Up to this point, the girls in the shelter had taken some
comfort from the fact that the lights were still working. Now,
they suddenly snapped out, plunging the cellar into darkness. The town's electricity station had received a direct hit.
Seconds later, equally abruptly, the wireless went dead. The
girls clutched each other, terrified by the prospect of death.

The bombs and incendiaries were by now causing incal-
culable damage. Entire quarters of the city had collapsed
into rubble. Leopoldstrasse, Pforzheim's busiest street, had
received dozens of direct hits and its elegant façades had
already collapsed by the time the firestorm took hold. Alone
in escaping the destruction was the Golden Adler, a hotel-
cum-tavern. Its windows had melted, its roof had collapsed,
yet its damaged façade was to remain standing until the
end – a lone survivor amid a heap of ruins.

On Goethestrasse, nothing remained intact. It was a
mountain of burning masonry. Museumstrasse lay in
rubble. Baumstrasse had ceased to exist. Even the medieval
heart of town on the Schlossberg had been lost. By 8.05
p.m. the centre of Pforzheim had already been obliterated,
yet less than a quarter of the total quantity of explosives
that would be dropped that night had fallen on the town.

The loss of life was to be disproportionately high because
no one had expected Pforzheim to be a target. It was only in
the last year of war that shelters had begun to be built, but
there were never enough and, when the big raid finally
arrived, many people had only their cellars for shelter.

Hannelore Schottgen was one of thousands who was

trapped underground; falling masonry had blocked the entrance to the shelter. 'The walls were moving and chunks of plaster kept falling into the room. Dust and smoke. We put wet cloths over our mouths and noses.'

Although the ceiling of the cellar was still holding up, it had been dangerously weakened. 'We must find a way out,' said the air-raid warden. 'The ceiling is not going to bear up for much longer.'

In total darkness, the man groped for his hammer and began knocking on the wall, listening for the hollow sound that would indicate the exact location of the adjoining cellar.

'He was knocking everywhere, looking everywhere, getting really desperate.'

As he tapped the walls, the first trickle of smoke began filtering into the cellar. Soon, more and more smoke was pouring in. The girls realised that the building must be burning on top of them. In this they were correct. The streets were a cauldron of fire.

Even the warden recognised that they were doomed either to be burned alive or to suffocate from the asphyxiating gases. 'The only thing we can now do is pray,' he said. 'Come on, let's make a circle.'

The girls drew together and listened as the man praised God. Hannelore pinched herself to see whether she was still conscious. 'We had given up and were waiting for the end.'

On the other side of town, Martha Luise Rodi's mother and sister had also sought refuge in their cellar and were listening to the roar of the flames. For them, as for so many in Pforzheim, the greatest danger was hidden. As the firestorm tore through the old town, it poured forth a cocktail of poisonous gases that seeped into the underground shelters and snuffed out the lives of all those trapped inside.

The two ladies were saved by the quick-thinking owner of the building who had taken shelter with them. He was aware of the hidden danger and insisted they leave the cellar, even though the streets above presented many additional hazards.

Clambering out of the shelter presented considerable difficulties for Martha Luise's mother. With crippled feet, she found it hard to climb up the small ladder. It was even more difficult for her to crawl out through the burning house. They emerged at last to find the entire neighbourhood on fire. However, the two ladies were fortunate that their apartment stood next to the River Nagold, which created a barrier of sorts to the flames.

On the previous day, the river had been in high flood because of all the melting snow, but that very morning, the water level had dropped. They were therefore able to make their way along the muddy banks and eventually reach the Rodi family house.

By this point, Martha Luise and her children had crept into the garden to see the extent of the destruction in the valley below. As they stood there, watching the glow of the town on fire, they became aware of two familiar figures struggling up the hill.

'I'll never forget the first image of them arriving,' wrote Martha Luise in a letter to her absent daughter. 'There was a background of flames that filled the sky. Grandmother had her typical silhouette – it was unmistakably her – but the backdrop of flames was extraordinary impressive.'

*   *   *

Hannelore Schottgen had given up all hope of survival. The cellar was by now insufferably hot and smoke was pouring in from the outside. The warden suddenly got his strength back and began to bang on the wall with renewed effort, trying to smash a hole through to the adjoining cellar. As he did so, Hannelore and the others became aware of faint noises through the wall from people next door. 'We could hear them knocking. A stone gave way, and then a second, and they helped from the other side until the opening was big enough for us to squeeze through.'

No sooner had they reached safety than there was a tremendous crash. The ceiling of the cellar they had just vacated slumped in on itself, bringing down tons of rubble from the building above.

Acutely aware of the dangers of toxic gas, the warden in charge of the new shelter forced open the iron door that led to the street and poked his head outside. 'Quickly!' he said to the girls. 'Come immediately, it's burning everywhere. Soon there won't be any air left to breathe.'

The girls were fearful of stepping into the conflagration but the warden insisted. 'You know that we're not allowed to stay in the cellars when it's burning,' he said. 'There are no more bombs falling. Come on! Quickly!' Hannelore followed him but the others were too scared and stayed behind.

The sight of the town burning from end to end was deeply shocking. 'Massive flames everywhere – a sea of fire, like a hot tempest. Walls completely red hot and enormous pieces of rubble that were also red hot.'

Hannelore lost all feeling of orientation; she was concentrating on trying to escape the heat, but wherever she turned, the streets were blocked with burning masonry.

In the midst of the chaos there were incongruous scenes. One side street that had not yet been touched by the fire-storm was filling with people trapped by the fire.

Some of them ran towards her, saying: 'You can't get through here. It's too hot.' She and the warden turned back, only to be met by more refugees milling about in complete despair. 'There's no way out; there's just heat, heat.' Hannelore was suddenly struck by the awful realisation that they were going to be burned alive.

'Come on,' someone shouted. 'Right, down the side street. We must go down *there*. You won't get through that one, you'll burn.'

A loud scream announced the arrival of yet another crowd, bringing news that all avenues of escape were now closed.

The warden with Hannelore now took a decision that was ultimately to save both their lives. He told her to cover her hands and face with her coat and make a charge through the burning street towards the river. It was their last hope of survival.

Hannelore could not longer think, but just blindly followed the shouts of the leader: 'Come on, keep going, step by step.'

Hannelore begged him to tell her how much further it was to the river.

'Come on, keep going,' he shouted in answer. 'Step by step.'

They pressed on doggedly through the burning rubble until they felt a faint breath of air. At long last they had reached the river and slumped on to its bank where they were shielded from the worst of the heat. Hannelore lay on her front, placed her nose just above the water and focused on simply trying to get oxygen into her lungs.

*   *   *

In Eutingen, Wolfram's parents once again emerged from their cellar and stepped out into the garden, to be met by an awesome sight. 'To our horror,' wrote Marie Charlotte in a letter, 'we could see the entire town in flames. A gigantic black cloud of smoke was drifting along the Enz valley.' The acrid-sweet stench of burning houses, furniture and corpses hung in the air.

Although they were three miles from the epicentre, the flames were so bright that Marie Charlotte had to shield her eyes. The moon, so pristine and beautiful an hour earlier, was now hidden by a ghastly wreath of smoke. There was an unreality to the scene. 'The sky was completely red,' she wrote. 'Black smoke shaded the soft light of the moon and made Eutingen appear as a peaceful and sleepy little village.'

Marie Charlotte experienced a feeling of helplessness, for nothing could be done for friends down below so long as the inferno raged. 'We felt so anxious and worried about all the people we knew who must be trapped in the flames.'

There was also a feeling of guilt that their own little world had been saved. 'We had a deep feeling of gratefulness that we had been spared. Nothing is broken and there is no sign of any damage around the house, except for one window in the workshop which is smashed.'

As she and Erwin watched the fire sweep a path along the Enz valley, they heard a curious cracking and rumbling noise: it was the sound of buildings collapsing into themselves.

Both of them would later recall being paralysed by a sense of helplessness as they gazed across the valley below. The only practical thing to be done was to prepare the house for any survivors. 'We stayed up very late in expectation of homeless people turning up,' wrote Marie Charlotte. 'Finally, the doorbell rang and Ysole and Gunthe were outside, together with her fiancé, a very nice Flemish man.' They had picked their way across burning rubble and witnessed the most harrowing scenes. All three were singed and blackened with soot. 'They were desperate to get their breath back and to quench their thirst.' After washing their blackened faces, they told Marie Charlotte and Erwin how they had managed to make their escape.

In the lower village of Eutingen, Sigrid Weber and her sisters had also emerged from their shelter, crowds of soot-covered people coming from the direction of Pforzheim, picking their way along the banks of the river.

They walked in silence, the shock of the bombing having robbed them of speech. Homeless, blackened by fire and grieving for loved ones who were still caught in the inferno, they poured into the village in search of shelter from the February chill.

Hannelore Schottgen remained slumped on the river bank for many hours, waiting for the fire to burn itself out. Much later that night, when the inferno was a spent force, she found her way along the bank of the river to her parents' house. Miraculously, it had been spared by the fire.

The entrance door had been ripped off, all the glass had gone from the windows, the curtains were hanging in the trees and the garden was hittered with roof tiles. However, the house was still standing. She called out for her parents but was met with a ghostly silence. No one answered.

She made her way to the Stollen, where small groups of

dazed survivors were beginning to congregate. Then, unexpectedly, she experienced her second miracle of the night. Her parents were among the crowd. 'My mother screamed when she saw me. My hair and clothes were completely black.' But she was still alive.

For Hannelore, the sight of her mother also provoked a welling-up of emotion. She collapsed out of tiredness. Someone helped her on to a chair, wiped her face and gave her something to drink. It was dawn before she would see the grim reality of what had happened to Pforzheim.

Thirty miles away in Stuttgart, Captain Max Rodi had been first alerted to the fact that something was seriously awry by the distant drone of aircraft. Drafted back into the reserves as an officer some months earlier, and charged with tracking the path of enemy planes, he had climbed to the top of his Stuttgart watchtower shortly before 8 p.m. As he gazed in the direction of the town that was home to his beloved wife and children, he was shocked by what he saw. A dull orange glow hung in the sky and seemed to grow in intensity with every minute that passed.

He immediately realised that the aircraft were attempting to create a firestorm in the centre of Pforzheim, just as they had done in Dresden. The distant flames were already so bright that they hit up the pall of toxic black smoke, visibly hanging in the air. As Max stood there, desperately anxious for the safety of his family, he felt a curious tingling sensation on his face and arms. It was ash. Ash was pouring from the heavens. 'A massive rain of ashes,' he later wrote. 'Even in Stuttgart, I got ash on me, falling from the sky.'

Soon after, he noticed that the glow in the sky had

suddenly become much brighter. It was clear that a fire of cataclysmic proportions was devouring Pforzheim. He made repeated attempts to get news of his family but without success. The wires were down, the lines were dead. In desperation, he begged his commanding officer, Oberleutnant Steller, to allow him to return home. This was immediately granted.

With no vehicles available, Max climbed on to his trusty bicycle and set off on the four-and-a-half-hour ride. As he neared the town, he was met by the acrid stench of burning.

He was still some distance from Pforzheim when he came across the first survivors. They told him that the entire town had burned down and that only the outskirts were still standing. This last bit of news brought some comfort: although he feared for his extended family, there was still hope that his wife and children had survived.

He pushed on towards Pforzheim until his path was blocked by rubble. Leaving his bike in a house by the waterworks, he started walking through a biting black smoke.

There was not a single building left standing. Every house had been consumed and had collapsed in on itself. The rubble stood metres high, making it very difficult for Max to get through the blocked streets.

He was hoping to pass his mother-in-law's house on Nagoldstrasse on his way home, but it proved impossible to orientate himself in the tangle of ruins. When he arrived at what he thought was the correct place, he found that nothing was standing.

Although it was not easy to locate the right heap of rubble, he eventually managed to find the remains of what he thought to be her flat. The trapdoor to the cellar was open, suggesting that whoever had been inside had also been able to get out.

Max was by now desperate to get to his own house and check on his wife and children. In the light of both the moon and the fire, he began the slow climb up the hillside until he at long last reached the garden gate. He was greeted by a sight that brought him the greatest possible comfort. His little home was unharmed, peaceful and quiet in the moonlight.

He and Martha Luise sat up into the early hours, reliving everything they had experienced over the previous few hours. It was too awful for words. 'You just cannot imagine it,' Martha Luise would later write in a letter to her daughter. 'A catastrophe without name.'

Two miles away in Eutingen, Wolfram's mother was in full agreement. It was clear from a glance across the valley, which was still glowing a dull orange, that their lives would never be quite the same again.

'The English definitely made a proper job of it,' she wrote. 'I now know the meaning of rubbing something out.'

As the night wore on, a steady trickle of people began appearing at the Aïcheles' home. Wolfram's father lit a bonfire in the garden and dusted off an iron cauldron that was normally stored in the cellar. Marie Charlotte then began preparing food for more survivors who were sure to appear in the hours to come.

'People have been turning up to say that they're still alive,' she recorded in a letter written on the following day. 'And every time, you hear yet more horror stories of what happened.'

CHAPTER FIFTEEN

COUNTING THE COST

'No body. Not even a bone. The whole street had disappeared.'

Pforzheim was still smouldering when dawn broke on the following morning. A thick veil of dust hung in the air and black smoke drifted across the valley. It was eerily silent and would remain so for days. 'Everything is deathly quiet,' wrote Martha Luise Rodi to her absent daughter. 'Everyone is paralysed and speechless and dumb.' The only noise to be heard was the occasional rumble of a crumbling building.

Hannelore and her parents had returned to their damaged house at some point during the early hours of the night. Utterly exhausted, they tried to snatch some sleep in the basement kitchen, which had lost its windows and patches of plaster but had otherwise survived the bombing intact.

Others, too, began to take refuge here, grateful for shelter from the winter chill. It became very cold in the small hours and everyone huddled together. From time to time, Hannelore's mother made some malt coffee or peppermint tea to keep them all warm.

As it grew light, small groups of acquaintances also began to fetch up at the house. Some had little parcels with them: something they had managed to save from their former lives. One had an old violin. Another was clutching a pair of ski boots.

At one point, a close friend, Ferdinand von der Sanden, arrived at their kitchen door. The joy of seeing him alive was quickly checked by the expression on his face. Hannelore immediately realised that something terrible had happened. 'He looked really depressed. When we enquired after his wife, he pointed at the bag he had with him and which he had put on the kitchen floor. "What's left of her is here."'

He showed them the ashes and remains. 'But I recognised her.'

He was in a highly distressed state, gasping for air and trying to regain his composure. He just managed to tell them: 'Her face and shoulders were cut off. They lay under a big beam of wood. That's probably what stopped her burning completely. It must have fallen on her.' He paused for a moment before asking them if they would accompany him to the cemetery, then collapsed in tears.

Hannelore made her way outside. In the half-light of a new dawn, she gazed across the ruined town. Almost nothing was left standing: the familiar townscape of old had been obliterated. The British Bombing Survey Unit would later calculate that 83 per cent of the town centre had been destroyed, concluding that it was 'probably the greatest proportion in one raid during the war'.

One of the few structures left standing, alone and incongruous, was the conical spire of the Stadtkirche. Its tiles had been blown off and its windows were shattered but its internal structure of beams was intact, pointing accusingly at the sky from whence the destruction had come.

Hannelore picked her way through the smoking rubble, passing little groups of people, silent and shell-shocked, who were heading towards the ruined centre of Pforzheim. Survivors were working frantically, trying to clear paths through the debris and look for friends who might still be alive.

Many were in despair, tears streaming down their cheeks as they pulled the corpses of loved ones from the ruins. 'On the roadside there were bodies which had been dug from the rubble, put there in order that people could identify them. Everywhere there was an awful smell of decomposition and smoke.'

Hannelore and her mother were making their way along what remained of Durlacherstrasse when they bumped into Gretel, an old family friend. 'There were two tiny blackened corpses lying on the street like bits of burned wood. Gretel pointed to one of them and said: "That's what's left of my mother."' As she said this, a Nazi block-leader approached and started haranguing the women for being so unpatriotic as to commiserate over their dead.

Death was everywhere on the morning of 24 February. There were carts filled with corpses; there were even people pushing wheelbarrows containing dead bodies, sometimes with an arm or a leg dangling over the side.

Three miles away in Eutingen, Marie Charlotte was bracing herself for what she knew was going to be the most distressing day of her life. She, like so many other of the village inhabitants, was getting ready to head down the hillside into town to find out which of her friends had survived the catastrophe.

'A horrible sight,' she would later write in a letter to Wolfram's older brother, Reiner. 'Climbing over rubble, walking over corpses. There is no end to the horror.'

She had tried to prepare herself for terrible scenes, yet it still came as a huge shock to see the entirety of Pforzheim in ruins.

'Just rubble,' she wrote, 'where once there had been such beautiful grand houses. All the people in the Marktplatz, Langstrasse, Schlossberg, Leopoldstrasse and Sedansplatz – all died in their cellars, a sacrifice to the smoke and flames. In the Schlossberg, in the big cellars of the hotel restaurants, everyone died.'

As she clambered over the ruins, she watched dazed survivors attack the rubble with picks and shovels, desperately hoping to find friends or family alive in the cellars below. A lady with a big dog, a German shepherd, was crying and telling the animal: 'Look! Look! Your master's lying underneath.' And the dog was whining and trying to sniff him out.

Marie Charlotte was deeply shaken by the number of dead. 'Whole families have died, but there are also children without parents and parents without children . . . We went to see Trudel: her mother-in-law and brother-in-law have died. Frau Muller and Frau Kropt have died; her daughter at the fish shop has died. So many people have died.'

Overwhelmed by despair, Marie Charlotte made her way up the northern hillside to Spichernstrasse, to see whether her church friends, the Rodis, were still alive. Here, at least, was some good news. The immediate family had indeed survived. Martha Luise explained to Marie Charlotte that her mother and sister had managed to clamber out of their cellar and make their way along the river to their house on the hill.

While the two women exchanged stories of what they had seen, Max was busily writing a letter to his absent daughter, Ev-Marie. He felt the need to tell her of his experiences when he had ventured into town earlier that morning.

'We went to Uncle Hermann's in front of the Bohnenberger Castle,' he wrote. 'There were corpses everywhere. Almost impossible to locate the café – everything is destroyed, reduced to rubble and very hot. What happened to all the people? Can no one give us any information?'

Max had returned briefly to the family home to fetch a pickaxe, then headed back into town to check on the house of a close friend. This building too was in ruins. 'I tried to free one of the windows of the cellar but the stones got hotter and hotter the deeper I dug. No one could possibly be alive under there. Just to think that two weeks ago I went there with your mother and Trudel and Elizabeth for Holy Communion.'

Giving up his search, he walked slowly towards Durlacherstrasse where he bumped into his cousin, Walter Brenner, who told him that he had lost his wife, his parents and his close family. 'The two of us clambered over heaps of rubble and managed to get into one of the cellars where we found what was left of his family. But we didn't stay to identify them because Walter couldn't cope with it.'

Everyone who visited Pforzheim that day would return home with tales of suffering and tragedy. Sigrid Weber, former home-help to the Aïcheles, had gone into town in search of her grandmother. She saw dead bodies everywhere. A terrible, bitter-sweet smell hung in the air from the burned corpses.

The most terrible sight of all was the public air-raid shelter: everyone inside had perished. Endless shrunken and carbonated bodies had been brought out and stacked up on the pavement. Sigrid turned around and walked home to Eutingen, her clothes and hair carrying the sickly smell of charred flesh. She washed and changed as soon as she could.

Sigrid's father, accompanied by a few others, headed back into Pforzheim to resume the search for Sigrid's grandmother. He dug at the area where the house had stood but unearthed nothing except for a little bag with her keys in it. Sigrid was devastated. 'Nothing else was found. No body. Not even a bone. The whole street had disappeared. My favourite grandmother, not quite sixty, was gone without me being able to say goodbye or go to her funeral.'

By the end of that terrible Saturday, Marie Charlotte felt as if she were trapped inside an all-encompassing nightmare, tormented by what she had seen and wondering why humans had to do such horrible things.

'As I was making my way back home, I heard so many tales of horror that I couldn't take it in any more. Then I noticed that the first tentative buds of spring were emerging into the sunshine and I suddenly felt a hidden natural force that was more powerful than any of the destruction I witnessed.

'I have this strange feeling of the strength in nature. The first crocuses are in flower and are already surrounded by bees. It feels to me as if some sort of miracle is taking place – there's a beauty that envelops these miraculous blooming flowers.'

The burial of the dead created severe logistical difficulties for the Pforzheim authorities. The corpses needed to be interred as quickly as possible but the town did not even have a working bulldozer. One was eventually borrowed from Heilbronn, some forty-five miles away, and a mass grave was excavated.

The scorched corpses were placed in layers and then quicklime was poured over them in order to speed up the decomposition. German soldiers in charge of the operation were given cognac to protect them from infection. There was no time for funeral arrangements. Priests of the two denominations stood there for days and days on end, blessing the dead.

It made for a forlorn and tragic scene. The cemetery was piled high with heaps of the dead and just one official had to register them all. When people spoke to him with their hands over their noses, he told them irritably that *he* couldn't spend all day with his nose covered.

Many of the extended Rodi family lost their lives in the bombing. Among them were a great-aunt and a cousin who had decided to remain in their cellar. They were later found as tiny heaps of ashes and could be identified only by their keys. Another of the family's cousins went to the cellar with a blanket, collected up the remains and took them to the cemetery on his handcart.

Frithjof was putting his own handcart to good use, searching for firewood in the burned-out shells of buildings. There was no electricity or gas in the aftermath of the bombardment and his mother needed fuel because she was constantly cooking for all the homeless people that were staying with the family.

Wolfram's mother listened to the radio every evening in an attempt to find out news about the Allied advance. At the end of March, Marie Charlotte heard a report that American troops had fought their way into Frankfurt. A few days later, she learned that the Ruhr was completely encircled by Allied forces, trapping 325,000 German soldiers.

'The Germans must stay on their feet, no matter how,' said Goebbels in a defiant radio broadcast to the nation. 'Just stay on their feet, and then the moral and historical superiority of the German people can manifest itself.'

Wolfram's parents still had their friend, Frau Weber, staying at their Eutingen villa. Now, just a few days after Goebbels' speech, Frau Weber's husband, conscripted into the army some months earlier, turned up unexpectedly at their front door. Attorney Kurt Weber told them that he was on leave but had decided not to rejoin his regiment. 'What's the point?' he said. 'It's nearly the end.'

He changed into civilian clothes lent to him by Erwin and hid the army uniform in a secret little alcove in the cellar beneath the house. He knew that if the villa were searched and the uniform found, he would be shot as a deserter. However, he also knew that the war could be over within weeks. Allied forces were advancing on every front.

'Six in the morning: there was an explosion. The bridge near the sawmill was blown up. The tiles of the roofs and the windows of the grocery store, two floors below our apartment, were damaged.' So wrote Max Weber, friend and neighbour of Wolfram's parents, on Friday, 6 April 1945. War had at long last arrived in Eutingen.

The explosion was not, in fact, caused by Allied troops. Local German forces had blown up the bridge in the vain hope of halting the Allied advance, an act of destruction that infuriated the village inhabitants. A group of men gathered in front of the village hall and cursed the senseless actions of the military.

The distant boom of artillery could clearly be heard coming from the north-west, fuelling speculation that the Allied arrival was imminent. The nearby villages of Kieselbronn and Enzberg were rumoured to have been captured and it was said that Eutingen was to be the next stop for the Allies.

Whilst most of the villages were by now desperate for them to arrive, the local Nazi functionaries remained belli-cose. One of them, Herr Issel, kept driving to nearby Dillstein to receive new orders and harboured vainglorious dreams of halting the Allied advance in the fields around his village.

To this end, he instructed all local boys born in 1930, and now aged fifteen, to assemble at the village offices. When none of them answered the call to arms, Issel was obliged to order a house-to-house search of Eutingen and the neigh-bouring area. He managed to gather forty-six young lads but forty of them slipped away before they could be deployed and only six were actually sent to the front.

On the evening of 6 April, Max Weber glanced out of his window and was surprised by what he saw. From the church tower opposite his house and from the town hall, white flags, as the sign of surrender, could be seen fluttering in the breeze. He hoped – prayed – that the waiting game was almost over, but just a few minutes after the flags' appearance, German soldiers swarmed into the main street and ordered them to be taken down immediately. Eutingen was not yet in Allied hands.

For the next four days, the village was caught in limbo. At one point, Allied troops were said to be arriving from Kieselbronn. A few hours later, it was rumoured that German troops in the valley below had surrendered. Most of those living in Eutingen were delighted to learn that French forces had been seen entering the neighbouring village of Niefern, which lay just two miles away. However, they were dismayed to hear that German soldiers had fought back, throwing hundreds of hand grenades into local houses and causing considerable carnage before they were finally defeated. From this point on, Max and his family spent most of their time in the cellar, even sleeping there at night.

The boom of cannon and artillery grew steadily louder. 'The fighter-bombers are bombarding the forest and the tank barrages. Our village is becoming the main fighting zone, the front line.'

As the Allies approached the apple orchards that surrounded Eutingen, the local Nazi leaders quietly fled their posts. There was no longer any leadership.

All the bridges into Eutingen had by now been blown up – a sad sight to local eyes – but still there was no sign of Allied forces.

Shortly after dawn on 11 April, Max was awoken by a cry from his landlord.

'Open the doors! They are coming!'

Max quickly obeyed and stood on the pavement with Mrs Heidigger, his neighbour, who was convinced that the Americans were about to arrive. However, to the great consternation of everyone in Eutingen, the troops marching up Hauptstrasse were Moroccan – allies of the French and widely reported to be brutal and poorly disciplined.

The occupying forces immediately began house-to-house searches. A Moroccan burst into the Webers' apartment, demanding: 'Soldier? Gun? Pistol?'

A group of them occupied the town hall and issued their first order: 'All radios, cameras and binoculars are to be brought to the church, along with any weapons.' It was a taste of things to come.

Wolfram's sister, Gunhild, was lying in bed when the Moroccan troops reached Eutingen. A soldier suddenly burst into her room, gun in hand. Gunhild was terrified, for the Moroccans were said to have raped many German girls when occupying other villages. She let out a piercing scream: *Raus! Get out!* The man was so startled that he ran straight back downstairs.

The other Moroccan soldiers who had pushed their way into the villa were rather less intimidated, surging into the kitchen to begin a careful search of the cupboards and larder, while on the lookout for any German soldiers who might have taken shelter in the house. Finding nothing untoward on the ground floor, they demanded access to the cellar.

Marie Charlotte reluctantly led them downstairs and watched in dismay as they rifled through her various store boxes and alcoves. Her dismay turned to alarm when she saw the thoroughness of their search: they were turning everything inside out and upside down. She knew that the family friend, Kurt Weber, had hidden his German uniform down there. If the Moroccans discovered this and realised that he was a deserter, they would shoot him on the spot.

Her anxiety grew as the Moroccans approached the alcove where the uniform was hidden. They were emptying everything as they searched for items to loot and were certain to find it within the next few minutes.

Suddenly (until her dying day she was never able to explain how), she began talking to them in French – an almost fluent stream of words and phrases that she had not used since her childhood in Alsace. The men were so taken aback, and so charmed to speak with someone who knew their own language, that they promptly abandoned their search and traipsed back upstairs.

Wolfram's father had anticipated that their house would be searched by the victorious Allies and had taken the precaution some days earlier of hiding his valuable Leica camera. He had placed it in the nesting box of his most aggressive female falcon, which had recently laid eggs and was very protective of her nest, allowing no one except Erwin near it. When one of the Moroccans peered into the cage, curious to see what was inside, the falcon hissed and flapped her wings in preparation for attack. The soldier rapidly beat a retreat.

It became apparent to the Aïchele family that the Moroccan forces were in no hurry to move on from Eutingen. Pforzheim had not yet been captured, for the Nazi leader,

Hans Knab, was determined to defend the ruined town and thereby stall the Allied advance. While a tense waiting game was played out in the valley below, many of the Eutingen houses became lodgings for the occupying Moroccans.

The Webers had eight soldiers billeted in their ground-floor apartment. The men killed all the family's chickens and rabbits, and threw them on the kitchen table, demanding that Frau Weber cook them. Max was disgusted by their slovenliness – it was so different to what he was used to in Germany. The garden had been reduced to chaos, littered with feathers from the chickens, the skins of rabbits and the intestines of all the animals, as well as boxes and tins of American provisions.

His daughter, Sigrid, was concerned that the soldiers would find the jars of oil that the family had buried in the garden. Max was rather more worried about the safety of his pretty teenage daughter. He persuaded her to disguise herself as an old lady, dressing in old-fashioned clothes and swathing herself in a headscarf.

Sigrid's younger sister, Doris, fearful that the Moroccans would kill and eat her pet rabbit, hid it in a big trunk in the kitchen, leaving the lid propped ajar with a wooden spoon. Whenever the Moroccans came into the kitchen, she would remove the wooden spoon and quietly close the box. Her ploy worked: they never realised it was there.

The Moroccan troops were poorly disciplined and became particularly unruly whenever they laid their hands on alcohol. They kept petitioning Max Weber for schnapps, but he told them that he did not have any. When they eventually found some elsewhere, they were soon completely drunk, going on the rampage and smashing all the shop windows in the village. A textile shop stood opposite the Webers' apartment; the Moroccans broke all the glass and took all the cloth that was red, white and blue, hanging it from the electric wires all down the street.

After four tense days, the Moroccan troops left abruptly and were replaced by Tunisian soldiers under the leadership of French officers. The new arrivals were better equipped than the Moroccans, with black tea, biscuits, mustard, sugar and bottles of wine from the Rhineland, and had no need to pillage for their food. They also had smoked ham and bacon, which they fried in the Webers' kitchen.

The French officers took their meals in the family dining room and, as they ate, they told Max about the extermination camps. They talked of the cruelties of the SS in France and of the concentration camp at Sachsenhausen, where, they said, they had found 700 French, Ukrainians, Russians, Poles and Jews lying on the ground, either dead and dying.

They also told him that the SS had been locking prisoners into ovens and gassing them to death. Max had difficulty crediting such stories, writing in his diary, 'Everything they said to me seemed unbelievable.'

The occupation of Eutingen became increasingly chaotic with every passing day. Troops came and left – Moroccan, French and Tunisian – although no one seemed in overall control. Finally, one afternoon, all of the occupying forces suddenly packed up and left. No one knew what was going on and rumours spread quickly.

Max was appalled to see German soldiers move back into the village, lining up around the town hall and arming themselves with hand grenades, but they quickly melted away when yet more Moroccans arrived. These new troops were jumpy and clearly expecting trouble. A burst of gunfire sent the Weber family scuttling into their cellar. When they emerged, they saw that the Moroccans were using two of their neighbours as human shields, making Mrs Morlock and Mr Keller walk in front of them, although it was not clear why. As the troops passed, they smashed all the windows and doors that remained unbroken.

Just a few hours later, the inhabitants of Eutingen faced yet another unwelcome surprise. Trucks of angry French soldiers began pouring into the village. An officer banged on the Webers' front door and shouted: 'Come on! Come out!'

He told Max that German civilians had shot at his troops, so the French were now going to have their revenge. 'In two hours,' he said, 'your town hall will be burned.'

Max was deeply alarmed, as his apartment stood next to the town hall and was likely to be consumed too. He hurriedly began to stow precious items in the cellar while his neighbours unrolled their hoses to spray the walls and roof with water.

When one of the French soldiers saw them doing this, he shouted hysterically: 'You didn't see my village burn. Here, everything – *everything* – must burn.'

Young Doris Weber was terrified. '*Alles muss brennen! Alles muss brennen!*' The words rang in her ears.

The French were indeed intending to burn the whole of Eutingen, but their plan was stopped in its tracks in a most unexpected fashion. For several years, the village had played host to a dozen or so French prisoners of war. They worked on local farms during the day and had been well treated by the Eutingen locals, forging a close relationship with several of those who spoke French. Now, learning that the village was to be burned, they remonstrated with their compatriots and begged them to reconsider.

Their intervention had the desired effect: the French soldiers agreed not to burn people's homes although they insisted on torching the village offices, because they stood as a symbol of Nazi officialdom.

They threw hand grenades into the building and it quickly caught fire. The Weber family was extremely fortunate that the wind was blowing a stiff easterly, which carried the flames away from their apartment. A few of the French troops, annoyed by this, threatened the assembled villagers, telling them that they would execute fifty inhabitants for every shot fired at them. 'A terrible day,' wrote Max. 'The worst.'

The air of uncertainty struck great fear into everyone in Eutingen. With unconfirmed reports of shootings and revenge killings in nearby villages, most people stayed firmly indoors. The Webers, like the Aïcheles, were praying for the arrival of the Americans, who were rumoured to be very close to Pforzheim.

The sound of the Allied artillery grew louder with every hour that passed. Soon, it was coming from just behind the Rodi house. Young Frithjof could hear four distant booms as each of the battery's guns were fired, followed by a long *sssscchh* sound as the shells traced through the sky. It was the second week of April and a new wave of Allied forces were approaching Pforzheim from the north.

They could have taken the town without a fight if the battle-weary German troops on the ground had got their way. Most wanted to lay down their arms or retreat southwards to the Black Forest, but the town's leader, Hans Knab, refused to countenance any retreat. He wanted what was left of Pforzheim to be defended at all costs.

The Allies stalled for time, besieging the town for a further ten days but declining to fight their way into the ruins. The French sent in very low-flying aircraft, which flew round and round, all day long. Frithjof watched them circle the town from the vantage point of the family's vegetable plot. Whenever the pilots saw troops, they would pass on the coordinates to the artillery, with instructions to bombard them.

On one occasion, the planes began firing on the ground as they circled the hilltop on which stood the Rodi house. Frithjof's grandmother, who had been sitting outside in the sunshine, was unable to make a quick retreat into the cellar on account of her crippled foot. When young Frithjof walked into the dining room once the all-clear had sounded, he was surprised to see both his grandmother and his aunt huddled under the table. It was a sight to remember: two normally composed and dignified ladies lying on the floor in terror. He knew, at that moment, that the old orderly world had come crashing down.

After a week of Allied bombardment, Hans Knab realised that further resistance was futile, as well as likely to lead to his capture. Throwing in the towel, he fled Pforzheim, taking with him all of the town's senior Nazi officials. Shortly before leaving, he ordered the destruction of the electricity generating plant – only recently repaired after the February bombing – as well as all of the town's surviving gas and water supply lines.

In giving this order, he was putting into effect Hitler's Decree on Demolitions on Reich Territory, the so-called Nero Decree, in which the German army was ordered to destroy all surviving infrastructure as it retreated eastwards.

'All military transport and communication facilities, industrial establishments and supply depots, as well as anything else of value within Reich territory, which could in any way be used by the enemy immediately or within the foreseeable future for the prosecution of the war, will be destroyed.'

Thirty miles away in Stuttgart, Max Rodi had also received this order. He was specifically charged with destroying all the bakery ovens in the city – an act of vandalism that he refused to undertake. Indeed, he was so incensed by the Nero Decree that he summoned the men under his charge, informing them that he was abandoning his post and returning to his home and family in Pforzheim. He added that they were free to do whatever they wanted; he was no longer their commanding officer.

Pforzheimers were as appalled as Max Rodi when they learned of the Nero Decree and were disgusted to discover that Hans Knab had left orders for it to be carried out to the letter. A small group remonstrated with the staff sergeant in charge of the operation and eventually persuaded him to refrain from such senseless waste. However, it was too late to save the town's remaining bridges from being blown up. Only the iron railway bridge was saved by quick-thinking inhabitants who pulled the fuses from the explosive devices and threw them into the River Enz.

The flight of Knab and his cortège left a power vacuum in Pforzheim. For a few hours there was no one in charge. Then, soon after they had fled, the sounds of different weaponry could be heard. Allied tanks could be seen circling around the Rodi family house and moving towards the town.

Martha Luise panicked when she saw the tanks. Her second daughter, Gisela, had only just gone into Pforzheim in an attempt to find some desperately needed food for the family. Now, fearful for her safety, she ran down the hill to fetch her and bring her home. Having done so, when the two women attempted to get back to the house, they found their path blocked by a German soldier.

He told them not to go any further because the road ahead had already been seized by French and Moroccan forces. Martha Luise brushed him aside. She and her daughter dashed up the street to the entrance gate and rushed along the long path to the front door, while the French, still hidden from view, kept up a constant barrage of fire. The bullets whistled passed their ears.

They made it safely inside the house and headed straight for the cellar, from where Frithjof, through an air vent, had been watching their lucky escape.

After a while the gunfire stopped. Martha Luise went outside again to see a single German soldier holding two guns and running along the garden path. It was the last vestige of German power in Pforzheim.

Although the German soldiers stationed on the hillside were under orders to defend their positions to the death, their commanding officer had foreseen the inevitability of defeat and decided that enough was enough. Calling at the house belonging to the Rodis' neighbours, the Elsässers, he asked for some civilian clothes. For the next couple of days, he lay low to avoid being caught and shot as a deserter. In the wake of his desertion, all the men under his command simply melted away.

The Moroccan troops were by now so close that Frithjof could hear noises coming from their encampment, yet it was a further forty-eight hours before he actually saw them, going from garden to garden stealing hens and rabbits. On the third day, a young French officer knocked at the front door to commandeer the family's camera. He was deeply disappointed when Martha Luise handed over a cheap box camera, clearly having hoped for a Leica.

The arrival of the regular French army brought a semblance of order to Pforzheim. By 18 April, the last of the German snipers had been captured or killed and the entire town fell into Allied hands. The French commander, General Jean de Lattre de Tassigny, made a triumphant entrance through the ruins. Posters went up everywhere, claiming that the glorious French army had not only crossed the Rhine but had also reached the Danube.

The French were still in the process of establishing their military headquarters when on 28 April an announcement came on the radio that was as dramatic as it was unexpected.

It was the voice of Admiral Donitz, speaking gravely and slowly.

'Comrades,' he said, *'der Führer ist gefallen.'*

Adolf Hitler was dead.

CHAPTER SIXTEEN

ESCAPE TO FREEDOM

'Is it really true? Can it really be true?'

Wolfram knew nothing about the capture of Pforzheim by Allied forces. Nor, indeed, was he aware that the town of his childhood lay in ruins. It was not until May 1945, fully three months after the bombing raid (and a week after Hitler's suicide), that he first learned of the devastation.

He was glancing through one of the German-language newspapers published in America when his eye lit upon an article about the February bombardment. It contained a graphic description of the destruction, written by a businessman who had been staying in the suburbs on the night of the raid.

Wolfram was greatly alarmed by what he read. His father travelled into Pforzheim almost every day in order to work at the School of Decorative Arts. His mother also made regular shopping trips into town. It was quite possible that they, and perhaps his sister, had been caught in the firestorm.

It was not until October, eight months after the

bombing, that he finally received the news that his parents had survived when a card came from an uncle in Switzerland, saying that they were alive and well.

In his prisoner-of-war camp at Pont d'Ain in France, Peter Rodi was similarly ignorant of the fate of Pforzheim. He never received any news about the war. Indeed, he was lucky to pick up the occasional rumour from newly captured prisoners. The first he knew about the firebombing was when he received a postcard from his mother, telling him that the immediate family had survived.

By this time, Peter was himself extremely lucky to still be alive. He had given himself just two weeks to live when confined to the camp infirmary. He had been suffering from acute oedema and had lost so much weight that his skeletal frame could be clearly seen through his skin.

A stroke of luck was to save his life. One morning, the camp's cook entered the makeshift infirmary and cast his eye over the wan faces of the sick and dying. Alighting on Peter, he peremptorily ordered him out of bed. He needed someone to help out in the kitchen and Peter was in marginally better shape than the other men.

The job was a godsend. Peter was able to help himself to scraps of fatty meat and the occasional potato when the cook was not looking. He was ravenously hungry and his famished body took advantage of every little morsel. Within a month, his oedema had disappeared and he was declared fit enough to start manual work once again.

This time, his spell of good fortune was to continue. He and a few others spent several days as volunteer drivers, transporting to the camp's storeroom the confiscated clothes of newly arrived prisoners. For a brief time they lived like princes. Peter had the opportunity to jettison the old rags he had been wearing for months and replace it with a new set of clothes. He was also able to lay his hands on food and cigarettes.

When the work came to an end, he was sent as part of a team to a nearby farm. For the first time in months, he found himself on the receiving end of kindness as well as huge quantities of food.

The farmers ate five big meals a day. In the morning, Peter tucked into fried potatoes, bread, eggs and two different types of meat, and in the evening, he would be given omelettes made with six eggs. The farmers, watching him wolf this down, would say: 'My, you've got a cavernous belly!'

In the first week of May 1945, the German prisoners at Pont d'Ain, in Oklahoma, and elsewhere in America and Europe began to hear whispered rumours of the impending collapse of the Werhmacht. It was said that armed forces everywhere were about to capitulate to the Allies. These rumours proved correct. On 7 May came the announcement that German soldiers on the western front had surrendered. A day later, troops on the eastern front also laid down their weapons. After five and a half years of conflict, the war in Europe had at long last come to an end.

Later that day, Wolfram and his fellow prisoners were summoned to a camp meeting. An American officer read out a statement telling them that Germany had surrendered.

There was no wild celebration on the part of the prisoners, no cheering or jubilation. Most of them were simply relieved that the fighting would finally cease. All hoped and prayed that they might soon get to go home to their families and loved ones.

For Wolfram it was a day for inward rejoicing. The war was over and it had been his good fortune to survive. The outcome could so easily have been different. Diphtheria had almost cost him his life in the Crimea, yet it had also saved him from certain death in Stalingrad. Almost all his conscripted comrades from the 1942 call-up had died in that epic winter battle. Many of those fighting alongside him in Normandy had also been killed. Among the dead was the soldier who had been sheltering inches away from him in the roadside ditch near Le Vretot.

Wolfram was surprised to discover that his feeling of quiet elation was not shared by the American soldiers in charge of the prisoners, who told him they regretted the outbreak of peace. He could hardly believe what they were saying and asked them why. They replied that the end of the war meant that they would all soon be unemployed again. The conflict had not only brought them jobs and salaries, but had also enabled many of them to make a fast buck through private profiteering. Now, the good times were coming to an end.

There were big changes at Camp Gruber within days of the German surrender. The thousands of American troops still based there were told to pack up their possessions in preparation for being sent home. The months of military training had been for nothing; now that all hostilities had ceased, their services were no longer required.

The day for the soldiers' departure came soon enough. One morning, Wolfram awoke to the sight of a huge fleet of pick-ups pulling up outside the camp gates. For the next few hours, the entire encampment was alive to the cries of men and the crash and clatter of equipment as the trucks were loaded, driven away then, one by one, with the men on board. The vast camp complex fell eerily silent. The only Americans left behind were those in charge of the German prisoner-of-war camp.

Its inmates were informed that the whole place was going to be dismantled and the land sold off to local farmers. Before that could happen, however, all the unexploded mines in the woodland areas, which had been used as a training ground, had to be removed or detonated.

Wolfram and his comrades spent the next month searching for mines in the swampy land that surrounded the camp. It was dangerous work and not just because of the mines. There were bird-eating and black widow spiders, as well as poisonous copperhead snakes. One prisoner focused entirely on trying to catch these snakes so that he could turn them into snakeskin shoes when he returned to Germany.

Once a week the prisoners were allowed to watch a movie in the camp cinema. These were almost always westerns and, after many months of seeing such films, most of the men were so bored by them that they had stopped attending. An afternoon came when they were assembled together and told that they were obliged to watch that week's screening. They shuffled their way into the auditorium, wondering what they were going to be shown.

There was a whirring noise as the projector started to turn. Seconds later, a black-and-white image flickered on to the screen. It immediately became apparent that this was no cowboy film. Rather, it was a horror movie of such intensity and human cruelty that it would be etched into their minds for the rest of their lives.

On 15 April, the British 11th Armoured Division had entered Bergen-Belsen extermination camp. 'Here, over an acre of ground, lay dead and dying people,' reported the BBC broadcaster, Richard Dimbleby, who was accompanying the army. 'You could not see which was which . . . The living lay with their heads against the corpses and around them moved the awful, ghostly procession of emaciated, aimless people, with nothing to do and with no hope of life, unable to move out of your way, unable to look at the terrible sights around them.'

Similar scenes greeted Allied forces that entered the other extermination camps: sickness, death and abject human misery on an unimaginable scale. Now, the German prisoners were to watch a film of the scenes that had greeted these Allied troops.

Wolfram was shocked to the core by what he saw. He was no less shocked by the scale of the suffering. In Bergen-Belsen alone, Allied soldiers had found 55,000 prisoners in the camp – cadaverous, wan and suffering from typhus, dysentery and malnutrition. There were 13,000 corpses, unburied, in various states of putrefaction. Corpses in piles and cadavers on carts. The living looked little different from the dead. The staring eyes of a bewildered child; the blank expressions of men and women who had been witness to mass killings for months on end.

The German prisoners watched the film in complete silence. They were left reeling by what they saw. So profound was their stupefaction that when the film finished and the men were back outside, blinking in the sunshine, no one could bring himself to speak. There was nothing to be said.

Their silence on the subject was to endure for many weeks. Once or twice, a few lone voices dared to venture that it could not be true – that the Allied film was a fake. However, most of the men knew better than to challenge the evidence of the eyewitnesses and the victims. It was a truth that would have to be borne.

All of the prisoners were hoping that they would be repatriated to Germany as soon as the minefields were cleared. As the weeks passed and turned into months, there was still no talk of their being sent home. Indeed, many of them were taken back to work as labourers on the local farms. Then, the day came when they started seeing returning American soldiers. The nearby towns were soon full of them.

The troops would call over to the German prisoners as they were being transported to their workplaces. They had letters from girlfriends and sweethearts in Germany but very few men were able to understand them. One of Wolfram's friends spoke good English and so he translated for them.

Summer passed in a blaze of heat and then, in the first week of September, the leaves started to colour once again. Wolfram was struck by the realisation that fully five months had now elapsed since the capitulation of the German army and an entire year had passed since he had first arrived in Oklahoma. Yet whenever the prisoners asked when they would be going home, their guards simply shrugged their shoulders. No one seemed to know.

The first that Peter Rodi knew of the armistice was when it was announced on the camp's loudspeakers. Shortly afterwards, the French guards went around hanging up photographs of emaciated people in extermination camps.

It quickly became apparent that the end of the war was not going to bring about his early release. The French intended to use their German prisoners to help rebuild the country that they had done so much to destroy.

Peter worked on farms for many months before he and his fellow prisoners were moved to Camp 142 near Bourg-en-Bresse. Life there was not a pleasant experience. There was never enough food for everyone and the prisoners were constantly hungry. The hunger and their aching, empty bellies drove them to distraction. On several occasions, Peter woke up at night and bit into his finger, thinking it was a piece of bread.

The debilitating hunger provoked black humour. The prisoners used to joke that if anyone found any fibres of meat in the watery soup, they had to be gathered up and returned to the kitchen to be reused.

The only good news in these grim times was the announcement that prisoners would henceforth be allowed to write letters to loved ones – some of whom had no idea that their husbands and sons were still alive. The prisoners were also told that they would be allowed to receive parcels.

Peter knew that his parents in bombed-out Pforzheim would not be in a position to send him sorely needed items. He wrote instead to his uncles in America, asking them for help.

'My dear ones, I have been a prisoner since November 1944 . . . Pforzheim is destroyed. Our home is still standing . . . if you would like to send me something, please send underwear, sewing kit and cigarettes. I hope you are well and I'm very grateful that the family has survived the war.'

Peter's uncles responded generously to his request: their first parcel arrived in January 1946 with tinned food, shirts and underwear, as well as ten packets of Chesterfields.

Overnight, Peter's life was transformed. Suddenly he found himself king of the camp. He gave a whole packet of cigarettes to the camp commander, and another to his deputy and an orderly. His generosity was much appreciated – it was very rare for anyone to be given a whole packet.

As parcel followed parcel, Peter realised that the cigarettes and food could be put to good use. Hitherto, he had never seriously considered trying to escape from the camp. Now, however, he had the means and the potential resources to consider making a break for freedom.

He knew that any attempt would carry great risks. Escaping prisoners who were caught were thrashed by three or four of the most brutal guards, followed by thirty days' confinement with half-rations and constant punishment exercises.

Peter was himself witness to one of these beatings because it was carried out in the camp supply depot where he was working at the time. Four guards set on the recaptured prisoner and kicked him to within an inch of his life.

The punishment ought to have deterred Peter, but he was sick of being a prisoner and the idea of escaping brought a renewed sense of purpose to his life.

He made a list of the five requirements that needed to be met if he was to have any hope of successfully reaching Germany: civilian clothes, identity papers, money, food to last for several days and good enough French to pass himself off as an Alsatian. He also needed to obtain an official paper-of-discharge that authorised his release from the camp. Without this, he risked being handed over to the Allied authorities if and when he reached Pforzheim.

Language was the easiest hurdle to overcome. He already spoke good French and felt sure he could convince people that he was from Alsace, thereby explaining his German accent.

The four other requirements for his escape were more difficult to arrange. Civilian clothes, shoes and official papers had to be laboriously made – and to a high standard – if Peter was to avoid being rumbled.

He had at least half a dozen people working in secret on his behalf. A former tailor in the camp made him a convincing overcoat from a waterproof French cape. Another prisoner, a cobbler by trade, repaired a pair of leather shoes. The same man also crafted him a holdall out of pigskin so as to make his civilian disguise more convincing. A third prisoner, a smithy, made a suitcase out of an old box that had previously contained hand grenades.

Peter's greatest challenge was to lay his hands on convincing identity papers. He knew that these would be inspected four or five times on his journey home and would be subjected to particular scrutiny as he attempted to cross into the American-occupied zone of Germany.

He managed to acquire a blank identity card – a stroke of good fortune. He then asked a fellow prisoner, a graphic designer named Göppert, to produce the necessary official-looking stamp. Göppert revelled in the challenge, carving it from the cork lid of an ink bottle. It was done with such skill that the resulting stamp was indistinguishable from the real thing.

Only the identity photograph was now missing. This was to prove the biggest hurdle, for none of the prisoners possessed a camera. One day, Peter was told that the camp's Moroccan cook had an old box camera. The cook agreed to help, in return for cigarettes, smuggling his camera into the camp and taking a picture of Peter in broad daylight. A few days later, the developed photo was safely delivered and inserted on the fake identity paper.

Peter now had his principal requirements in place. Then, unexpectedly, he got a bonus. He managed to get hold of a blank dismissal form that authorised permission for a prisoner to leave camp.

There remained one major obstacle to overcome: how to get himself and his new belongings out of the camp. The solution, settled upon by Peter and the camp leader (a fellow prisoner), was for him to enrol on an external work mission. This would take him to a farm in the nearby countryside. Once he was there, the camp leader would contrive to have one of his parcels from America forwarded to him – but, in reality, the parcel would contain everything he needed for his escape.

The plan worked perfectly. Peter was sent to work on a farm as an interpreter. It turned out to be the perfect location for launching his bid for freedom, being far enough from the camp to require him to sleep there at night. The farmer, a sullen individual, did not want a German prisoner inside his house, telling Peter to bed down in an outhouse that lay at some distance from the main building.

By 16 June 1946, Peter had successfully received his parcel and decided that the time had come to make his break. It was a Sunday. He heard the clock tower of the nearby village strike ten o'clock and felt it was now or never.

He changed out of his prisoner-of-war uniform, put on his newly made civilian clothes and gathered together his belongings. A few minutes later, he set out on the road to what he hoped would be his freedom.

While Peter was hatching his plans, Wolfram had received news that he and his comrades would soon be on the move. At the beginning of June 1946, after twenty-one months in captivity, all the prisoners at Camp Gruber were to be transported back to Europe.

The men packed their few possessions and were put on a train to New York. It was a painfully slow journey, taking an extremely circuitous route, looping north into Canada before heading back towards New York. When they finally arrived, they were transferred on to a ship that was awaiting them in the harbour.

The return voyage across the Atlantic was to prove a storm-tossed ordeal for Wolfram and his comrades. The skies darkened as they left behind the Manhattan skyscrapers and the wind began to whip up a gale. Within hours, mountainous waves were pitching the prisoners from their bunks and hurtling them to the floor, leaving them bruised as well as feeling dizzy and queasy.

Wolfram had never had good sea legs. Now, after a head-spinning night of constant motion, he developed serious seasickness. For the next five days he was violently ill and desperate to set foot on dry land.

He was delighted when one of his friends reported that the ship was nearing the French coastline and that the roofs of Le Havre could already be seen through the spray. However, the good news was tempered by bad: the men, it was rumoured, were not going to be allowed home to Germany. Instead, they were to be imprisoned once again when they landed in France.

After the ship docked in Le Havre, the men were lined up in front of a doctor and given a quick medical. Wolfram looked dreadful; he had been constantly sick for the duration of the voyage and had not slept for almost a week. When the doctor saw his pale face and learned that he had suffered from serious diphtheria in Russia, he immediately declared him unfit for work. Wolfram was free to return home to Germany.

He was one of the fortunate ones. Most of his fellow comrades were declared to be in robust health and were told, to their abject dismay, that they were to remain prisoners of war. The French were in desperate need of manpower to clear minefields and bombsites. The easiest source of labour was the tens of thousands of German prisoners still on French soil. Many of these men would continue to be kept in prison camps for a further two years.

The small group of men who had been set free were told to make their way to a nearby station where there would be a train waiting for them. Wolfram clambered aboard in great excitement. There were no guards – that was the first thing that struck him. The men had not travelled on their own for more than two years. There had always been someone watching their every movement.

Although they were not given any food for the journey, most of them still had the tins of peanut butter that had been supplied to them on leaving America. For once, the lack of food did not bother them. There was just a wonder-ful, exhilarating feeling that they were finally on their way home.

Wolfram's mother had seen little of Martha Luise Rodi during the long captivities of their two sons. Both women were kept extremely busy in the aftermath of the Pforzheim bombing. Catering for their homeless house guests, along with the endless search for food and fuel, took up the greater part of each day.

The two mothers met occasionally at church services and impromptu coffee parties. On one occasion, Martha Luise attended a house concert given by local musicians at the Aïchele villa in Eutingen.

Her spirits had been raised by the unexpected return of her husband, Max, who had abandoned his post in Stuttgart in disgust at the Nero Decree. He had made his way back to Pforzheim and a reunion with his wife and family, but his return to civilian life was to prove short-lived. The newly arrived French army announced that any family found hiding German soldiers would be severely punished. Max, who had no official papers of discharge, reported himself to one of the commanders of the occupying forces, along with a fellow officer who had also fled his post.

The Frenchman to whom they addressed themselves took one look at the shiny boots worn by Max's comrade and ordered him to hand them over. The German officer protested and was subsequently beaten black and blue. What particularly appalled both him and Max, apart from the savagery of the beating, was the fact that a French officer could thus treat a German soldier of equal rank, in complete disregard of the conventions of military etiquette. Only later, when the two men learned of the atrocities committed by the German army, would they realise that their outrage had been somewhat misplaced.

Max would live to regret his decision to surrender himself to the French. He was immediately taken prisoner and transported to France. For the next twelve months, his wife and family received almost no information as to his whereabouts.

In the dying days of the war, Marie Charlotte had learned that her eldest son, Reiner, had been captured and briefly held prisoner by the Soviet army. As the Russian colonel in charge had found himself unable to feed so many prisoners, he announced one day that they were all free to go. He even stamped their papers, officially releasing them back into civilian life. Reiner made his way back to Pforzheim for a euphoric reunion with his parents and younger sister.

Whilst his return was a source of great joy to Marie Charlotte, there was on the other hand a complete silence about Wolfram. The family had heard nothing from him for many months and were growing increasingly concerned for his safety.

Martha Luise was relieved to have had contact with her eldest son, Peter, who had managed to write her a number of letters but without revealing his attempted break for freedom. His mother's ignorance was, as he knew, a blessing in disguise. She would have been worried sick if she had known.

It was a lovely moonlit night as Peter set out along the country lane that led away from the French farmhouse. The nearby villages were completely silent and not a single light could be seen. Everyone was already in bed.

Peter's first destination was the railway station at Bourg-en-Bresse, which lay some eighteen miles to the north-west of the farm. He had decided to stay on the roads, rather than cross the fields, reasoning that there was little danger of being seen. Only a couple of cars passed him during the night and he was able to hide himself in a roadside ditch long before the drivers spotted him.

Adrenalin and fear enabled him to cover the long trek to Bourg-en-Bresse in just three hours and forty minutes. He glimpsed the station clock in the distance: it was exactly one-forty in the morning. He was now about to face his first serious hurdle: to buy a ticket and board a train, any train, heading east.

There was a nervous moment when he approached the ticket office. *'Le prochain train pour Dijon,'* he said, *'quand est-ce-qu'il part?'* The guard passed no comment about his German accent, saying only that the next train would not leave until the morning. Peter bought a ticket and snatched a little sleep on one of the station benches. His one consolation was the fact that he had not aroused any suspicions.

The Dijon train drew into the station long before its scheduled departure and Peter clambered aboard immediately. He knew that he would be reported missing within a few hours and that the hunt would be on to recapture him. It was with great relief, therefore, that he heard the welcome rumble of the engines starting up. Soon after, the train set off.

He experienced his first attack of nerves on arriving in the city. News of his escape would by now have reached the camp authorities and search parties would have been sent to track him down. His nervousness increased still further at the sight of two policemen observing passengers arriving at the station. Having some money, he planned to lie low in a hotel for a few hours, but the place was so disgusting and the mattress smelled so bad that he decided to visit the town instead. It was not until later that evening that he went back to the station and boarded the train to Metz.

This leg of the journey posed a particular challenge. Peter found himself sharing his compartment with a French army officer who was returning home to his family. Keen for company, he engaged Peter in conversation, asking him where he had been and where he was heading. The two talked for a while until eventually the heat of the compartment sent both of them to asleep.

At some point, the compartment's fold-away table fell down and woke them. For months Peter had prepared for just such an eventuality, training himself to say, '*Nom de Dieu*' if woken in a start. It was all in vain. Startled, and not thinking straight, he mumbled an apology in German.

The officer must surely have been surprised – suspicious, even – but he passed no comment, inviting Peter to join him in a glass of beer at the station bar once they had pulled into Metz at around midnight.

It was while they were drinking it that the military police asked to see their papers. This was the first time that Peter had had to show his identity card and he did so with trepidation, pulling it out of his pigskin pouch and handing it over. The policemen gave only a cursory glance at the paper and then handed it back. The fake ID had passed its first test.

It was while Peter was chatting to the Frenchman that he

picked up important information: the Americans had built a temporary bridge over the Rhine close to the town of Boppard. As this was in the French zone of occupation, there were fewer controls than in other places. When he heard this, he decided that that was where he would cross the Rhine.

The two of them eventually finished their beers and settled the bill. Peter bade farewell to the French officer and joined up with a group of people looking for hotel rooms for the night.

Peter had been a free man for twenty-seven hours and almost 200 miles now separated him from the prison camp. He was tantalisingly close to home: Pforzheim lay just eighty miles to the east of Metz. Yet a world of difficulties stretched between these two places. He still had to cross the frontier into Germany, as well as the Rhine, and then get himself into the American-occupied zone.

All the hotels in Metz were full but he bribed the receptionist in the Hôtel Bon Pasteur, who allowed Peter to sleep in a bathroom at the top of the building. Then, after a good night's rest, he boarded a train to St Avold, just six miles from the German border, before continuing on foot to Freyming-Merlebach, a little market town right on the frontier. He had been given the address of an Italian who had previously been held in the same prisoner-of-war camp and who he hoped would help him to cross the border.

The Italian was not at home when he rang the bell, but his mother invited Peter in and, without asking any awkward questions, offered him food and a bed. He felt able to relax until the evening, when the woman's two sons returned from work.

Peter was now about to have a further stroke of good fortune. The family's youngest son was engaged to a girl who lived just across the border in Germany. She was due to visit the family that very night, using a path that was unknown to the authorities. It was decided that she would guide Peter back across the border when she returned home. He would still have to cross the Rhine (for the girl lived in the German Palatinate, on the river's western shore) but he would at least be inside Germany for the first time in almost two years.

They crossed the frontier in darkness and it was late by the time they arrived at the girl's parents' house. Peter was once again given a bed for the night and on the following morning the family changed his remaining francs into Reichsmarks. They then took him to the station and put him on a train to Saarbrucken, some fifteen miles to the north-east.

On arriving here, he had no problem buying an onward ticket to Boppard, where the French-controlled bridge spanned the Rhine. However, when he went to board the train, he was stopped by an officious inspector who announced that everyone travelling to Boppard required not just a ticket but a special pass as well.

As Peter remonstrated with the man, he was acutely aware that the train was inching slowly out of the station. There was not a moment to be lost – it was make or break time. He pushed passed the inspector and made a dash for it, chasing along the platform and throwing himself aboard the moving train. He glanced back and saw to his immense relief that the inspector was still at the barrier, having neither the energy nor the inclination to raise the alarm.

After a long journey, the train pulled into Boppard on the banks of the Rhine. Peter now had to face his greatest hurdle – crossing the bridge on foot without being rumbled. He was in luck: although he was extremely nervous and covered in goose pimples, he was not stopped by a single guard. When he was at last on the far side of the river and safe, he headed to a local inn for food.

It was while he was eating that a man sat down at his table and said to him: 'You're an escaped prisoner of war.' Peter was so taken aback that he admitted it.

The man showed no signs of wanting to report him, telling Peter that a number of escaping prisoners had passed through Boppard as they attempted to make their way home. He then offered Peter some advice, informing him that there were two possible ways to enter the American zone: either on foot or by train. Peter heard him out before settling on the latter.

Boarding the train brought him none of the problems he had faced at Saarbrucken, but when it reached the border between the French and American controlled zones of Germany, all the passengers were told to get off. Their papers would be scrutinised and their bags searched before they would be allowed back on the train.

Everyone got out except for Peter. He had decided to hide in the toilet, an old trick, except for the fact that he left the door open and clung to the hook at the back. He hoped that the guards and military police would see the empty cubicle and not investigate further.

Once again, his luck held. A guard poked his head inside and, satisfied that no one was there, continued down the corridor. After an agonising wait, but no more inspections,

Peter heard the passengers getting back on board. Soon after, the train lurched forward, carrying him finally into American-controlled Germany.

He now took a train to Frankfurt and Heidelberg before continuing on towards Karlsruhe and Pforzheim. He had prepared himself for what he might expect in his home town, yet it still came as a massive shock to see the ruins. Although more than sixteen months had passed since the bombing, Pforzheim remained a gigantic heap of debris.

Peter bumped into family friends as he walked through the town. Two of them rushed off to find his parents, who were on their way to a concert in nearby Brotzingen. The third ran home to alert Peter' siblings.

His youngest sister, Barbara, was sitting in the garden, reading a children's classic about a happy child, when the family friend rushed up the path and told her that she, too, was about to become a very happy child.

As she said this, Barbara spied her eldest brother sauntering along the road. He had changed enormously in the two years he had been away. He had became a man, and was smoking.

Elation, disbelief and sheer joy: Peter experienced a wave of emotion as he made his way up the garden path. Above all, he felt a deep pride in his achievement and could not quite believe that his bid for freedom had been successful. He had been blessed by good luck, of that there was no question, but he had also put enormous effort into the planning. He was one of the few German prisoners to successfully escape and make it home alive. And he was fêted as a hero by everyone in the family.

*   *   *

Wolfram stared out of the train window as the French countryside flickered past, trying to catch glimpses of places he might recognise. At one point he saw towers and spires astride a hilltop, which he thought might be Luxembourg. Not long afterwards, the train crossed the Rhine and the men found themselves back in Germany. As they pulled into Saarbrucken, hundreds of women and children poured on to the station platform to greet them.

The ex-prisoners soon discovered why they were being given such an enthusiastic welcome. The women had learned that soldiers returning from America often brought with them huge quantities of cigarettes, which happened to be true in the case of Wolfram and his comrades. Having no idea how precious these packets were, they were extremely gencrous in giving them away. Only later did they realise that cigarettes were a valuable currency on the black market.

Their journey became painfully slow once they were back on German soil. They stopped in Marburg, where they were registered and given official papers declaring them free to go. As the damaged rail network was undergoing repair, Wolfram had to take a circuitous route, passing through Frankfurt, Wurtzburg and Heilbronn before catching an onward train to Stuttgart. Now, at long last, he felt he was nearing home.

At one point the train passed through a most beautiful village where he had once gone for a long hike with his mother. He rejoiced that not everything had been destroyed.

After another long stop in Bietigheim, twenty miles to the north of Stuttgart, Wolfram finally boarded a train bound for the village station in Eutingen. He was excited as well as a little anxious to think that he would soon be back in the family villa that he had not seen for two years and wondered what changes he would find. He had received almost no news from his parents since he had left for Normandy in January 1944. A lone postcard, which reached him at Camp Gruber, had informed him that they were still alive, but these prisoner-of-war cards, issued by the state, allowed the sender to write just twenty-five words.

The train slowed as it pulled into Eutingen station. There was a squeal of the brakes and then it jolted to a halt. Wolfram gathered together his few belongings and stepped down on to the platform. As the train's conductor gave a shrill blast on his whistle, signalling its departure for Pforzheim, Sigrid Weber, who had just climbed aboard, glanced back down the platform as the train drew out of the station. She saw Wolfram's familiar figure, and recognising him instantly, realised that his parents had no idea of his imminent return.

As soon as she arrived in Pforzheim, she ran straight to the school where Erwin was teaching to pass on the good news.

Erwin found it hard to believe what she told him. 'Is it really true?' he asked breathlessly. 'Can it really be true?'

When Sigrid confirmed that it was definitely Wolfram she had seen, Erwin clapped his hands and called for silence in the workshop, then made an apologetic speech to his students. 'I'm so sorry,' he said, 'but I have to leave immediately. I've just been told that my son, whom I haven't seen for two years, has arrived home.' Hardly daring to believe it, Erwin lost no time in catching the first train back to Eutingen.

Wolfram was meanwhile climbing the Hohe Steig – the High Path – which led to the family house. At the end of the long climb he reached the top to stand once more in front of the familiar plate-glass windows and low porch. A light could be seen shining from the kitchen and a familiar figure stood at the sink. His mother, Marie Charlotte, was preparing lunch.

Wolfram rang the bell and waited. For a few seconds there was no sound, then he heard the shuffle of feet in the hallway. The door opened slowly and he stood face to face with his mother.

She let out an excited shriek, flung her arms around him and pulled him into a huge embrace. She had been in the middle of making pastry and was so enthusiastic in her hugs that Wolfram's dark American army shirt was soon white with flour.

Half an hour later, Erwin arrived from Pforzheim to be reunited with his son. It was a moment to be savoured for years to come. Wolfram looked older and thinner than when he had first left home and his face was still pale from the long sea voyage. But he was alive – *alive!* – a lucky survivor of both the eastern and western fronts.

When the time was right, he would tell his parents of his experiences: his hellish months in Normandy, his brush with death and his extended captivity in America.

For now, on the day of his homecoming, it was time to celebrate. Almost two years after he had been taken prisoner – and fourteen months after the German army had surrendered to the Allies – Wolfram's war was at an end.

EPILOGUE

Wolfram spent just six weeks at home before returning to Oberammergau. He had been longing to restart woodcarving ever since his studies had been abruptly terminated by war in the spring of 1942. Now, almost four and a half years later, he finally got the chance.

He set off for Bavaria in July 1946 in order to be certain of having a place for the autumn term. Once this was assured, he spent the summer months hiking in the spruce forests of the high Wetterstein and chopping wood for the winter months ahead. He also crafted spinning wheels, still much in demand at the time, and trudged with them from farm to farm, exchanging them for food and supplies. The interiors of these farmsteads, furnished with rare examples of Bavarian folk art, were to inspire him far into the future.

The war had left Oberammergau untouched but it had taken its toll on the students. Wolfram learned that several of his comrades had lost their lives and many more were now disabled, having lost feet and legs. A high proportion of the newly enrolled students had been farmers in peacetime. Now, missing limbs and unable to do hard physical work, they had turned to woodcarving in the hope of scratching a living.

Wolfram excelled at his studies. When the three-year course drew to an end, each student was set the challenge of carving a miniature processional church staff – a final showpiece. The creator of the best sculpture would be granted the honour of donating a full-size version to the village's glittering baroque church. Wolfram clinched the prize with a deftly carved Christ on a donkey. It remains in the church to this day.

In Pforzheim, life remained fraught with daily challenges as people adjusted themselves to not only living amid a heap of rubble but under an occupying army. The French forces had left Pforzheim within two months of their triumphant entry into the town, to be replaced by American troops in the second week of July 1945.

Most Pforzheimers were glad to see the back of the French. They had fleeced and exploited the local population with all the enthusiasm of a medieval army, looting and requisitioning food, cameras and electrical equipment.

The French were still looting on the day that the Americans moved into Pforzheim, obliging these newly arrived soldiers to frisk and search their departing allies. 'All convoys of French vehicles were halted and the property not authorised to leave the area was taken from them,' reads the first official report issued by the new occupying forces. The Americans found themselves the unexpected custodians of a large collection of farm animals that were being smuggled out of town: 'hogs, cattle, sheep, goats, ducks, chickens and a few automobiles'.

The French had further offended the local population by exhuming the decomposing corpses of resistance fighters – Frenchmen executed by the SS – and requiring everyone in Pforzheim, young and old, to view them. This policy of deliberate humiliation was a serious misjudgment. Although there was widespread revulsion, the reaction of the populace was not 'How terrible that this happened,' but 'What a disgrace that we're being forced to look at such things.'

The French had mounted these gruesome displays out of a concern that people might refuse to believe the enormity of the atrocities carried out in the name of Nazi Germany. The truth was indeed too ugly for ordinary Germans to comprehend. When the full horror of Auschwitz was made public, many Pforzheimers dismissed it as Allied propaganda.

The Americans displayed boundless energy from their very first day and expressed surprise that the French had repaired so little of the damaged infrastructure. 'Nothing has been done towards clearing the city,' wrote one newly arrived officer, 'except the removal of the rubble and debris from the main roads.'

The Americans undertook a comprehensive survey of the local population's most basic needs, which revealed that two of the town's three hospitals had been flattened and there was a total lack of medical supplies. Not only was there almost no coal, gasoline or other fuel but there was an acute shortage of flour, oil, meat, sugar and oats.

Acquiring basic supplies was indeed a real problem for families such as the Aïcheles and the Rodis. Barbara Rodi, nine years old at the time, would accompany her mother on long walks in the hope of getting a little flour, milk or oil. Her sisters would wait for hours in long queues just to get a tiny loaf of bread.

American efforts to improve the lives of the local populace were hampered by a general lassitude that had settled over Pforzheim. People were still trying to make sense of the magnitude of their loss. Their loved ones, their town and the war itself – everything had been lost.

It was particularly traumatic for young children. Destruction and death had become so commonplace that it was hard to escape them. Young Barbara Rodi would often play an imaginary game of funerals, making miniature figurines out of flowers and digging little tombs in the garden. Having solemnly buried the figurines, she would decorate and tend the tombs.

The general sense of loss made a deep impression on the occupying American forces. '[The people] believed their situation was hopeless,' concluded one report, 'so why try to improve themselves?'

When the Americans tried to conscript labourers to help clear the ruins, only 800 men of working age reported for duty, which was deemed 'unusually low for a city of 40,000 people'. Eventually several teams of workers were assembled and for the next two months they dug corpses out of buildings and transported them to the cemetery. This task had by now become pressing: cadavers were rotting inside the ruins, creating a very real risk of spreading disease and infection.

The Americans also brought a sense of urgency to the most essential reconstruction work. The town's electricity generators were restored, the crippled gasworks repaired and underground telephone cables that had melted in the firestorm were relaid.

Schools also began to reopen – an essential step on the path to normality. Many children had received no formal education since the summer of 1944, when their teachers were drafted to work in munitions factories.

At first these new educational establishments were rudimentary affairs, often run out of private homes. The Rodi dining room became a classroom for one group of youngsters; Trudel, the family's aunt, spent her days teaching them to read and write.

Wolfram's father had also started teaching art again, albeit in the cramped conditions of his atelier in Eutingen. When the weather was fine, he and his students painted outside in the garden.

One of the key concerns of the American occupiers was to capture and prosecute all who had been involved in the organisation and running of the local Nazi Party.

Robert Wagner, the fanatical gauleiter of Baden, had been seized soon after the war's end, taken into American custody and interrogated. He continued to display 'a ferocious fidelity to Nazi ideology', according to those who questioned him, a fidelity that remained undiminished until the last. His final action before being executed was a defiant salute to the unholy trinity that had given his life purpose for more than two decades. 'Long live Greater Germany,' he shouted as the noose was placed around his neck. 'Long live Hitler. Long live National Socialism.'

Pforzheim's leading Nazi official, Hans Knab, was also tracked down and captured, then put on trial for a specific crime of which his guilt was assured. Fifteen months earlier, he had ordered the execution of seven RAF airmen who had bailed out of their stricken Lancaster and landed in newly destroyed Pforzheim.

Knab had instructed them to be taken to the nearby village of Huchenfeld, well out of sight, where they were murdered by a group of Hitler Youth. The killings were bungled: on the night of the bloodshed, two of the airmen had miraculously managed to escape.

Now, in the aftermath of the war, these two survivors gave evidence at the War Crimes Proceedings in Essen-Steele. It was enough to convict Knab and his accomplices. Knab himself was hanged, along with two fellow function-aries; fourteen others were given lengthy prison sentences. Little by little, the Nazi hierarchy was made to pay for its crimes.

The Americans did not want to punish only those in senior positions of responsibility: they wanted everyone to account for themselves during the previous twelve years of Nazi rule. 'Denazification and demilitarisation comprises the main effort of all offices . . .' reads a report written just three months after the arrival of the Americans. 'The only way [for Germans] to rid themselves of Nazi influence is by the ruthless removal from office and power [of] all who might seek in the future to reinstate in part or in full the Nazi system.'

To this end, they instituted a sweeping denazification programme in which everyone in Pforzheim and Eutingen, along with all other towns and villages in Germany, had to complete a detailed *fragebogen* or questionnaire that touched on every facet of their lives.

The Americans placed all Germans into one of five categories to determine their level of involvement in the Nazi regime. The worst offenders were the *hauptschuldige* – those who had played an active and organisational role in the Nazi hierarchy. At the other end of the scale were the *entlastete* or exonerated – men like Wolfram's father and Max Rodi who had managed to avoid joining the party.

Special law courts were established to determine the level of a person's complicity. These courts relied not only on information contained in the questionnaires, but also on testimonies of neighbours and family.

They were presided over by local individuals, laymen, who were untainted by the previous regime. Both Erwin Aïchele and Max Rodi (the latter had been released from his prisoner-of-war camp in the summer of 1946) were asked to serve as presidents of one of the impromptu Pforzheim courtrooms.

The American system was imperfect because it relied, to a large extent, on honesty. This was often in short supply in the aftermath of the war, prompting the wry comment that there seemed to be more Germans who had helped Jews than there were Jews themselves.

One section of the questionnaire required people to declare whether they had been a member of 'any association, society, fraternity, union, syndicate, chamber, institute, group, corporation, club or other organisation of any kind'. This caused problems for many. One of the Rodis' neighbours was a passionate horseman. His riding club was, like all the others, transformed into a Nazi organisation, which meant that he became, by default, a member of the SS, even though he never played an active role.

However, the Americans failed to make any distinction between active and non-active members and the man was imprisoned for two years. Such cases of injustice created a bad atmosphere in Pforzheim.

It quickly became apparent that the majority of Germans belonged in the same category – *mitläufer* or passive followers. This included most teachers, who had joined the Nazi Party because it was almost impossible to retain a teaching job without being a card-carrying member. Only a small minority of these people had been committed to propagating a Nazi education.

This led to a vigorous debate among Pforzheim's American officials about the extent to which individuals should be penalised for finding themselves in situations beyond their control. There was a feeling that if the punishment was too harsh, it could easily backfire '[and] drive them either in the arms of Communism or anarchism or back to National Socialism'. And that was to be avoided at all costs.

One solution was to entice exonerated locals into positions of public responsibility. The Americans had been in the town for only a few weeks before appointing a Pforzheimer, Adoph Katz, as acting mayor. Elections followed within nine months, bringing a degree of democracy that was deemed an essential ingredient in rebuilding the new Germany. One report concluded, 'before democracy can work ... a sound education in democratic procedure must be given to the German people.'

A key figure in post-war Pforzheim was a dynamic young American named Nicholas Semashko. Appointed Public Safety Officer on his arrival, he proved himself so efficient that he was soon promoted to the post of director of Pforzheim's military government, despite being just twenty-eight. He requisitioned a large villa in the leafy suburbs of Pforzheim that belonged to a close relative of the Rodi family and began to direct the town's reconstruction with impressive vigour.

It so happened that several paintings by Wolfram's father hung on the villa walls. Semashko, a commercial artist by training, admired them greatly and enquired about the artist. When he heard that Erwin lived in nearby Eutingen, he paid him a visit. This was not only a great success but would prove beneficial to both parties, promoting a regular exchange of goods. Wolfram's father would give him the occasional painting and, in return, Semashko would have flour, milk and other necessities delivered to the house.

Semashko also lent his support to Erwin's long-term goal of reopening the School of Decorative Arts, along with all the other educational institutions of Pforzheim. Indeed, the American was an enthusiastic advocate of a large-scale building programme that would eventually see an entire new town rise from the debris of the old – another critical step forward in the path to normalisation.

It took three years to clear the worst of the rubble. At first, simple wooden shacks went up in front of the ruins of former stores, but by 1948 a few of Pforzheim's larger companies had started rebuilding their offices. Private individuals, too, began reconstructing their houses with financial aid given by the state and paid for by the American Marshall Plan.

When locals looked out of their newly glazed windows, they saw a dramatic change to the landscape. A monumental new outcrop had appeared on the skyline just outside Pforzheim.

Rubble Hill was created from the wreckage of the destroyed city.

The American occupation was a time of heady excitement for many in Pforzheim and Eutingen, particularly the teenage girls, a number of whom welcomed the Americans with open arms. These young men were well groomed and handsome, but, best of all, they came bearing gifts: soap, good food, biscuits, coffee and cigarettes – king-size Pall Mall.

Among the hundreds of soldiers based in the Pforzheim barracks were two officers who made regular visits to the Webers' family home in Eutingen. Frau Weber did their washing and ironing for them and they would come to the house on most days to pick up their clean shirts and trousers.

One of them was a jazz musician from Puerto Rico who, with endearing naivety, suggested that the Webers' eldest daughter, Sigrid, accompany him back to the States. The only drawback to his plan was that he did not speak a word of German. The two of them spent hours at the table, poring over a German–English dictionary and attempting to converse.

While they improved their linguistic skills, Sigrid's father, Max, would walk along Hauptstrasse holding a long stick with a nail in one end. Whenever the Americans threw their cigarettes out their jeeps, half smoked, he would pick up the butts with his stick and make hand-rolled cigarettes with the tobacco he collected.

After years of war and misery, there was at long last a

reason not only to be cheerful but to dress up. One day, Sigrid found a gigantic swastika flag and cut it up to make a red skirt, a white blouse and a black bolero out of the material – an exercise in needlecraft for which she would have been executed just a couple of years earlier.

Several of the local girls had a particular admiration for the black Americans, who brought gifts, jazz music and an enviable coolness to rural Eutingen. To Sigrid's younger sister, Doris, they seemed like exotic creatures from another planet. She asked one of them if she could touch his hair, never having seen anything quite like it in her life.

The arrival of these American troops transformed daily life in Eutingen; they were so different from the Moroccans who had preceded them. At least one local girl would fall pregnant from these exciting liaisons. Another would follow her American lover back to Honolulu.

Wolfram did not feel at ease in the new, post-war Germany. In 1949, the Western Allies handed over some of their powers and Konrad Adenauer became the first chancellor of the new Federal Republic. There was a sudden emphasis on wealth creation and financial success – a drive towards prosperity that held neither interest nor importance for Wolfram.

After leaving Oberammergau he signed up for three years of additional studies at the Academy of Fine Art in Stuttgart. It was while he was living in the city that his interest in Orthodoxy, first kindled as he lay dying in the Ukraine, was suddenly reignited. Back in 1942, it had been the beauty of the polyphonic music that had captivated him. Now, it was the intensity of the religious art.

The Russian parishioners in Stuttgart were surprised to find a German in their midst and were no less so when they saw the icons that Wolfram was starting to paint. They were nothing like the sentimental, nineteenth-century icons so popular in Russia. Wolfram had turned instead for inspiration to the great medieval masters like Andrei Rublev, whose work had first come to his attention in a Pforzheim bookshop when he was just six years old. This return to tradition was also taking place elsewhere in Europe – in Greece, in Serbia and among the large Russian émigré community in Paris. It would lead to an extraordinary renaissance in Orthodox iconography that endures to this day.

In 1954, Wolfram undertook a three-month pilgrimage-of-sorts through Serbia and Greece, where he visited Mount Athos. It left him hungering for a more stimulating milieu than was offered by provincial Swabia. He decided to move to Paris, where he lived as a struggling artist among an international community, many of whom were impoverished White Russians. His new-found friends were refugees and émigrés like him – displaced theologians, bohemians and artists from the aristocratic dynasties of St Petersburg and Moscow.

It was to prove a turning point in his life, for his artistic skills now began to metamorphose into a style that was uniquely his own. Far from Germany and filled with ideas, he sought inspiration in everything he had seen over the previous decade: Russian icons, Bavarian folk art, the domes and minarets of Serbia and the works of Kandinsky, Klee and other modern artists.

His first important exhibition was in his native Germany,

but as his reputation grew, so his works were shown to a wider public – in Paris, New York, Zurich and other cities across Europe.

He still made occasional trips to Eutingen to see his family and it was during one of these visits that he again met Barbara Rodi, the youngest of the Rodi clan, whom he had last seen as a small girl. Now twenty-eight, she was working as a teacher in Eutingen, in the same primary school that Wolfram had once attended. Wolfram's young nephew was one of her pupils and she was often invited to eat at the Aïchele villa, having become good friends with Gunhild, Wolfram's sister.

Wolfram was captivated both by her interest in art and by her striking good looks. Barbara was no less entranced by his tales of life in bohemian Paris. Thus began a court-ship that was followed, in 1964, by marriage. The couple then returned to Paris where Barbara would later give birth to a daughter, Alexandra – my wife – and a son named Benedikt. The children were half Aïchele, half Rodi: in them, two families truly became one.

Wolfram and Barbara still live in Paris, in an apartment that is filled with exquisite works of art, all of which have been created by his own hands: a *hinterglas* or glass paint-ing of St Florian; a wooden sculpture of an angel; an icon of the prophet Elijah ascending to heaven in a ball of bright-red flame. There are also more recent works that draw the eye by their dazzling complexity of form and colour. Hanging on the wall of the salon is a semi-abstract water-colour of near-liquid luminosity, in which a sun-shot Alpine winterscape merges with a block of cobalt sky.

Wolfram, now eighty-six, still makes frequent visits to

the family villa in Eutingen. Last summer, he travelled to Oberammergau and renewed contact with the ninety-year-old Werner Lang with whom he had been a Morse code operator in Normandy.

Sixty-five years after last having seen him, Wolfram was able to tell Lang the touching story of Babei, the Turkmen, with whom he had been imprisoned on Utah Beach. Babei had originally intended to give his precious blanket to 'good Herr Lang', his commanding officer, because he had been one of the few Germans to treat the Turkmen auxiliaries with dignity and respect. When Lang was nowhere to be found, he had given it instead to Wolfram, whom he also liked.

Babei's end was not as fortunate as that of Wolfram and Lang. All the Asiatic soldiers serving with the German army were eventually repatriated to the Soviet Union, where they were either shot as traitors or died of starvation in Stalin's Siberian prison camps.

The Second World War brought catastrophe to every country that participated. Yet it is Nazi Germany that will carry for all time the stigma of genocide and mass murder, enthusiastically carried out by party functionaries. The War Crimes testimonies of men like Otto Ohlendorf, head of the killing squads in the Crimea, make for particularly chilling reading. One finds an intelligent and rational voice speaking with pride about murder on a truly grand scale.

There were a few Germans, of course, who lifted themselves out of the moral void and performed acts of dazzling courage. The students, Hans and Sophie Scholl, gave lead to an active, non-violent resistance, distributing anti-war leaflets at Munich University. It was short-lived. Both were arrested, convicted and swiftly beheaded, along with their fellow 'conspirator', Christoph Probst.

There were other Germans who performed less public but no less dangerous acts of charity: sheltering friends and neighbours who were Jewish or who had fallen foul of the regime.

There were also large numbers of Germans who found themselves unwillingly ensnared in this Mephistophelian nightmare – one that was not of their making nor within their control. The Aïchele and Rodi families retained a deep attachment to Germany throughout the twelve long years of the Third Reich, but it was a very different Germany from the one that Hitler was attempting to create. Theirs was the Germany of Goethe and Schumann, Heine and Bach.

Overnight, these two families discovered that the Nazis had wrapped their beloved Fatherland in a web of darkness. They despised Hitler for what he had done and they despised his entourage, but they also, naturally enough, wanted to preserve their own lives. They had young children to protect; they were scared of the Gestapo. They did not want to end their days in Dachau.

Under the Third Reich, they had precious little room for manoeuvre, being forced to compromise their morals, their ideals and their beliefs. 'Heil Hitler' never tripped lightly off their tongues.

'*Meine Ruh' ist hin*,' wrote Goethe, '*mein Herz ist schwer*.' My peace is gone, my heart is heavy. The Aïcheles and the Rodis would have given anything to have opted out. Instead, they were impotently sucked into a regime and a war that would lead to the darkest hours of Germany's history.

*   *   *

Thus it was that the eighteen-year-old Wolfram, much against his will, found himself a conscripted soldier in the Wehrmacht, travelling to Russia, to Normandy, to Britain and to America.

His story is not one of heroics on the battlefield, nor is it one of courageous resistance. It is simply an account of how an idiosyncratic young artist, whose only desire was to sculpt and paint, became trapped in a nightmare not of his making.

NOTES AND SOURCES

*'You're right to hurry up . . . in a few years
time there won't be any of us left.'*

Wolfram: The Boy Who Went to War is a true story based on
the eyewitness testimony of Wolfram Aïchele, a young
German conscript serving in the Wehrmacht.

Sixty hours of recorded interviews with Wolfram – together
with family letters and diaries from the time of the Third
Reich – form the heart of this narrative.

Other members of the extended family were also
interviewed, along with close friends and contemporaries
from Pforzheim. I wish to express my heartfelt gratitude
to the following family members: Wolfram and Barbara
Aïchele, Gunhild Aïchele, Peter Rodi and Frithjof Rodi.

Frithjof Rodi has written his own book about his
childhood – an autobiographical account entitled *Das Haus
auf dem Hügel: Eine Jugend am Rande des Kraters*. It
shows the profound dilemma of a middle class German
family that, despite its disgust with Hitler, was influenced
by patriotism and conservative traditions.

I am deeply grateful to Hannelore Schottgen (née
Haas) for allowing me to quote from her autobiography

and for kindly inviting me to her home in Taufkirchen near Munich. Her book is called *Wie Dunkler Samt um mein Herz: Eine Jugend in Der Nazizeit*. It is only available in German: for more information, see the bibliography.

Thank you to Sigrid and Doris Weber, friends and neighbours of Wolfram's parents, for spending time and effort recounting memories of their childhood in Eutingen. They also made available their father's manuscript diary covering the final few days of the war.

Thank you also to Doug Hicks, who I interviewed by telephone on 18 January, 2009. Hicks has written his own account of the bombing of Pforzheim. This can be found at *www.contact550.theraf.co.uk/hismemoirspforzheim.htm.*

I am grateful to Wing Commander Jack Harris, RAF 550 Squadron and North Killingholme Association for putting me in touch with other veterans.

A warm word of thanks is due to Dr Christian Groh of Pforzheim Stadtarchiv: he helped me locate a vast amount of hitherto unused material including newspaper reports, Nazi decrees and records of the town's post-war American military government. Thank you to Emilio Diebold for helping me in my research at the Stadtarchiv.

Lastly, I owe a debt of gratitude to my wife, Alexandra, who translated from German into English huge piles of documents and family letters, as well as many hours of taped interviews.

Unpublished manuscripts and papers:

Aïchele, *Family Letters, 1940-1947*, (various).

Aïchele, Marie Charlotte, *Erinnerungen von Marie Charlotte Aichele, geb. Boedicker* (family archives).

Aïchele-Rodi, Barbara, *Lettre à mes petits-enfants, de leur grand-mère Barbara Aïchele-Rodi* (family archives).

Barth, Arthur, *Ortsgruppenleiter Arthur Barth's decree on how the populace of Pforzheim is to celebrate the Anschluss with Austria* (family archives).

OMGUS, *Papers of OMGUS, Office of Military Government (USA)*. These are housed in Pforzheim city archives.

Rodi, Max, *Briefe von Max Rodi an seine Tochter Evmarie* (family archives).

Rodi, Max, *Tagebuch von Max Rodi, 1945–1946* (family archives).

Rodi, Peter, *Gefangenschaft und Flucht, 1944–1946* (family archives).

Weber, Max, *Diary of Max Weber* (in German).

Published newspapers, books, articles and websites:

(i) Newspapers

The following newspapers were consulted in the Pforzheim city archives: *Das Reich, Frei Presse, Pforzheimer Anzeiger, Pforzheimer Morgenblatt, Pforzheimer Zeitung, Volkischer Beobachter.*

(ii) Books, articles and websites

Badsey, Stephen, *Utah Beach*, Sutton, 2004, Stroud.

Bastable, Jonathan, *Voices from Stalingrad*, David & Charles, 2006, Newton Abbot.

Beevor, Anthony, *Stalingrad*, Viking, 1998, London.

Beevor, Anthony, *D-Day*, Viking, 2009, London.

Bielenberg, C., *The Past is Myself*, Chatto & Windus, 1968, London.

Brandle, Gerhard, *Die jüdischen Mitbürger der Stadt Pforzheim*, 1985, Pforzheim.

Bruhus, Wibke, *My Father's Country: The Story of a German Family*, Cornerstone, 2009.

Burleigh, Michael, *The Third Reich*, Macmillan, 2000, London.

Carell, Paul, *Invasion: They're Coming*, Transworld, 1963, London.

Dimbleby, Richard, http://www.bbc.co.uk/archive/holocaust/5115.shtml. Dimbleby's description of Belsen, recorded for the BBC in 1945.

Evans, Richard, *The Coming of the Third Reich*, Allen Lane, 2003, London.

Evans, Richard, *The Third Reich in Power, 1933–1939*, Allen Lane, 2005, London.

Evans, Richard, *The Third Reich at War, 1939–1945*, Allen Lane, 2008, London.

Gilbert, Martin, *Second World War*, Weidenfeld & Nicolson, 1989, London.

Grill, John Peter Horst, *The Nazi Movement in Baden, 1920-1945*, University of North Carolina Press, 1983, Chapel Hill.

Haffner, Sebastian, *Defying Hitler*, Weidenfeld & Nicolson, 2002, London.

Hagen, Louis, *Follow my Leader*, Allan Wingate, 1951, London.

Harrison Gordon, *Cross Channel Attack: US Army in World War Two*, United States Army, 1951.

Hastings, Max, *Overlord: D-Day and the Battle for Normandy*, Michael Joseph, 1984, London.

Hunt, Irmgard, *On Hitler's Mountain: My Nazi Childhood*, Atlantic, 2006, London.

Kershaw, Ian, *Hitler, 1889–1936: Hubris*, Allen Lane, 1998, London.

Kershaw, Ian, *Hitler, 1936–1945: Nemesis*, Allen Lane, 2000, London.

Klemperer, Victor, *I Shall Bear Witness: The Diaries of Victor Klemperer, 1933–1941*, Weidenfeld & Nicolson, 1998.

Koch, H. W., *The Hitler Youth: Origins and Development, 1922–1945*, Macdonald & James, 1975, London.

Laharie, Claude, *Le Camp de Gurs: 1939–1945*, Infocomp, 1985, Pau.

Lower, Wendy, *Nazi Empire Building and the Holocaust in the Ukraine*, University of North Carolina Press, 2005, Chapel Hill.

Mann, Thomas, *Reflections of a Nonpolitical Man*, Ungar, 1983, New York.

Maschman, Melita, *Account Rendered*, Abelard-Schuman, 1965, London.

Metelmann, Henry, *A Hitler Youth*, Caliban Books, 1997, London.

Metelmann, Henry, *Through Hell for Hitler*, Patrick Stephens, 1990, Wellingborough.

Middlebrook, Martin and Everitt, Chris, *The Bomber Command War Diaries: An Operational Reference Book, 1939–1945*, Viking, 1985, London.

Mitcham, Samuel, *Retreat to the Reich: The German Defeat in France, 1944*, Stackpole Books, 2007, Mechanicsburg.

Noakes, Jeremy and Pridham, Geoffrey, *Nazism 1919–1945, (vol 1): The Rise to Power; Nazism 1919–1945 (vol 2): State, Economy and Society; Nazism 1933–1939 (vol 3): Foreign Policy, War and Racial Extermination;* University of Exeter, 1983–2005, Exeter. An invaluable source, these volumes contain hundreds of translated documents and decrees from the period of the Third Reich.

Rodi, Frithjof, *Das Haus auf dem Hügel. Eine Jugend am Rande des Kraters*, Königshausen and Neumann, Würzburg, 2006.

Rubenstein, Joshua and Altman, Ilya, *The Unknown Black Book: The Holocaust in the German-Occupied Soviet Territories*, Indiana University Press, 2008, Indiana.

Ruppenthal, Ronald, *Utah Beach to Cherbourg*, Center of Military History, United States Army, 1990, Washington.

Schottgen, Hannelore, *Wie Dunkler Samt um mein Herz: Eine Jugend in Der Nazizeit*, Wartberg, 2003, Gleichen.

Schulte, Theo, *The German Army and Nazi Policies in Occupied Russia*, Oxford University Press, 1989, Oxford.

Shirer, William, *Twentieth Century Journal: A Memoir of a Life and the Times* (3 vols), Little Brown, 1984–1990, Boston.

Smelser, Ronald and Zitelmann, Rainer, *The Nazi Elite*, Macmillan, 1993, Basingstoke.

Steelman, Danny, *German Prisoners of War in America: Oklahoma's Prisoner of War Operations During World*

War Two, The Oklahoma State Historical Review, vol 4, 1983.

Stephenson, J., *Hitler's Home Front: Wurttemberg under the Nazis*, Hamblesdon Continuum, 2006, London.

Wiernik, J., *A Year in Treblinka*. An English translation is available at: http://www.zchor.org/treblink/wiernik.htm.

Wood, James (ed.), *Army of the West: The Weekly Reports of German Army Group B from Normandy to the West Wall*, Stackpole Books, 2007, Mechanicsburg.

Zaloga, Stephen, *D-Day 1944: Utah Beach and US Airborne Landings*, Osprey, 2002, Oxford.

PICTURE ACKNOWLEDGEMENTS

Courtesy of Wolfram Aïchele: 1, 2, 3, 4, 5, 7 left and below right, 8 below, 13 centre, 16 below. AKG-Images: 6 above/ Bildarchiv Pisarek, 11 above left and right/Ullstein Bild, 12 centre, 13 above, 13 below/Ullstein Bild,14 above. Bildarchiv Preussischer Kulturbesitz: 12 above. Corbis/Bettmann: 15 below. Getty Images: 7 above right/Time & Life Pictures, 10 above left and right, 14 below, 15 above and centre/Time & Life Pictures. Courtesy of Peter Rodi: 8 above. Schoeningh & Co., Luebeck: 6 below. Stadtarchiv Pforzheim – Institut für Stadtgeschichte: 9, 10 below, 11 below, 12 below, 16 above.

INDEX

Academy of Fine Art, Stuttgart 313
Adenauer, Konrad 313
Aïchele, Alexandra 315
Aïchele, Benedikt 315
Aïchele, Erwin (Wolfram's father) 9,
    11–12, 13–14, 15, 18, 20, 22, 27, 39,
    63, 237–8; after end of the War
    291, 309; as artist/art teacher 16,
    54, 83, 307, 311; attitude to Hitler
    and the Nazis 32, 34, 42–3, 45,
    47–8, 51, 67–8; draftings after
    Allied landings in Normandy
    218–19; and the English 90; job at
    Fine Art School, Karlsruhe 68;
    and Kraft 68; at start of War 104;
    and a tramp 45; visit to Wolfram
    at Marienbad 160–1; on Wolfram's
    return from prison camp 300,
    301; and Julius Zorn 209–10
Aïchele family 317 see also
    individual family members;
    flying the Nazi flag 77–8; and the
    Nazis in the mid-30s 67–8, 77–8,
    79–80; and refugees 166–7;
    traditions 52; and wartime
    household management 165–7

Aïchele, Gunhild (Wolfram's sister)
    63, 87, 107–8, 165, 166, 268, 315
Aïchele, Marie Charlotte (Wolfram's
    mother) 9, 11, 14–15, 17–18, 19, 23,
    26, 28, 40, 62–3, 147, 148–50;
    1942 122–3, 127–8; 1943 165–9;
    1944 187, 188, 207, 208, 219; 1945
    236–7, 238, 245, 253–4, 257,
    260–2, 263–4; after end of the
    War 292; attitude to Nazism 69–71;
    depression 167; on Elsässer's
    memorial service 168; feeding the
    family 165–6, 219; and the Gestapo
    79–80, 149–50, 167; and the
    Moroccan occupation of Eutingen
    268–9; and the Pforzheim
    bombing 245, 253–4, 257, 260–2,
    263–4; visit with Wolfram to
    Tiefonbronn 34–6; on Wolfram's
    return from prison camp 301
Aïchele, Reiner (Wolfram's brother)
    9–10, 16, 70, 148, 292
Aïchele, Walter (Wolfram's uncle)
    54, 57, 72–3, 166
Aïchele, Wolfram: in 77th Infantry
    164, 183–7, 191–200; art see under

art; birth 8; in Brittany 178, 179;
call-up 161; childhood life, early
8–13, 23–7, 28–30, 38–9, 44–5,
62–4, 71–2; Crimean posting
132–47; death of maternal
grandparents 61; diphtheria
142–7, 151–3, 281; early attitudes
to Nazism and Hitler 49, 51; and
Hitler Youth 73–5, 118; at
Marienbad sanatorium 156, 160–1;
marriage to Barbara Rodi 315;
move to Paris 314, 315; in
Normandy 170–8, 185–7, 188–90,
191–206; and the Normandy
Campaign 183–7, 188–90, 191–206;
in Oberammergau 116–20, 303–4,
316; as prisoner of war 211–18,
224–35, 278–9, 280–4, 289–91;
Reich Labour Service *see* Reich
Labour Service; resumption of life
after the war 303–4, 313–16;
return home from American
prison camp 289–91, 299–301;
surrender to the Americans 205–6;
teenage employment 89; teenage
interests 81–2, 88–9; training as a
funker (wireless operator) 161–4;
transported to America 224–34;
transported to England 216–18; in
the Ukraine 133–46, 151–3, 155
Alsace 123, 218–19
America *see* United States of
America, World War II
anthroposophical movement 65–6,
67, 149
anti-Semitism 18, 55–60; in 1930
Nazi political programme 22, 23;
deportation of Jews 101, 111–14;
German underestimation of Nazi
23; Goebbels' call for the
elimination/extermination of
Jewry 157–8; Kristallnacht 91–4;

mass executions 136–8, 158–60,
283; Nazi extermination
programme 103, 136–8, 158–60,
283; Reich Citizenship Law 58–9;
Russian Jews under Hitler's
invasion 134–8; SS orders against
103; taught in universities and
schools 128–9; Wagner and 40–2
Aron, Gustav 113
art: books 38–9; folk art 82–3;
influence of maternal
grandmother on Wolfram 61;
Nazism and 83–5; Orthodox
313–14; present exhibited work of
Wolfram 3–4; Wolfram's
childhood art 13, 24, 30, 36;
Wolfram's father and 16, 54, 83,
307, 311; Wolfram's post-war
pursuit of 313–15; Wolfram's
teenage passion 88
Audrieu 170–1
Auschwitz 114, 305
Austria: incorporation into German
Reich 85–8; Wolfram cycling in
97

Babei (a Turkmen) 213, 316
Bacherer, Col. Rudolf 164, 197, 198,
199, 203, 235
Bad Wimpfen 63–4
Baden state, Wagner and 40–1, 42–3
Bader, Franz 163
Barbarossa, Frederick 63
Barneville-sur-Mer 192
Barth, Arthur 85
Baum, Otto 84–5
BBC 220, 283
Becher, Otto 47–8, 51, 64, 123; and
Rust 70, 71
Becker, August 137
Becker, Werner 55
Beckmann, Max 85

Index

Beer Hall Putsch 21
Bergen-Belsen extermination camp 283
Berlin 14, 32–3; Olympic Games 72
Bible 53
Bloch, Margot 55
Boedicker, Herr, Wolfram's grandfather 61–2
Boedicker, Johanna, Wolfram's grandmother 61–2
Boedicker, Marie Charlotte *see* Aïchele, Marie Charlotte
book burning 45–7
Brenner, Walter 262
Brest-Litovsk 134–5, 136
Briquebec 192
Britain: British requirements for settlers in Palestine 57; declaration of war on Germany 102; German pre-war attitudes to the British 89–90; RAF *see* Royal Air Force
Brittany 178, 179
brownshirts *see* SA
Brüning, Heinrich 22
Bulge, Battle of the 232

Caen 170, 173–4
Chamberlain, Neville 89, 90, 97
Cherbourg 189; Fortress 184, 191
Cherson 143–6
Christianity: Christian community of Pforzheim and the Nazis 52–3, 65–6; closure of churches under Stalin 138; Nazi assault on Christian teaching 53, 128–9; Orthodoxy 313–14; paganising/ replacement of Christian festivals 49, 51–2
Christmas traditions 51–2
Clara (maid) 16, 47–8, 64, 68

Communism 23; and Hitler 37–8; and the Nazis 37–8, 54
Cotentin peninsular 184, 190, 192–3, 202
Coutances 203
Crimea 127–8, 139–43

D-Day 178, 179–84
Dachau concentration camp 67, 92, 159, 229
Danzig 96, 101
Decree of the Reich President for the Protection of People and State 38, 46
Decree on Demolitions on Reich Territory (Nero Decree) 275, 291
democracy 14, 15, 22, 310
Demolitions on Reich Territory, Decree on (Nero Decree) 275, 291
Dimbleby, Richard 283
divorce, on racial grounds 59
Dix, Otto 85
Dollman, Gen. Friedrich 180
Donitz, Admiral Karl 277
Dorothea, Sister 147
Dresden 156; air raid 238, 240, 245
Driffield 217–18
Ducy 212

Eberstadt 93
Ebert, Friedrich 15
educational propaganda 53–4, 90, 129–30
Elsässer, Rolf 168
Emsheimer, Blondine 113
ethnic cleansing 103, 136–8 *see also* Nazism: extermination programme
Ettal kloster 119
Ettal, Mount 116
Eutingen: American occupation 313; blowing up of bridge 265–6;

French prisoners of war 272–3; Hitler Youth branch 105–6; Hitler's visit to 50–1; murder of a British pilot 209–11; Nazi Party in 51, 76–80; and the Nazi revolution 76–80; occupation of 268–71, 272–3, 313; and the start of war 98; surroundings 29–30, 71; Tunisian occupation of 271; villa 9–11, 23, 24, 25–6, 34, 40, 62, 66, 79–80, 165–8, 207, 236–7, 265, 268–9; village 24–5, 50–1, 168–9, 208–11, 265–73

Falley, Gen. Wilhelm 180
farms, Swabian 29–30
Feodosia 140–2
flags 33, 40–1, 67, 77–8, 313
folk art 82–3
Frank, Hans 103
Freemasonry 17–18, 42–3; Reuchlin Masonic lodge 111
French prisoners of war 272–3
Frey, Adolf 93

German art 83–5 *see also* art
German economy 19, 29, 64
German Infantry: 1st Battalion, 1050th Infantry Unit 198–9; 77th Division 5–7, 164, 183–7, 191–200, 203
German patriotism 99
German prisoners of war: and the end of the war 280–5; in France 221–3; French post-war plans for using 285; Peter Rodi 221–3, 279–80, 284–9; Wolfram and his comrades 211–18, 224–35, 278–9, 280–4, 289–91
German Sixth Army 153, 156–7, 169
German war casualties (World War II) 122, 156–7, 163, 166, 195–6, 281; Pforzheim bombing 247, 248, 261, 263
Germanic traditions 49–50
Gestapo: 1937 78–80; deportation of Jews 113; and the Rodis 67, 150–1; and Wolfram's mother 79–80, 149–50, 167
ghetto, Pforzheim 94, 113
Glasser, German officer 177–8
Gleiwitz 98
Goebbels, Joseph 21, 32–3, 36, 48, 84, 123, 157, 265; presentation of Kristallnacht 92; Propaganda Ministry 99, 102, 103, 156–7
Goering, Hermann 21, 38, 43, 65, 102, 153
Goesser (a prisoner of war) 215–16
Goethe, Johann Wolfgang von 317
Göppert, Herr (prisoner of war) 287
Gradenwitz, Herr 58
Gretel (friend of the Haas family) 260
Gruber, Camp 229–35, 280–4, 289
Guggenheim family 17, 57–8
Gurs, Camp 114

Haas, Frau 56, 76, 87, 96
Haas, Hannelore *see* Schottgen, Hannelore
Haas, Herr 58, 92, 96, 99, 105
Halder, Fritz 121
Hallig island 54
harvest festivals 71–2
Hebel, Mr 231, 233
'Heil Hitler' salute 48, 69–70, 317
Hennecke, Admiral Walter 181
Hess, Rudolf 122–3
Heydrich, Reinhard 43, 66, 103, 113, 149
Hicks, Sgt Doug 239–41, 244, 246–7
Hillenbrandt, Dr 25, 39, 81–2
Himmler, Heinrich 79, 136

Hindenburg, Paul Ludwig von 12, 20, 31–2
history, Nazi version of 129–30
Hitler, Adolf 12, 20, 21, 47–8; 1930 election 22–3; 1933 election 36–7, 38; adulation of 48, 50, 52, 87; and the Allied Normandy Campaign 189, 190–1; and art 83–5; assassination attempt 202; assurances of avoiding war 95; and Austria's incorporation into German Reich 85–8; birthday 48, 95; and Chamberlain 89; and the Communists 37–8; Crimean campaign 132 *see also* Crimea; cult of the Führer 50, 52, 87; death 277; decree on Hitler Youth 73–4; 'Heil Hitler' salute 48, 69–70, 317; invasion of Soviet Union 120–2, 134–8, 153, 155, 156–7; *lebensborn* (racial breeding programme) 107–10; in mid-1930s 64–5; monologues 100; Nero Decree 275; and the Olympic Games 72; order of mass executions 136; and the outbreak of war 99; and Poland 95, 96–7, 98–9, 101; Reich Citizenship Law 58–9; rise to chancellorship 31–4; signing of Decree of the Reich President for the Protection of People and State 38; SS orders against enemies of Nazism 103; Sudetenland crisis 89; visit to Pforzheim 50–1; War advances 106–7
Hitler Youth 8, 45–7, 60, 73–6, 105–6, 118, 308
Hoch, Frau 147

Ilse (maid) 16
Issel, August 76–7, 266

Jahnke, Lt. Arthur 181, 182–3
Jews: anti-Semitism *see* anti-Semitism; deportations 101, 111–14; emigration to Palestine 57–8; Jewish immigrants in England 216; law concerning declaration of Jewish origins 59–60; of Pforzheim 17, 18, 54–8, 59, 91–4, 111–15; Reich Citizenship Law 58–9; Russian 134–8; yellow stars 115

Karlsruhe 50; court 59, 78; Fine Art School 68; Organisation I 68
Katz, Adoph 310
Kerch 142
Kiev 120, 121
Knab, Hans 270, 274–6, 307–8
Kraft, Herbert 20–1, 23, 68
Krakow 101
Kristallnacht 91–4
Kuppenheim, Lilly 111–12
Kuppenheim, Rudolf 110–12
Kursk, Battle of 169

Lang, Werner 162, 178, 316
Lattre de Tassigny, Jean de 277
Le Havre 290
Le Vretot 6–7, 193–7
League of German Girls 76
lebensborn (racial breeding programme) 107–10
Lehman, Frau (cleaning lady) 37, 38
Lemberg (Lvov) 155
Leningrad 120, 121
Lieutenant W. 162–3
Lubbe, Marinus van der 37
Lvov (Lemberg) 155

Maginot Line 107
Malicious Gossip Law 79
Mann, Thomas 46, 80

Marienbad 156, 160–1

marriage legislation, Reich Citizenship Law 59

Marshall Plan 311

Mayer, Rupert 119

Melchior, 'Captain Melchior' 233

Miggel, Erwin 162, 172, 174, 178, 199, 200, 201

Milton, Madeleine 1

Minsk 121, 135

Moroccan occupation of Eutingen 268–71, 272

Moscow 120, 121–2

Moser, Lusas 35–6

Moses, Dr 55

Munich Agreement 89

Münsingen 161–4

Mussolini, Benito 170

National Socialist Party *see* Nazis

Nazism *see also individual Nazis*: 1928 election 21; 1930 election 22–3; 1930 political programme 22; 1933 election 38, 117; American action against Nazis after the war 307–10; anti-Semitism *see* anti-Semitism; assault on Bible and Christian teaching 53, 128–9; and Austria's incorporation into German Reich 85–8; brownshirts *see* SA; and Communism 37–8, 54; criminalisation of non-participation 78; and the culture of secrecy 160; death squads 136–7; early days of Nazi Party 20–3; extermination programme 103, 136–8, 158–60, 283; flag 33, 40–1, 67, 77–8, 313; and German art 83–5; and Germanic traditions 49–50; Gestapo *see* Gestapo; Hitler Youth 8, 45–7, 60, 73–6, 308; ideology

48, 53–4, 68, 78, 128–30; *lebensborn* programme 107–10; Malicious Gossip Law 79; Nazi Party in Eutingen 51, 76–80; Nazi Party in Pforzheim 33, 40, 41–3, 48–9, 52–3, 66–7, 94, 307–10; Night of the Long Knives 65; propaganda *see* propaganda, Nazi; public holidays and festivities 48, 49, 51–2, 71–2; Reich Citizenship Law 58–9; renaming of streets and schools 48–9; SA *see* SA (Sturmabteilung, brownshirts); SS *see* SS (Schutzstaffel); torchlit parades 32–3

Nero Decree 275, 291

New York 225–8

Niederbayern 125–7

Night of the Long Knives 65

Nikolaev 146, 151–3, 154–5

Nikolaus, St 52

Normandy 5–7, 170–8; Campaign 179–200

Nuremberg trials 137

Oberammergau 115, 116–20, 303–4, 316

Oeschelbronn 50

Ohlendorf, Otto 137–8, 316

Olympic Games 72

Omaha Beach 184

Operation Uranus 153

Orthodoxy 313–14

Otto the Great 130

pagan festivals 49, 52

Papen, Franz von 32

Paris 107, 314

patriotism 99

Paulus, Gen. Friedrich Wilhelm von 153, 154, 156

Peenemunde 131

Index

Pforzheim 10, 14, 14–21, 23, 26, 30–1; after Allied landings in Normandy 218–19; after end of the War 304–13; Allied advance on 273–5; Allied arrival in 276–7; bombing and aftermath 238–57, 258–65; burning of books by Hitler Youth 45–7; Christian community of 52–3, 65–6; ghetto 94, 113; Hitler's visit to 50–1; Jewish community 17, 18, 54–8, 59, 91–4, 111–15; Kristallnacht 91–4; Nazi Party in 33, 40, 41–3, 48–9, 52–3, 66–7, 94, 307–10; Nazi renaming of streets and schools 48–9; and the Nero Decree 274–5; picture house 44; public morale 168–9; surroundings 81–2; and the vote on Austria's incorporation into German Reich 86–8; War years 105, 106

Pforzheimer Anzeiger 46, 52–3, 83, 102, 103

Pforzheimer Rundschau 96, 102–3

Philip, Hulde 8, 30

Poland 90, 95, 96–7, 98–9, 101; SS orders against Poles 103

Probst, Christoph 317

propaganda, American 197–8

propaganda, Nazi 32–3, 50, 64–5, 90, 99; in German education 53–4, 90, 129–30; Goebbels' Propaganda Ministry 99, 102, 103, 156–7

public holidays and festivities 94

race: anti-Semitism *see* anti-Semitism; Nazi ideology 72, 128–30

RAF *see* Royal Air Force

rationing 96, 104–5

Reich Citizenship Law 58–9

Reich Labour Service 8; medical exam for 119–20; Niederbayern camp 125–7; Wolfram's Crimean posting 127, 132–47

religious festivals 49, 51–2

reparation payments 19

Reuchlin Masonic lodge 111

Riemenschneider, Tilman 88

Ritzy (a *funker*) 162, 178

Rodi, Barbara 151, 160, 245, 305–6, 315

Rodi, Ev-Marie 242

Rodi family 52, 53, 66–7, 78, 104, 317 *see also individual family members*; American uncles 285–6; on Hitler's birthday 95; and the Pforzheim bombing 249–50, 261–2, 264–5

Rodi, Frithjof 27, 30–1, 53, 66–7, 98, 100, 107, 124–5, 130, 218, 264–5, 273, 274

Rodi, Gisela 219, 276

Rodi, Martha Luise 26, 67, 100, 104, 123–4, 159, 220; after end of the War 291, 292; and the Allied arrival in Pforzheim 276, 277; and the Gestapo 150–1; and the Pforzheim bombing 242, 250, 257, 258, 262, 265

Rodi, Max 26, 53, 67, 95, 98, 100, 114, 123–4, 159–60, 275, 291–2, 309; and the Pforzheim bombing 255–7, 262

Rodi, Peter 27, 30–1, 75, 90–1, 95, 100, 125, 160; conscription into infantry 219–20; drafting into home defence 130–1; escape from prison of war camp 292–8; escape plans 286–9; as prisoner of war 221–3, 279–80, 284–9, 292; reported missing in action 220

Röhm, Ernst 65

Romanian Third Army 153
Rommel, Erwin 180, 184, 191
Rothfuss, Werner 208, 209, 211
Rothschilds 17, 93–4
Royal Air Force 131; Pforzheim
  bombing 238–41, 244–7 *see also*
  Pforzheim: bombing and
  aftermath
Rublev, Andrei 314
Rundstedt, Gerd von 191
Rust, Bernhard 69–71

SA (Sturmabteilung, brownshirts)
  31, 32–3, 40–1, 42, 56, 65, 86, 92,
  111–12
St Maria Magdalena church,
  Tiefonbronn 35–6
Salamon family 58
Sanden, Ferdinand von der 259
Schaaff, Dr and Mrs 25
Schenkel (Hitler Youth leader) 46–7
Schiller, Friedrich 90
Schleicher, Kurt von 31
Schlieben, Gen. Karl-Wilhelm von
  180
Schloss Linderhof 117–18
Schnurmann, Dr 25, 58
Scholl, Albrecht 158–9, 160
Scholl, Hans 316–17
Scholl, Sophie 316–17
School of Decorative Arts 278, 311
Schottgen, Hannelore (née Haas)
  33, 49, 50, 52, 56, 57, 76, 95–6,
  99, 110, 129; and the Pforzheim
  bombing 243–4, 247–9, 251–2,
  254–5, 258, 259, 260
Schulz, Herr 114
Schulz, Kathe 113
Semashko, Nicholas 310–11
Shakespeare, William 90
Shirer, William 106
Siebert, Herr 45

Soucrain family 149
Soviet Union 120–2, 153–4, 155,
  156–7 *see also* Crimea; Ukraine;
  Russian Jews under Hitler's
  invasion 134–8
Speidel, Hans 191
SS (Schutzstaffel) 33, 65; Death's
  Head regiments 103; Gestapo *see*
  Gestapo; *lebensborn* programme
  108–10; and the vote on Austria's
  incorporation into German Reich
  86; and Wagner 40–1
Stalin, Joseph 138
Stalingrad 144, 153–4, 156
Stauffenberg, Count Claus von 202
Stegmann, Maj.-Gen. Rudolf 183,
  196
Steiner, Rudolf 26, 53, 66;
  anthroposophical movement 65–6,
  67, 149
Stern, Susanna 93
Strongpoint W8 fortification 181–2
Stuttgart 89, 275; Academy of Fine
  Art 313
Sudetenland crisis 89
swastikas 1, 4, 31; flags 33, 40–1, 67,
  77–8, 313

Thälmann, Ernst 37
Tiefonbronn 34; St Maria
  Magdalena church 35–6
Tiehl, Herr 24
Treblinka concentration camp 158–9
Trutz, Hildegard 108–9
Tunisian occupation of Eutingen
  271

Uffhausen 61–2
Ukraine 120, 133–9, 170; Crimea
  127–8, 139–43; Wolfram's
  experiences in 133–46, 151–3, 155
unemployment 64

United States of America, World War II 124, 183, 184, 189–90, 191–9, 205–6, 232, 236; American action against Nazis after the war 307–10; American rebuilding efforts after the War 305–7; Marshall Plan 311; Rainbow, 42nd Infantry Division 229; US Third Army 236; and Wolfram's experiences as prisoner of war 211–18, 224–35, 278–9, 280–4
Utah Beach 180, 184, 212–14

Verschuer, Otmar von 59
Vilnius 121
Vögtle, Dr 8, 74–5
Voluntary Labour Service 64

Wagner, Robert Heinrich 40–2, 50, 59, 94, 113, 307
Warsaw 101
Weber, Doris 98, 208–9, 210, 270, 272, 313
Weber, Frau 207, 237, 238, 265, 312
Weber, Karl 25
Weber, Kurt 207, 265, 269
Weber, Max 219, 265–7, 270, 272, 273, 312
Weber, Sigrid 106, 167–8, 242, 254, 262–3, 270, 300, 312, 313
Weill, Dr 58
Weimar Constitution 15
Weimar Republic 31

Wiernik, Yankel 159
Windgassen, Wolfgang 169
Wolfram *see* Aïchele, Wolfram
World War I, Wolfram's father in War and aftermath 13–14
World War II: Allies, 1943 170; Allies, autumn and winter 1944–45 232; Allies, final months 265, 276–7; America *see* United States of America, World War II; Battle of Kursk 169; blackouts 105; Britain's declaration of war on Germany 102; D-Day 178, 179–84; end of 280; food and rationing 104–5, 122, 163, 165–6, 201, 219; German casualties *see* German war casualties; Hitler's advances 106–7; Hitler's death 277; Hitler's invasion of Soviet Union 120–2, 134–8, 153–4, 155, 156–7; Normandy Campaign 179–200; Normandy, spring 1944 170–8; outbreak 98–100; prisoners of war *see* French prisoners of war; German prisoners of war; RAF bombings 238–41, 244–7 *see also* Pforzheim: bombing and aftermath

Yellowfin, Operation 239–41 *see also* Pforzheim: bombing and aftermath

Zorn, August 25
Zorn, Julius 209–10, 211